'Inward and Outward Health'

'Inward and Outward Health'

*John Wesley's Holistic Concept of Medical
Science, the Environment and Holy Living*

Edited by
Deborah Madden

WIPF & STOCK · Eugene, Oregon

Wipf and Stock Publishers
199 W 8th Ave, Suite 3
Eugene, OR 97401

'Inward and Outward'
John Wesley's Holistic Concept of Medical Science,
the Environment and Holy Living
By Madden, Deborah
Copyright©2008 by Madden, Deborah
ISBN 13: 978-1-62032-127-0
Publication date 8/1/2012
Previously published by Epworth, 2008

Contents

Contributors

Dr Deborah Madden is a Postdoctoral Research Fellow in the Theology Faculty at the University of Oxford. She has written several articles on religion and culture in the eighteenth century, as well as a monograph examining John Wesley's medical activity: *'A Cheap, Safe and Natural Medicine': Religion, Medicine and Culture in John Wesley's Primitive Physic* (2007).

Randy L. Maddox is Professor of Theology and Wesleyan Studies, Duke University, Durham, North Carolina. He is the author of *Responsible Grace: John Wesley's Practical Theology* (1994), a contributor to *Wesley and the Quadrilateral* (1997), and editor of *Aldersgate Reconsidered* (1990) and *Rethinking Wesley's Theology for Contemporary Methodism* (1998). He also serves as the Institute Secretary of the Oxford Institute of Methodist Theological Studies, General Editor of the Kingswood Books Imprint of Abingdon Press, and Associate General Editor of the Wesley Works Editorial Project. He is a past president of the Wesleyan Theological Society, and past co-chair of the Wesley Studies Group of the American Academy of Religion.

Margaret G. Flowers is Professor Emerita of Biology, Wells College, Aurora, New York, and Research Fellow and Adjunct Associate Professor of Science, Theology and Ministry at Northeastern Seminary, Rochester, New York. As an ordained Elder she serves as co-pastor of the Clarion Free Methodist Church, Clarion, Pasadena. She holds the AB in Biological Sciences from Mount Holyoke College, the PhD in Botany from the University of Texas, and the MDiv and MA in Theological Studies from Northeastern Seminary. She is the author of numerous publications in science and theology.

Dr Laura Bartels Felleman is a graduate of the Wesleyan and Methodist Studies PhD programme at Drew University, Madison, New Jersey. She is adjunct faculty at Cazenovia College, Cazenovia, New York, and pastor of Forest Home Chapel in Ithaca, New York. An ordained elder of the United Methodist Church, her recent articles appear in *Wesleyan Theological Journal*, *Epworth Review*, *Methodist History*, and *Perspectives on Science and Christian Faith*.

Linda S. Schwab is Professor Emerita of Chemistry, Wells College, Aurora, New York, and Research Fellow at Northeastern Seminary, Rochester, New York. As an ordained Elder she serves as co-pastor of the Clarion Free Methodist Church, Clarion, Pasadena. She holds the BA in Chemistry from Wells College, the MS and PhD in Organic Chemistry from the University of Rochester, and the MDiv and MA in Theological Studies from Northeastern Seminary. She is the author of several publications in science and theology.

Dr Robert Webster obtained his DPhil, 'Methodism and the Miraculous: John Wesley's contribution to the *Historia Miraculorum*' (2006), in the Theology Faculty at the University of Oxford. He has published several historical and theological articles in the area of Methodist studies. More recently, he edited a special volume of essays about Charles Wesley for the *Bulletin of the John Rylands University Library of Manchester*. Currently he is completing research for a book that examines the place of dreams and visions among Methodists in the eighteenth and nineteenth centuries.

Abbreviations of Wesley materials

John Wesley   *John Wesley*, ed. Albert C. Outler, New York, Oxford
                      University Press, 1964.

Letters (Telford)   *The Letters of the Rev. John Wesley, A.M.*, ed. John
                      Telford, 8 vols, London, Epworth, 1931.

Works   *The Works of John Wesley*; begun as *The Oxford
                      Edition of The Works of John Wesley*, Oxford,
                      Clarendon Press, 1975–1983; continued as *The
                      Bicentennial Edition of The Works of John Wesley*,
                      Nashville, Abingdon, 1984–; 16 of 35 vols published
                      to date.

Works (Jackson)   *The Works of John Wesley*, ed. Thomas Jackson, 14
                      vols, London, 1872; Grand Rapids, Zondervan, 1958.

Works (Pine)   *The Works of the Rev. John Wesley, M.A.*, 32 vols,
                      Bristol, W. Pine, 1771–74.

Introduction

Saving Souls and Saving Lives:
John Wesley's 'Inward and Outward Health'

DEBORAH MADDEN

I have a sin of fear, that when I have spun
My last thread, I shall perish on the shore;
Swear by thyself, that at my death thy Sun
Shall shine as it shines now, and heretofore;
And, having done that, thou hast done,
I fear no more.

John Donne, 'A Hymn to God the Father' (1623)[1]

Hereby the great physician of souls applies medicine to heal *this sickness*; to restore human nature, totally corrupted in all its faculties . . .
'in Adam ye all died;' in the second Adam, 'in Christ, ye all are made alive' now 'go on' from 'faith to faith', until your whole sickness be healed . . .

John Wesley, 'Sermon on Original Sin' (1759)

On 13 January 1738, John Wesley was forced to face his own mortality during a spectacular and dramatic sea-storm, which threatened to break into pieces a ship that 'would not obey the helm' and risked drowning everyone on board. As the *Samuel* made its voyage, heading out from 'Charles-Town', South Carolina, across the Atlantic Ocean towards Deal in Kent, this stormy experience must surely have reiterated to Wesley the terrifying power of nature – God's immediate commissioner. To 'perish on the shore' was a thought that struck deep fear into his heart, and Wesley, clearly terrified, cried out to God for help. Travelling back to England after a two-year missionary trip to Georgia, Wesley noticed that the ship was battered by violent waves breaking over the vessel continuously. The quivering motion, he observed, resembled that of a large cannon or earthquake:

The Captain was upon deck in an instant. But his men could not hear what he said. It blew a proper hurricane . . . at the same time the sea running (as they term it) mountain high, and that from many different points at once, the ship would not obey the helm; nor indeed could the steersman, through the violent rain, see the compass. So he was forced to let her run before the wind . . .[2]

Being tossed and thrown upon the high seas certainly gave one time to repent at leisure; the storm, which began at 10 p.m., finally passed by noon the following day, though, even a week or so later, as the ship approached Land's End, the Captain continued to feel uneasy about being taken by the wind 'unawares into the Bristol Channel', or crashing during the night against the rocks of Scilly. Shaken by the storm, the very next day Wesley resolved to preach 'to every single soul' on board. The difficult journey meant that everyone, including Wesley, was also looking for more tangible signs of relief, observing at all times wind direction and cloud formations, hoping to catch sight of land ahead:

Sat., 28 was another cloudy day; but about ten in the morning (the wind continuing southerly) the clouds began to fly just contrary to the wind, and to the surprise of us all, sunk down under the sun, so that noon we had an exact observation; and by this we found we were as well as we could desire, about eleven leagues south of Scilly.[3]

Reflecting on how he had felt during the storm, Wesley castigated himself for crying out to God in fear, which, he thought, indicated a superficial, lukewarm and purely 'rational' faith. This lack of spiritual depth had been directly responsible, so he believed, for the disappointing outcome of his missionary efforts in Georgia:

I went to America, to convert the Indians; but oh! Who shall convert me! Who, what is he that will deliver me from this evil heart of un-belief? I have a fair summer religion; I can talk well; nay, and believe myself, while danger is near; but let death look me in the face, and my spirit is troubled. Nor can I say, 'To die is gain!'
'I have a sin of fear, that when I've spun
My last thread, I shall perish on the shore.'[4]

The fragment from Donne's 'Hymn to God the Father' is interesting; this work formed part of a corpus written in 1623 when the poet was gravely ill with a 'relapsing fever'. Donne used his illness to structure the poem and another, 'Hymn to God My God, in My Sickness', as well as *Devotions upon Emergent Occasions*, a work which was comprised of twenty-three meditations, expostulations and prayers, following progress of the poet's fever. In this corpus Donne mined the symptoms of his disease, which were linked to bigger theological questions about corporeal and divine health. Perhaps Wesley chose to cite from this corpus because, throughout, Donne repeatedly invoked sea-faring metaphors to draw out important differences between spiritual and physical health when meditating upon his mortality and the afterlife. For example, Donne compared his physicians to sailors who, navigating through the 'sea' of his illness, searched for a sign in the 'clouds', which would indicate when the long and tempestuous voyage was nearing its end. Here, the word 'cloud' clearly alluded to the medieval devotional and mystical text, *The Cloud of Unknowing*, written some time during the mid-fourteenth century, but referred also to the 'outward' appearances of Donne's physical symptoms: those fevered 'vapours' and 'clouds' that his physicians were busily scrutinizing to determine the extent of his illness.

Meditating upon a tempestuous voyage that was literal rather than metaphorical, Wesley concluded that to all 'outward' appearances he was a good Christian. He believed in the Gospels and engaged in acts of charity, the latter of which, he argued, were a practical outworking of faith via good works. Yet during the storm Wesley had also asked himself 'what if the Gospel be not true? Then thou art of all men most foolish':

For what has thou given thy goods, thy ease, thy friends, thy reputation, thy country, thy life? For what art thou wandering over the face of the earth? A dream, a cunningly devised fable? O who will deliver me from this fear of death! What shall I do? Where shall I fly from it?[5]

This, Wesley lamented a few days later, was the sum total of all he had learnt on his travels to 'the ends of the earth'. Deeply troubled by this thought, but advised to 'be still, and go on', Wesley embraced the doubts and fears crystallized by his stormy experience as a necessary cross he had to bear – a burden, he hoped, that would quicken his resolve to do good works in a spirit of humility and, aided by unceasing prayer, lead to greater spiritual enlightenment. The storm had highlighted the extent of his shortcomings, which was that yawning gap between things as they really are, and the demand God places upon us as Christians living in the Spirit. Currently, Wesley remarked, he had only the faith of a servant and not a son. But Wesley wanted 'that faith which St Paul recommends to all the world, especially in his epistle to the Romans; that faith which enables every one that hath it to cry out "I live not; but Christ liveth in me; and the life which I now live, I live by faith in the Son of God, who loved me, and gave himself for me"'.[6] Those who had this faith were fully reconciled to God through Christ. As such, in spite of life's storms and travails, they were freed from the sickening 'sin of fear'.

Wesley's oft-cited 'Aldersgate' conversion experience, which, of course, took place several months later in May this same year, had a profound impact on the way he regarded his trip to Georgia, but also those spiritual agonies he endured whilst on board the *Samuel*. These thoughts were recorded and published in the immediate aftermath of the fierce theological rush and spiritual glow of Aldersgate. A great deal of scholarship has devoted much time and attention to tracking these developments, usually by way of ascertaining whether or not Wesley's conversion experience represented a decisive and radical break from his inherited High Church Anglicanism. Fear of sailing into choppy or even stormy waters on this subject means that, for now, we will put these scholarly debates to one side, not least because Henry D. Rack has summarized this period of Wesley's life so well:

> If the retrospect after his conversion led him to believe that he had never had faith in God, never been a Christian, the more exactly contemporary reflections, though troubled and severe enough, suggest something less clear-cut theologically, but more practical and experimental. What haunted him was the fact that he had only a fair-weather religion, and the fear in storms had not in fact been dispelled. He persisted in his discipline and the ideal of complete dedication of life and thoughts and feelings, but felt he lacked peace of mind in face of trouble, danger or emotional disturbances.[7]

Wesley's lack of peace, both in mind and spirit, led him to think that he was deficient in faith. This, Rack observes, was exaggerated until it finally mutated into a notion that he had no faith at all. The Moravian teachings Wesley encountered during and after his missionary trip to Georgia had already exposed the inadequacy of a purely 'rational', intellectual faith, which needed to be more personal or 'inward'. This 'inward' religion should also be accompanied by assurance, something, Rack says, that Wesley realized he was without.

In this respect, the missionary trip to Georgia, followed by the terrible storm on board the *Samuel*, were important events in developing his theological understanding of Primitive Christianity and its practical application.[8] Georgia, in fact, was an experience that tested, through a lived experiment, the extent, but also the limits, of those early Christian ideals expounded by the Methodist Holy Club in Oxford. As Rack remarks, this 'primitive' and 'natural' habitat, which, by turns, was also a difficult and inhospitable environment, served as a 'theatre' for individual piety – a life of piety that frequently threw man back upon his 'naked self', forcing him to confront 'inward problems', thus offering a 'disturbing challenge' and reminding him of what he lacked. For the Christian, as Wesley became painfully aware on board the *Samuel*, these trials and tribulations needed to be cherished, like treasure, as the challenge involved brought man closer to God and could, by steady degrees, lead to a truly holy (whole) and happy (sinless) state of perfection – as it was in the beginning, before the slow, languid poison of original sin had worked its pernicious influence. Wesley states in the 'Preface' to his medical manual, *Primitive Physic* (1747), that man first came out of the Creator's hands, 'clothed in body as well as in soul, with immortality and incorruption'. In this state of sinless perfection, there was no place for physic or the art of healing.[9]

When sailing on the stormy seas of life, a deeply committed 'inward' faith in God was the only secure ship that could be relied upon; those who 'abide in the ship' (Acts 27:31) would be brought to safe ground. The affliction of original sin, in the form of doubt (spiritual malaise), fear (mental illness), or sickness (bodily disease), meant that people should try to find refuge in God's ark or ship. As Donne reminded himself during his fever, 'in this sea, in sickness, thy ship is thy physician'. This ark was God's 'seal' or promise, which had saved the world from drowning, indicated not in 'clouds' or 'vapours', but in a rainbow.[10] If there was risk of drowning at sea, however, water, the elixir of life on earth and, as indicated in *Primitive Physic*, a panacea for so many physical ills, could also provide a powerful remedy for sin in the form of baptism. The water of baptism was a living (divine) element that initiated Christians into the Church, bonding them to the body of Christ, which necessitated spiritual well-being. Furthermore, Methodism was a movement that sought to bring a new influx of living waters into the dry channels of Britain's established Church and, in doing so, hoped to revive its Spirit by drawing this precious element from the original source, which could sustain inspiration and spiritual nourishment.

This nourishment, or 'inward' faith, equated to spiritual equilibrium, which also had a bearing on the physical health of mind and body. In his 'Sermon on Original Sin' (1759) Wesley asked followers to call on 'the great physician of souls', who could apply his efficacious medicine to heal the sickness caused by our first parents. This medicine would restore human nature 'in all its faculties'; through Christ, our 'whole sickness', spiritual, emotional and physical, would be healed with human beings returning to their pristine state. When writing to his friend, Alexander Knox, who was suffering from melancholia, Wesley thought it was crucially important to give the following advice: 'it will be a double blessing if you give yourself up to the Great Physician, that He may heal soul and body together. And unquestionably this is His design. He wants to give you . . . both inward and outward health.'[11] In this context taking due care of the body and 'outward' health also became a spiritual act of vindication; looking after God's exquisitely wrought machine demonstrated the true wisdom and beauty of God's creation. This exquisitely wrought machine was merely on loan until that time when God judged it best to resurrect the whole of humankind at the end of our temporal existence.

Emphasis in *Primitive Physic* upon looking after the body and preventing illness by a sensible or moderate regimen shows that Wesley did not simply spiritualize disease. It was, in fact, essential for the sick to follow the very best medical advice available. As I suggest in Chapter 3, *Primitive Physic* was a manual designed to help the labouring poor stave off disease by regulating their lifestyle through regimen, as well as self-medicating safely when they became sick. This testifies to a rationally verifiable empirical method for treating illness, which was fully conversant with Georgian medical practice. The remedies listed in *Primitive Physic* can be traced to contemporary 'orthodox' medical sources and Wesley was not merely peddling 'kitchen-physic' recipes from a bygone era. His empirical, experimental method sought to restore an 'ancient standard' in physic, which was also the intellectual corollary to those trials and tribulations faced by Christians as they struggled for spiritual wholeness in a post-lapsarian world. Wesley's practical treatment and Christian compassion when treating the deathly distress of 'consumption', for example, therefore provides an extremely useful heuristic device for a fuller understanding of his enlightened medical holism. Wesley's recovery of an ancient empirical standard, combined with an integrated approach to treatment and patient care are, I think, potentially valuable tools for clinicians, governments and aid agencies today when attempting to deal with the alarming numbers of individuals dying of tuberculosis in sub-Saharan countries.

Viewing nature with one eye firmly fixed on the eternal realm means 'seeing' or 'blind seeing' the presence of God in every aspect of the material world. As Laura Bartels Felleman suggests in Chapter 4, rather than simply relying on the physical senses or outward appearances to alert them to things that seem good, Christians like Wesley focus on developing their 'spiritual sense', which they use to 'discern what has lasting, eternal value'. Wesley, she argues, taught that the sanctified regulated their will so that its actions were perfectly consistent with this spiritual sense: 'as long as the Methodists followed a regimen that kept the avenues of their souls open and clear, Wesley expressed optimism that they would enjoy spiritual health forever'.[12] Wesley's concept of the supernatural, divine and invisible realm as a means of comprehending healing sprang from current medical theories about the body–soul connection that were elaborated by the physician George Cheyne. Bartels Felleman suggests that when tracking this 'necessary' relationship, however, Wesley stopped short of conflating their interdependence altogether. In her careful reading of Wesley's *Thoughts Upon Necessity* (1774), she conveys the complexity of his natural philosophy, depicting a theologian who reflected contemporary medical science in his belief that the operations of the human soul correlated with the functioning of the brain and nervous system, but who, in the end, did not believe that this interrelationship proved beyond doubt that the human will was necessarily determined by bodily functions.

Unlike the practice of following a rationalized mode or regimen for physical health and long life, regulating the will was not something that could be worked out intellectually. A spiritual sense, which is discerned by the soul and felt in the heart, flows through faith and is fuelled by love: God can only be truly 'known' through love. Attention to this spiritual sense produced the fruits of faith, which, in turn, leads to humility and charity. This 'holistic' vision of salvation encompassed the whole of God's creation. Moreover, acknowledgement of nature's divine author means that human beings are just guardians, custodians or caretakers of the world's natural resources. As Randy L. Maddox points out in a recently published article, Wesley's emphasis upon God's care of the whole creation – and our calling to participate in this care – was not tangential to his interests, but central to his intellectual and theological convictions.[13] In Chapter 2 Margaret G. Flowers sees how Wesley envisioned enlightened Christians using their spiritual senses to respect this divinely created order, with its carefully calibrated and richly variegated habitats, vegetation, ecological systems and animals. In *Survey of the Wisdom of God in the Creation* (1763), Wesley's microscopic examination of the planet's flora and fauna, with its manifold developments, illustrates how his concept of environmental change fits into a theological framework of salvation that breathes life into St Paul's image of the creation groaning and travailing in pain (Romans 8:22).

Flowers also provides a very convincing case for representing Wesley's ideas concerning environmental stewardship to ecologists and Christians today. By reconciling scriptural authority with Georgian scientific thinking, Wesley's intellectually rigorous but delicate balance of competing interests can speak to modern ecologists, scientists and Christians working in their respective academic communities. This approach would also help Christians across the political spectrum in the United States to take a theologically irenic stance, while transcending their distrust of a scientific community that has historically excluded them from making valuable interventions on issues concerning the environment. This exclusion can be directly attributed to the longstanding tension or 'conflict' between science and religion, a clash that has, in recent years, been exposed by scholars like John Hedley Brooke, David C. Lindberg and Ronald L. Numbers, as being more apparent than real. The 'conflict', originally documented in Andrew Dickson White's *History of the Warfare of Science with Theology in Christendom* (1896), and picked up again by Lynn White Jr's article 'The Historical Roots of our Ecological Crisis' (1967), which was featured in the prestigious journal *Science*, continues to set the tone for current environmental debates. Andrew Dickson White's disregard for Wesley's theology and Lynn White Jr's scathing denunciation of western Christianity as the cause of ecological crisis have found much support in the scientific community.

Flowers notes that Christians, on the other hand, have been sharply divided, not only on the issue of whether the Church has been complicit in environmental degradation, but also regarding the need for environmental stewardship. At the heart of this debate, she says, is a scientific demand for concrete, verifiable data in the fields of ecology and environmental studies. By contrast, there is often suspicion or wholesale rejection of scientific findings in some quarters of the Christian community because of its perceived 'liberal' agenda and non-Christian affiliations among those making up the environmental movement. Flowers outlines the debate between science and faith, drawing attention to the fact that little mention has been made of Wesley's theoretical or practical writings on environmental stewardship. This, she says, might usefully serve as a critical bridge between scientific and faith communities. Looking specifically at the ethically loaded issue of environmental stewardship, Flowers dismantles the thesis which pits science against faith by identifying how Wesley used a practically oriented scientific method to understand and appreciate God's created order. One of Wesley's greatest strengths, Flowers argues, was to negotiate those 'big' scientific questions of his day, without undermining biblical precepts or religious beliefs.

Wesley's concept of salvation was all-encompassing, though its practical effect in the form of charitable works was focused primarily on the missionary impulse to save the souls of human beings. Empathy for the physical, psychological and spiritual suffering of others brought one's own earthly mortality into consideration while strengthening sacred bonds with God – the bell that rings out for the deathly affliction of another also rings out for our own. Maddox sees how the High Church Arminian strains of Wesley's theology, which rejected Calvinism, saw him emphasize, along with other Anglicans such as Bishop Gilbert Burnet, medical care as part of his pastoral tasks.[14] Wesley's holistic understanding of salvation took him, in fact, to the very heart of human anguish. He spoke out against slavery, campaigned for prison reform and gave alms – as well as medicines – to the poor. As this volume amply demonstrates, Wesley's concept of nature and the environment, which underpinned his active participation in medical science, sprang from this holistic framework of holy living, but also, as Robert Webster shows in Chapter 6, of holy dying.

The important place of prayer and supernatural healing when all medical techniques and powers had been tried and tested is, as Webster sees it, an inviolable Wesleyan and Methodist principle. It is for this reason, he argues, that Wesley's view and use of prayer for healing should be given more serious scholarly consideration. For Wesley, the relationship between body and soul highlighted an important intersection of visible and invisible realms of existence. Orthodox medicine was always complemented by prayer and joined too with other religious disciplines, such as fasting and receiving the Eucharist, which, Wesley insisted, produced powerfully healing results. Webster suggests that Wesley saw prayer as a means of accessing a divine energy when rational medical techniques were no longer viable. Throughout the Methodist literature of this period followers testified to the success of using prayer as a means to complete health and wholeness. This was used, not only in death-bed healings like that of John Pawson, which Wesley recorded in his extremely successful *Arminian Magazine*, but also in documented exorcisms and supernatural or 'miraculous' restorative healings. The dispensing of medicines after Society meetings, with the application of electrical healings on preaching tours, was combined with the use of prayer to cure the infirm – all of which, Webster argues, fits into a symbiotic understanding of human nature and divine grace. Wesley's supernatural healing, he says, took place 'within a grid that embraced a polyvalent hermeneutic for understanding the means of grace'.[15]

When Wesley successfully managed to integrate the latest medical and scientific discoveries into his overall spiritual and theological mission, there is little doubt that he regarded this as a personal triumph. Evidence of this can be seen in his repeated endorsement of other pietistic endeavours that were medically and scientifically grounded – practitioners and experimenters he referred to as 'lovers of Mankind'. A more concrete example, however, can be seen in the obvious personal satisfaction Wesley gained from his own experiments with electricity, which, as Linda S. Schwab observes, was driven by a concern for universal access to an inexpensive, non-invasive form of medical treatment. In Chapter 5 Schwab re-evaluates some of the scholarly misconceptions that have grown out of Wesley's scientific work, *The Desideratum: Or, Electricity Made Plain and Useful* (1760). Schwab sees how almost all of the available studies examining Wesley's *Desideratum* focus on its relationship with the medical practice of its day. She suggests, however, that it is equally important to understand its setting in the context of electrical research and technology.[16]

Schwab argues, far from dismissing the philosophical and scientific considerations of electricity, or being opposed to theory because of a lack of interest in mathematics, Wesley clearly commented on the state of electrical research, which he believed was still dogged by many inexplicable observations. That Wesley did not dismiss theory in favour of practice is obvious, Schwab says, when reading the main body of *The Desideratum*. She is also keen to challenge the 'persistent and critical misunderstanding' of Wesley's experiments here; namely, that the only useful application of electricity in medicine was electro-convulsive therapy (ECT), used primarily for psychiatric illnesses. She argues instead that the recent growth of electrotherapy for disorders associated with the peripheral nervous system should set *The Desideratum* in a new context that is worth exploring in more depth.

Anyone reading Wesley's medical and scientific works, but also his journals, diaries and letters, quickly realizes that he fully embraced the daily realities of flesh and blood existence. The explicitly missionary content of charitable Methodist works means that although there was nothing programmatic about his theology, Wesley did provide followers with a compellingly straightforward moral compass, which helped them to navigate their way through high and low tides; steering hitherto lost souls in the right direction whilst promising always to reveal paradise waiting at journey's end. This compass was an essential prerequisite for making those necessary moral readjustments when coping with the crosscurrents of sin and temptation, but also with worldly attacks in the form of scorn, criticism and even physical violence. A useful example of how Wesley himself responded to sectarian, political and *ad hominem* attacks can be seen in the way he handled contemporary criticism of his medical interests. In Chapter 1, Maddox traces the development of this criticism, noting too Wesley's strategy for fending off attacks in an age when medicine was becoming increasingly professionalized.

The ghosts of critics past have continued to haunt modern scholarship and an important feature of this volume's significance lies in the fact that Maddox's detailed investigation of the reception, influence and legacy of Wesley's engagement with medicine, science and natural philosophy – a hitherto neglected area. Maddox examines the historiography of Wesley's medical and scientific practice, looking at the distorted caricatures, but also those attempts early in the twentieth century to rehabilitate his influence, while providing a survey of the scholarly work in this field that has taken place in very recent years. Indeed, for anyone wishing to have an entrée into Wesley's medical interests as a whole, Maddox's bibliography highlights the rich and eclectic nature of this research to date. Maddox places Wesley's consuming passion for medicine and natural philosophy into its historical context, showing how his publications and other efforts in these areas were 'deeply congruent with his understanding of God's mission of truly holistic healing'. Following the historiographcial fortunes of Wesley's medical activity within the ecclesial tradition he founded, Maddox reveals how its reception is largely one of non-acknowledgement or embarrassed dismissal. He sees several factors contributing to these reactions, including the emergence of disciplinary specialization within science and medicine itself and, as a result of this, the role of populist sentiments in North American Methodism.

Changes in Enlightenment historiography, combined with eighteenth-century studies conducted by social, cultural, or socio-cultural historians of medicine and science, particularly that which contains a New Historicist inflexion, have been extremely valuable for developing methodological tools to deepen our understanding of John Wesley's complex theology, but also the historical specificity of his medical and scientific knowledge – the context in which this knowledge emerged, and how it changed over time. With emphasis now upon the equality of historical discourses, social and cultural historians of medicine have long since identified different dynamic contexts in which a variety of individuals, 'professional', 'lay' and 'quack', take an active role in medical practice. These scholars have searched for meaning well beyond the core of established medical orthodoxy, looking for answers in 'marginal' texts, or discursive practices operating at the fringe of society – practices hitherto neglected by traditional historiographies of medicine.[17] Examining medical and scientific texts in the context of their own specific vocabularies promises to uncover, as John Hedley Brooke suggested some time ago, interesting and surprising relationships between apparently conflicting discourses in the past.[18] Wesley's medical and scientific interests, which relied heavily upon a thriving commercialized intellectual print culture, are therefore not anomalous or extraordinary; they reflect the views of a controversial religious figure who, in many ways, personifies many of the Enlightenment's contradictions.

Despite the enormous changes that have taken place in Enlightenment historiography, both generally and also within the sub-disciplines of histories of medicine and science, John Wesley continues to be represented as an irrational religious leader who spiritualized healing and peddled 'home-made' folk remedies or 'simples' for his Methodist followers. Moreover, attention to the purely populist strains of his medical and scientific works obscures a rich variety of sources, which not only sought to meet the immediate practical needs of its readership, but reflected in several significant theological and intellectual debates.[19] This volume deals with an important subject that has been neglected by scholars of eighteenth-century history, religion and medicine; taken together, these essays convincingly correct a persistent view of Wesley as an irresponsible religious 'enthusiast' who confused medicine and theology. The reader here is given instead a picture of someone who was a critical admirer of Enlightenment principles: a deeply pious individual who could minister to the physical and spiritual welfare of the poor, applying remedies for the body or prayer for the soul when appropriate.

The aim of this volume is threefold. Its first objective is to correct an enduringly stubborn caricature of Wesley as an anti-Enlightenment, anti-science theologian. This view, despite recent scholarship to the contrary, still persists amongst scholars and, as Maddox shows in his chapter, within the Christian tradition that Wesley actually founded. The second objective here is to collate and publish the research and scholarship undertaken by those wanting to modify this caricature. There has, in the last decade, been something of an upsurge of interest in Wesley's medical and scientific activity with a number of scholars, including the contributors to this volume, publishing a steady stream of articles and chapter-length studies on the topic. Currently, however, there is no edited volume of scholarly essays which can address those issues concerning academics working in this burgeoning field. Contributors to this volume wish to respond to these changes by opening fresh lines of enquiry. In this sense, the volume is also particularly well placed to complement a forthcoming critical edition of the entire corpus of Wesley's medical work. This corpus, co-edited by Randy L. Maddox and James G. Donat, is part of the Bicentennial Edition of the Works of John Wesley and is due for publication in the United States in 2008. The chapters collected in this volume reflect certain historiographical changes in mood-music and methodology that have taken place in recent years, whilst also examining these developments in their larger historical framework.

Wesley's medical and scientific practices are easily located in the religious and medical context of European enlightened thought. However, contemporary themes and resonances are explored here to cast fresh perspectives on issues that Wesley faced, but which also continue to confront us today. The third aim of this volume involves acknowledging the practical force of Wesley's intellectual knowledge and Christian piety. Our work in this collection, if it is to show fidelity to Wesley's practically engaged holism, cannot remain a purely theoretical project. Any analysis of the intellectual underpinnings of Wesley's practical piety must respond to his call for worldly action. Wesley posed uncomfortable questions about the medical, scientific and political practices of Georgian England – questions still relevant for us today. Indeed, it is precisely where medical, scientific, technological, political and socio-economic agendas are kept discrete that there is most need for the strength of Wesley's holistic vision. Contemporary western culture places the preservation of life, the population's health and safety, at the core of its secular value-system. Yet, in adopting a limited, partial view of human life, western culture often falls short of this very aim. As a pastor and physician Wesley recognized the importance of treating body and soul – the whole person. People today remember Wesley mainly for saving souls. Often forgotten is the fact that he also saved lives by offering accessible, cost-effective remedies for curing diseases of the flesh. Wesley's concept of the universal nature of salvation – an event that saved all of mankind – meant that he expressed joyful hope and anticipation for the new creation, while embracing the restive grief of a diseased, fallen world.

Notes

1 John Donne, 'A Hymn to God the Father' (1623), III, 13–18, in John Carey ed., *The Oxford Authors: John Donne*, Oxford, Oxford University Press, 1990, p. 333; Wesley, *Sermon on Original Sin* (1759), in *Works*, vol. 2, pp. 172–85 at pp. 184, 185.

2 Wesley, *The Journal of the Rev John Wesley* (4 vols, London, 1827), 13 January 1756, vol. 1, p. 68.

3 Wesley, *Journal*, 13 January 1738, vol. 1, pp. 69–70.

4 Wesley, *Journal*, 13 January 1738, vol. 1, p. 69.

5 Wesley, *Journal*, 13 January 1738, vol. 1, p. 69.

6 Wesley, *Journal*, 13 January 1738, vol. 1, pp. 71–72.

7 The best and most succinct summary of these debates remains Henry D. Rack's classic intellectual and theological biography, *Reasonable Enthusiast: John Wesley and the Rise of Methodism*, 1989, 2nd edn, London, Epworth, 1992, pp. 97, 133–6, 146–7.

8 There is a wealth of scholarship which charts and examines this development. For a shortcut see Rack, but also L.L. Keefer, 'John Wesley: Disciple of Early Christianity', *Wesleyan Theological Journal* 19 (1984), pp. 23–32 and Ted Campbell, *John Wesley and Christian Antiquity: Religious Vision and Cultural Change*, Nashville, Kingswood Books, 1991.

9 Wesley, *Primitive Physic*, 1747, 24th edn, London, 1792, p. iii.

10 Donne, 'Expostulation', XIX Meditation in *Devotions Upon Emergent Occasions* (1623) in Carey ed., *The Oxford Authors. John Donne*, p. 349.

11 'Letter to Alexander Knox, 26 Oct. 1778', in *Letters* (Telford), vol. 6, p. 327.

12 Laura Bartels Felleman, 'A Necessary Relationship: John Wesley on the Body–Soul Connection' (Chapter 4).

13 Randy L. Maddox, 'Anticipating the New Creation: Wesleyan Foundations for Holistic Mission', *Asbury Journal* 69 (2007), pp. 49–66, 52.

14 Randy L. Maddox, 'Reclaiming the Eccentric Parent: Methodist Reception of John Wesley's Interest in Medicine' (Chapter 1).

15 Robert Webster, 'Health of Soul and Health of Body: The Supernatural Dimensions of Healing in John Wesley' (Chapter 6).

16 James G. Donat's 'John Wesley on the Estimation and Cure of Nervous Disorders' also casts fresh perspectives on this. See his chapter in Harry Whitaker, C. U. M. Smith and Stanley Finger eds, *Brain, Mind and Medicine: Essays in Eighteenth-Century Neuroscience*, New York, Springer-Verlag, 2007, pp. 285–300.

17 For a summary of this historiography see Deborah Madden, 'Medicine, Science and Intellectual History', in R. Whatmore and B. Young eds., *Palgrave Advances: Intellectual History*, Basingstoke, Palgrave Macmillan, 2006, pp. 147–70.

18 John Hedley Brooke, *Science and Religion: Some Historical Perspectives*, Cambridge, Cambridge University Press, 1991.

19 For a corrective to this tendency see Deborah Madden, '"A Cheap, Safe and Natural Medicine": Religion, Medicine and Culture in John Wesley's *Primitive Physic*', *Clio Medica* 83, Amsterdam and New York, Rodopi, 2007.

Reclaiming the Eccentric Parent:
Methodist Reception of John Wesley's Interest in Medicine

RANDY L. MADDOX[1]

We had rather to sit at the feet of the venerable
Wesley as a divine, than as a teacher of physic.

So opined John Stamp in 1845 in the *Wesleyan Methodist Magazine*, after mentioning in a memoir of Charles Atmore some medical advice that Atmore had received from John Wesley.[2] Stamp was a leading minister in this largest branch of the British church, eventually serving as President of Conference. As such, we can expect that his sentiment was common among his peers. Yet his comment is likely to mystify readers in the early twenty-first century on several levels. To follow his contrast, we need first to recognize that 'divine' was the current term for a clergyman, while a 'teacher of physic' offered advice on medical treatments for specific ailments and on general practices for promoting health. At that point, many will wonder why anyone would have considered sitting at the feet of Wesley, the Anglican priest turned leader in the Methodist renewal movement, as a teacher of physic. By contrast, those who are aware of the prominence of medical advice in Wesley's writings might well wonder how this came to be considered eccentric so soon after his death. The present essay will summarize Wesley's emphasis on offering health advice and care, then explore in more detail how this emphasis was called into question and increasingly viewed with embarrassment or disdain, turning finally to a brief overview of the recovered appreciation among Wesley's heirs for this dimension of his ministry and its precedent for contemporary mission.

Centrality of Wesley's Ministry of Health Advice and Care

Recent scholarship has demonstrated that offering health advice and care was a central dimension of Wesley's ministry and of his model for the ministry of early Methodists.[3] For those who find this surprising, it is helpful to recall that study of basic medicine had become part of the training of Anglican clergy candidates in the seventeenth century. In the small villages that dominated England's landscape the priest was often the most educated person in residence. Thus it was a common expectation for priests to be able to offer informed advice about treatment of ailments and promotion of health as part of their overall ministry.

In keeping with this expectation, we know from sources like the diary that Wesley began at Oxford of several medical treatises that he purchased and/or read between 1724 and 1732. Diary entries for 1736, when Wesley was serving as a missionary priest in Georgia, show continued reading of medical texts, including one by John Tennent that focused on medicinal herbs that were available in North America. Similar reading continued through Wesley's life and included consultation of the *Philosophical Transactions* of the Royal Society and the *Medical Transactions* of the Royal College of Physicians.

While Wesley's Oxford studies prepared him to offer basic medical advice, his active ministry overlapped a period when the Royal College of Physicians in London was making efforts to monitor certification of medical practitioners. Clergy joined apothecaries, barber-surgeons, and various 'quacks' as groups targeted for exclusion. Like most in the other groups, Wesley resisted the suggestion that he should refrain from offering medical guidance, leaving it to those certified by the College.[4] But his motive for resisting was not to protect a source of income; it was grounded instead in his holistic understanding of salvation.

One of Wesley's deepest theological convictions was that the mediocrity of moral life and the ineffectiveness in social impact of Christians in eighteenth-century England could be traced to an inadequate understanding of salvation assumed broadly in the church. The root of this inadequacy, and the core of Wesley's alternative understanding, can be seen in his most pointed definition of salvation:

By salvation I mean, not barely (according to the vulgar notion) deliverance from hell, or going to heaven, but a present deliverance from sin, a restoration of the soul to its primitive health . . . the renewal of our souls after the image of God in righteousness and true holiness, in justice, mercy, and truth.[5]

The notion that Wesley was rejecting here reduces salvation to forgiveness of our guilt as sinners, which frees us from future condemnation. Wesley consistently encouraged his followers and contemporaries to seek the benefits of *truly holistic salvation*, where God's forgiveness of sin is interwoven with God's gracious healing of the damages that sin has wrought.[6] The scope of the healing that Wesley invited all to expect is captured well in pastoral letters, like his reminder to Alexander Knox: 'It will be a double blessing if you give yourself up to the Great Physician, that He may heal soul and body together. And unquestionably this is His design. He wants to give you . . . both inward and outward health.'[7]

While most Christians shared the conviction that God would provide full healing of body and spirit at the resurrection, Wesley's emphasis on the degree to which *both* dimensions of divine healing can be experienced *in the present* was less common. This is evident concerning the spiritual dimension even within the Methodist revival, where the Calvinist branch of the movement rejected Wesley's emphasis on Christian perfection, insisting that we can hope for only limited transformation of our fallen spiritual nature in this life. The assumption that we should expect only limited expression in this life of God's ministry to our bodies was more widespread, but it is notable that resistance to suggestions that clergy include medical care as part of their ministry in the English church during the reign of James I (1603–25) also came from the most Calvinist voices in the church. These objectors urged that labour for the souls of their parishioners, by preaching and counselling, should fill the full time of the pastor.[8] In contrast, the more Arminian 'high-church' voices, which gained in strength after 1625, elevated a model where, in addition to reverent leadership in defined times of regular worship, clergy were expected to spend a significant part of their time in ministries of good works – like offering medical advice and care – among the needy in their parish.[9]

As one who embraced the high-church Anglicanism of his upbringing, Wesley also embraced this holistic model of the pastoral office. When he accepted the offer to go to Georgia, one of his first concerns was to study physic 'properly' in preparation for his work as a parish priest.[10] On returning from Georgia, Wesley was drawn into leading a widely scattered spiritual renewal movement, never to serve as a parish priest again. He brought his pastoral heart to this leadership role and was quick to discern the paucity of holistic care in most parishes as he travelled around England and Wales. In addition to preaching in every locale he travelled through, Wesley also frequently offered medical advice to those with ailments whom he encountered. But he could not rest content with this haphazard approach for meeting either the spiritual or physical needs of those who responded to his call to renewal. So Wesley began gathering the laity who embraced the renewal movement into local support networks (called 'societies'), and he began seeking a more systematic means of offering care for the sick within these networks.

The Dimensions of Wesley's Ministry of Health Advice and Care

As an initial foray in providing care for the sick, in 1741 Wesley selected members within each society in London, instructing them to check regularly on the sick in their group and offer assistance.[11] This office of 'visitor of the sick' was formalized for all of the societies connected with the Wesley brothers at the first annual conference held for the connection in 1744; those holding the office were charged to visit sick members in their area three times a week, to inquire into the state of their souls and their bodies, and to offer or procure advice for them in both regards.[12] This special office supplemented the more general expectation of *all* Methodists to visit the sick as one of their ways of 'doing good' to *all* persons.[13]

In 1745, at the second annual conference, the lay preachers who assisted Wesley in riding around the connection, providing pastoral oversight of the societies, were instructed to visit the sick regularly as well.[14] The role envisioned for travelling lay preachers went beyond that of the local visitor of the sick; they were not just to *procure* medical advice, they were to be ready to *dispense* advice. Accordingly, the independent course of study for lay preachers (who generally lacked any university education) assigned at the 1745 annual conference included appropriate medical texts.[15] Wesley was clearly trying to expand his reach in offering the holistic care of the pastoral office within the Methodist movement. From this point, the ideal was that his lay assistants would not only preach and offer spiritual direction, but also be able to offer medical and health advice routinely.[16]

At the same time, Wesley recognized that even the most studious lay preachers would have a limited range of medical knowledge, while the local visitors of the sick might have little at all. So the third prong in his strategy for more systematic health advice in the movement was to publish a distillation of his study in this area. The earliest venture in this regard was a small pamphlet that was also released in 1745 – a *Collection of Receits* (or prescriptions) for some of the most common health ailments.[17] This pamphlet sold for 2 pence, so that it could be accessible to the poor.[18] The *Collection* was expanded in 1747 into the first edition of the *Primitive Physic*, which now sold for a shilling.[19] While this work is still occasionally dismissed as consisting of folklore prescriptions, current scholarship is demonstrating that, through its 23 editions during his life, Wesley drew a significant number of his treatments from standard texts of medical advice, including such authors as Hermann Boerhaave, Kenelm Digby, Thomas Dover, John Huxham, Richard Mead, Lazarus Riverius, Thomas Short, Thomas Sydenham, and Thomas Willis.[20] This recognition suggests that *Primitive Physic* should be seen as a parallel to Wesley's 50-volume *Christian Library*. In both cases he was distilling the fruits of broad reading for the benefit of his Methodist people.

In late 1746 Wesley felt compelled to attempt an even broader foray into providing medical advice and care for those among whom he was ministering; he opened perhaps the first free dispensary in London, dedicated particularly to those with the most limited financial resources.[21] As he described this decision later:

> I was still in pain for many of the poor that were sick: there was so great expense, and so little profit . . . I saw the poor people pining away, and several families ruined, and that without remedy. At length I thought of a kind of desperate expedient. 'I will prepare, and give them physic myself' . . . I took into my assistance an apothecary, and an experienced surgeon; resolving at the same time not to go out of my depth, but to leave all difficult and complicated cases to such physicians as the patients should choose. I gave notice of this to the society; telling them that all who were ill of *chronical* distempers (for I did not care to venture upon *acute*) might, if they pleased, come to me at such a time; and I would give them the best advice I could, and the best medicines I had.[22]

Within a few years Wesley found the expenses of running such a dispensary too great for his limited resources. But his decision to close it was not a retreat from concern to provide physic for the poor. Rather, this concern was channelled into frequent republication of the *Primitive Physic* at a price at which he hoped it could be afforded by every family.[23] He also published several other works related to maintaining or restoring health, including *A Letter to a Friend Concerning Tea* (1748); *The Desideratum, or Electricity Made Plain and Useful* (1760); *Thoughts on the Sin of Onan, chiefly extracted from [Tissot]* (1767); *Advices with Respect to Health, extracted from [Tissot]* (1769); 'Extract from [William] Cadogan on the Gout' (1774); and *An Estimate of the Manners of Present Times* (1782).[24]

These various programmatic efforts demonstrate that provision of health advice and care was a central element of Wesley's ministry. He strove to help his followers see that participation in God's present saving work involved nurturing both their souls and bodies, and addressing both as they reached out to others in mission. The remaining point to develop in this section is that, just as Wesley's commitment to care for the body was grounded in his conviction of the holistic nature of salvation, his suggested manner of caring for the body sought holistic balance.

The Balanced Character of Wesley's Health Advice and Care[25]

In the first place, Wesley refused to counterpose divine healing and medical healing. He was convinced of the possibility of miraculous healing, and highlighted apparent instances in his publications – partly to rebut deism.[26] But he rejected suggestions of the spiritual superiority of relying on divine healing alone. Even a brief perusal of Wesley's correspondence will show how quickly he encouraged medical treatments. Of course, he could characteristically add: 'as God is the sovereign disposer of all things . . . I earnestly advise every one, together with all other medicines, to use the medicine of medicines – prayer.'[27]

A second characteristic of Wesley's health advice and care is its appreciation for points of interconnection between physical health and emotional/spiritual health. Drawing on figures like George Cheyne, over the course of his life Wesley began to counter the dualistic tendencies present in strands of both Christian tradition and Enlightenment culture.[28]

Moving to a third dimension, Wesley's health advice was not limited to treatments for ailments; he placed strong emphasis upon measures like diet, exercise, and rest to prevent illness and promote well-being. If readers find this emphasis surprising, it is because the explosion of new knowledge and skills in surgical interventions and medications through the twentieth century tended to eclipse an earlier tradition that balanced such interventions with counselling people how to live in accordance with nature by proper diet and exercise, both to restore health and to retain it. Current emphasis on wellness and preventive medicine is best seen not as a new trajectory but as part of the recovery from this eclipse.

Turning to his specific prescriptions for ailments, Wesley's health advice is marked by strong preference for common plants and roots over chemical, exotic, and artificial compound medicines. On this point he was swimming against the stream of emerging professional medicine and is sometimes portrayed as a counter-champion of natural or 'alternative' medicine. But this contrast must not be overdrawn. It is true that Wesley offers some theological rationale for preferring the 'natural' cures that God has placed in creation. But he was also quick to cite current medical authorities for this preference. Moreover, while *Primitive Physic* focused on self-help advice, Wesley comments on several ailments that the best advice was to consult a good physician. This suggests an ideal of balancing natural and professional medical treatment.

This is not to deny that Wesley had concerns about 'professional' physicians in his time. In part, he worried that many unnecessarily protracted the cure of patients' bodies in order to derive the maximum fee, which is why he stressed finding 'honest' or 'God-fearing' physicians. A deeper worry undergirded his resistance to restricting authority for offering medical advice to those approved by the Royal College of Physicians. In 1746, as Wesley was gearing up his initiatives in health care, there were only 80 fellows and licentiates on the College's catalogue, a ratio of about 1 to 10,000 for London alone. Perhaps the most defining characteristic of Wesley's efforts in health care was his concern to make informed medical advice available for *all* – particularly the poor and those scattered through rural England who had no access to this elite faculty of physicians. As he stressed in a postscript to the preface of *Primitive Physic*, he sought there 'to set down cheap, safe, and easy medicines; easy to be known, easy to be procured, and easy to be applied by plain, unlettered men'.[29] Likewise, a key factor in his enthusiasm for the potential health benefits of electric shock was its broad availability and low cost (anticipating the spread of his inexpensive 'electrifying machine').[30]

Dynamics in the Shifting View of Wesley's Interest in Medicine

In light of the integral role that Wesley assigned to dispensing health advice and care in his ministry and in the initial mission of Methodism, how do we account for the reserve – even embarrassment – about this role among prominent members of the movement Wesley founded (like John Stamp) within a half century of his death?

By the mid-nineteenth century it was commonly assumed that systematic efforts to professionalize medicine in England were initiated in the early part of the eighteenth century, creating a setting of antagonism toward 'amateur' efforts like those of Wesley from the beginning. This assumption lies behind the surprise expressed in 1870 by Luke Tyerman, a Methodist biographer of Wesley, about the apparent lack of significant criticism of *Primitive Physic* over the first three decades of its publication.[31] The assumption continued to appear in scholarly settings into the 1980s. But it has been challenged by more recent studies. It is now generally agreed that a dynamic interplay between 'professional' physicians and lay medical practitioners continued through most of the eighteenth century, with more stringent efforts at asserting a professional monopoly on medicine emerging only in the last quarter of the century.[32] This revised account finds strong support in the example of the changing valuations of Wesley's efforts to provide medical care and advice.

Relative Acceptance through First Three Decades

There was little direct criticism of Wesley's various efforts to provide medical care and advice prior to the last quarter of his century (i.e., through the first three decades of these efforts). To be sure, Anglican opponents characterized the Methodists as 'young quacks in divinity' from the earliest years of the renewal movement.[33] But this was a use of the term in its general sense of 'pretending to knowledge that one does not have', and there is no specific criticism of offering medical advice in these attacks. Indeed, one would be surprised to find such criticism, as this was still an accepted role (even if not widely embraced) for Anglican clergy.[34]

One of the particular accusations aimed at the Methodists was that they were fanatics or 'enthusiasts'. Nathaniel Lancaster framed this attack in his 1767 satirical poem *Methodism Triumphant*, through extended ridicule of the claim of Wesley and others to offer 'ancient remedies' for healing 'distempered souls'.[35] While forceful, Lancaster's ridicule was analogical, focusing on evangelistic practices rather than treatment of physical ills.

Moving a bit closer to our topic, a common evidence cited by Lancaster and others to prove the fanaticism of Methodists was their reliance on *miraculous* healing.[36] But this implied no necessary criticism of the practice of offering *medical* care. Indeed, William Warburton, a bishop and leading critic, mentioned Wesley's embrace of that practice in an (ironic) positive light, suggesting that Wesley took up these efforts merely to demonstrate that he placed more emphasis on 'works' than did George Whitefield – thereby distancing himself from Anglican criticism of Whitefield's preaching of 'free grace'. Warburton also proposed that Wesley drew upon his Oxford training in producing *Primitive Physic* (in principle, apparently, a positive venture) primarily to counter earlier statements that seemed to imply that he disdained human learning.[37]

Developments moved even closer to explicit criticism of Wesley for offering medical advice in the early 1770s, in the context of debate between the Wesleyan and Calvinist Methodists. In 1771 John Fletcher published his *Second Check to Antinomianism*, in which he tried to defend Wesley against the charge of giving inconsistent *spiritual* advice by using the analogy of how a physician might dispense hot medicines to some patients and cool to others, depending on their condition.[38] Richard

Hill, an adamant Calvinist Methodist, challenged the appropriateness of the analogy rather sharply: 'Unless Mr. Fletcher can prove that the ability of the physician may be consistent with him sometimes administering a plentiful dose of hemlock or rats-bane, I fear we cannot allow Mr. Wesley any other title than that of an empiric, or quack doctor.'[39] In his reflections on Hill's response, John Wesley singled out this quote as an example of the ungentlemanly tone of the work.[40] Responding in turn to Wesley, Hill made clear that he was not attacking Wesley for giving medical advice, he was simply playing with Fletcher's analogy for Wesley's spiritual advice. Then Hill extended the analogical critique in a long satirical poem about Wesley as a quack offering spiritual 'nostrums'![41] Whatever the tone of this piece (Hill offered nothing more in this vein), it still did not breach the analogy to criticize Wesley for offering medical advice.

Ulterior Motives in Initial Direct Attacks?[42]

The first clear instance of that breach came in early 1775, from the pen of Augustus Toplady, a more rancorous Calvinist critic of Wesley. In the preface of his response to Wesley's tract *Thoughts upon Necessity*, Toplady drew a direct comparison between the dangers of Wesley's 'spiritual medicines' and a 'quack remedy' that Wesley recommended in the *Primitive Physic* for gout (applying raw beef steak to the part affected). Toplady noted that Dr Edward Townshend, dean of Norwich cathedral, died of gout in 1765, even though he had followed this prescription. While Toplady admitted that he had no evidence Townshend had found the remedy in *Primitive Physic*, he insisted that this instance 'demonstrates the unskillful temerity wherewith the compiler [Wesley] sets himself up as a physician of the body'.[43]

While Toplady was obviously challenging Wesley's qualifications for issuing medical advice, it is also obvious that this was not his primary concern – he invoked the issue in passing, in hopes that it would help discredit Wesley in their ongoing debate over predestination. As 1775 drew to a close, Wesley came under a more fierce attack for another prescription in *Primitive Physic*. He soon became convinced that in this case too the real goal was to discredit his stance on a different topic. I will sketch the running battle (highlighting some key phrases in **bold font**), then return to Wesley's suggestion about the possible ulterior motive.

The onslaught began with a letter to the editor in *The Gazetteer and New Daily Advertiser* in London, published 25 December 1775, by a person using the pseudonym of 'Antidote'.[44] The author mentions 'happening' upon the prescription in *Primitive Physic* for 'one poisoned' that read 'give one or two drams of distilled verdigris'. He then exclaimed: 'I could scarce believe my eyesight for some time, nor can at present by any means account for the ignorance and presumption of a man who deals out as an antidote one of the most active poisons in nature, in such an enormous dose.' Antidote goes on to show that the actual dose recommended for use of this drug is one or two *grains* (a grain being about 1/60th of a dram), and exhorted Wesley to recall 'these *firebrands and death*, that you have scattered so plentifully through the land' (i.e., copies of the *Primitive Physic*), suggesting that otherwise he will bring it to the attention of the College of Physicians.

Wesley responded quickly with a letter thanking 'the gentleman', though wishing he had drawn this obvious 'mere blunder of the printer' to Wesley's attention in a more obliging manner.[45] Wesley insisted he had written 'grain' rather than 'dram'. He ended his letter by begging everyone that had a copy of *Primitive Physic* to insert a correction in their copy.

Wesley's response was attacked immediately by a writer using the pseudonym 'Fly-Flap' (i.e., fly swatter), who argued that instead of apologizing Wesley's letter was 'a most crafty piece of evasion, and only worthy of an unfeeling quack, regardless of, and sporting with the health and lives of his fellow creatures'.[46] The writer dismissed the suggestion that the wording could have resulted from a printer's error and challenged Wesley to show any edition of the work in which the error was not present.

In the same issue of *The Gazetteer* was a second, much longer, letter protesting against Wesley's 'despicable apology', under the pseudonym of 'Civis'.[47] The author argued that Wesley ought to have reviewed personally every edition of *Primitive Physic* issued, and contended that the only reason he did not was his 'thirst for gain'. He then added, 'Or did more important avocations (**political ones perhaps**) render you totally forgetful of your duty in this particular?' Civis concluded by admonishing Wesley to publish the correction of the 'poisonous prescription' in papers throughout the kingdom and to revise *Primitive Physic* immediately.

Another letter signed 'Antidote' was published in the January 10 issue of *The Gazetteer*. This time the author said that he owned the 8th edition (1759) of *Primitive Physic*, which also contained the 'famous poisonous recipe', contradicting Wesley's 'artful' suggestion that the error had crept into only a few editions.[48]

This was followed three days later by a letter from 'A Friend to Truth'.[49] This writer suggested that Wesley's confession of the 'fatal blunder' of his printer was a reaction that betrayed Wesley's 'usual levity' about such serious matters. He continued:

How many thousands may have fallen by it is not easily estimated; but is hoped this, with **other** *fatal* **blunders and mistakes in politics**, will at last teach this Reverend Methodist Gentleman, Scholar, Christian, Physician, and **Politician**, to be more serious, and remember in his next *Calm Address* the adage of '*ne sutor ultra crepidam*', that

One science only will one genius fit,

So vast is human knowledge, so narrow human wit.[50]

He will therefore for the future [return] *to his pulpit and text*, as the cobbler should to his stall and *last* [i.e., 'stay'], lest by his pamphlets, sermons, and prescriptions, he brings his other foot, and grey hair, with sorrow to the grave.

In the middle of January at least one other anonymous letter appeared in a London newspaper which opined: 'Wesley may be a very good divine, but when he writes upon physic, he proves himself extremely weak and ignorant; and **when he writes upon politics**, he proves himself an artful knave.'[51]

Wesley's answer to this flurry of attacks came in a letter to the editor of *Lloyd's Evening Post*, published on 26 January 1776.[52] He began his response with the observation: 'The *Primitive Physic* might have escaped, had it not been for the *Calm Address*, but he[53] will shew no mercy to this poor tract, in order to be revenged on the other.' He then sketched the process that led to the publication of the *Primitive Physic*, stressing that his only motive was to be of benefit to others. He rebutted several accusations – such as that he considered all physicians to be ignorant knaves, or that he rejected all Galenical medicines. Most of all, he challenged the tone of the letters and their many exaggerations, asking: 'Who can account for these palpable, barefaced falsehoods, advanced without rhyme or reason? Only on this supposition; a **red hot American** will say any thing to blacken one that loves King George.' Wesley closed with an invitation for those who had authentic concerns about prescriptions in *Primitive Physic*, and who were willing to share these in a calm and dispassionate manner, to be in touch.

After Wesley had written this reply, but before it appeared in print, another attack was published in *The Gazetteer*, this time signed 'XXX'.[54] The writer opened: 'I find that Mr. Wesley is too proud, too self-sufficient, and too much wrapt up in his present supposed state of self-importance, to vouchsafe either **Mr. Caleb Evans**, or any other correspondent, any thing in the shape of an answer.' He then proposed that the real reason for the 'blundering prescription' was that Wesley mistook a 'dram' for a 'grain', because he did not recognize that apothecaries use a unique type of Troy weights. Broadening the charge, he suggested 'People who . . . generally *run as they read*, and fling books aside as soon as they fancy themselves possessed of what they were *prepossessed* in favour of *before*, are perpetually falling into great errors. Mr. Wesley's whole progress in life stands as a proof that he is one of that species of readers.' XXX closed by again challenging Wesley to point to a single edition of *Primitive Physic* without the error.

The next day, *The Gazetteer* carried yet another letter, from 'Antidote', with the heading 'O thou Man of God, there is death in thy pot' (2 Kings 4:40, revised).[55] The writer first claimed that intervening letters (since the first) under that pseudonym were by another author, but went on to say that he considered Wesley's reply to date unsatisfactory and evasive (Wesley's longer answer did not appear in print until the following day). He then bluntly dismissed the suggestion that the use of 'drams' in the prescription was a printer's error. More pointedly, drawing on the analogy of 2 Kings 4:38–41, Antidote charged that Wesley had raised a false alarm that there was a dearth of physic in the land, and then ostentatiously produced his great pot of *Primitive Physic*; which actually was a deadly mix, leaving the people now in need of a 'holy hand to cast in the healing meal, that there may be no harm in the pot'! The writer closed with the suggestion that Wesley's wisest course of action would be to stop offering medical advice.

Wesley replied to these final volleys over his prescription for 'one poisoned' in a letter published on 31 January in *The Gazetteer*.[56] He opened with a sarcastic entreaty to continue publishing their letters – since it was helping more people become aware of *Primitive Physic*. He next insisted that he had given public answers to **Caleb Evans**, Antidote and the others. Then Wesley turned to XXX's characterization of him as one who 'reads as he runs'. While admitting that he read while journeying, since his time at home was usually spent in writing, Wesley insisted that his study of Scripture was methodical and pled for some latitude given his age (72).

Having sketched the running battle, it is time to note a few details. The suggested dosage of 'one or two drams' appeared in the 2nd edition of *Primitive Physic* (ca. 1750), which was the first to contain this remedy; the prescription remained unchanged through the 16th edition (1774), current during the debate; hence there was no edition to which Wesley could point that did not contain the error. There is also no way to verify Wesley's suggestion that his original manuscript was correct, but misread by the printer. What can be verified is that Wesley revised the dosage to 'one or two grains' in the next edition of *Primitive Physic*, published in late 1776, as encouraged by his critics.

Turning to motives attributed by some of the critics, the suggestion (by 'Antidote') that Wesley exaggerated the dearth of physicians in order to create a market for *Primitive Physic* is ludicrous, particularly given his focus on the poor and those in the scattered villages. It is equally unconvincing to suggest that Wesley was motivated to publish by desire for financial gain; the *Primitive Physic* was still selling for only £1, while William Buchan had recently issued his *Domestic Medicine* at £6![57] Overall, there is little reason to doubt that Wesley's chief motive was to share his (limited) knowledge of medical matters with those in need.

Reversing the table, what about the ulterior motive Wesley attributed to his attackers? He was suggesting that they had latched onto this minor mistake in *Primitive Physic* and caricatured it, not because of a deep interest in the health of his readers but as another tool in their attempt to discredit his public stand in support of King George against the rebellion of the American colonists. Some background will help put this suggestion in context. From the beginning of their disputes with the British government about taxation and representation, through to mid-1775, Wesley had shown public sympathy for the stance of the American colonists. Then Samuel Johnson's tract *Taxation no Tyranny* (and the colonists' declaration of independence in July) changed his mind. In September 1775 Wesley published *A Calm Address to our American Colonies* (which digested Johnson's tract, without acknowledgement), publicly adopting the government's side in the dispute. Released when excitement over the colonies was at a fever pitch, Wesley's 'turncoat' *Calm Address* caused a furore. The next three months witnessed numerous critical letters to the editor in London magazines (particularly those with Whig connections) and no fewer than sixteen tracts published against Wesley.[58] Caleb Evans, a dissenting preacher and Whig, took the lead in attacking Wesley, seeking to discredit the *Calm Address* by exposing it as 'plagiarized' from Johnson (who could be dismissed as a pensioner – or paid propagandist – of the government).

In light of this background, the reader might review the **bold text** in the sketch of the debate above, noting the frequent allusions to *Calm Address*, Caleb Evans, and Wesley's political ambitions. It should also be noted that nearly all of the letters appeared in *The Gazetteer and New Daily Advertiser*, which remained a strong supporter of the American cause after the war began, reflecting its largely mercantile readership. Wesley's *Calm Address* had been a prime target for *The Gazetteer*, which included a couple of Caleb Evans's final letters attacking Wesley just prior to 'Antidote's' opening volley in the 'poisonous recipe' debate.[59] Another letter praising Caleb Evans for unmasking Wesley as a liar was published in the midst of the running debate.[60] One can well understand how Wesley could suspect that the primary motivation for attacking his prescription for 'one poisoned' was not medical but political – to *poison the (ink) well* of his *Calm Address.*

Targeted in Broadened Appeals for Professional Specialization

Whatever its original motive, the attack upon Wesley's 'poisonous recipe' played out just as a broadened basis for enforcing specialized training and certification of medical practitioners was taking form. In 1773 John Coakley Lettson, a Quaker physician and philanthropist, founded The Medical Society of London – the first *general* medical society of note in England.[61] Unlike the earlier Royal College of Physicians, it invited surgeons and apothecaries into membership as well. This act of inclusion, by drawing the line at these two groups, was also a major step in consolidating and intensifying efforts to define the boundaries of 'professional' medicine.

The 'poisonous recipe' debate helped to make Wesley a target in these intensified efforts. Actually, the initial debate was largely ignored by broader London society, with few of the letters in *The Gazetteer* being picked up and reprinted in other newspapers (as was commonly done with prominent topics). But it did draw the attention of William Hawes, a London apothecary, who published an advertisement in *The Gazetteer* on 3 February 1776 – three days after Wesley's last letter – announcing a book he was preparing that would analyse all of the prescriptions in *Primitive Physic*, exposing their many follies and dangers.[62] Hawes specifically thanked Antidote for his 'humane and sensible letter' pointing out the dangerous prescription for counteracting poison, which Hawes credited with convincing him of the need for this book.

Hawes, thereby, appeared on the scene as the 'holy hand to cast in the healing meal' that Antidote had called for a week earlier. Indeed, it is hard not to view Antidote's call as an intentional teaser, setting up Hawes's announcement. The possibility should even be considered that Hawes himself was 'Antidote'. We know that Hawes was an elder in Abraham Rees's Presbyterian Church of St Thomas in Southwark. Like most dissenting ministers, Rees was a Whig and strong supporter of the colonists in their revolt. From comments in the preface of Hawes's published *Examination of the Revd. Mr. John Wesley's Primitive Physick* it is clear that he shared this political stance. He speaks disparagingly of Wesley's character and conduct as a politician, specifically endorsing Caleb Evans's attack upon Wesley.[63]

Divergence from Wesley on the most burning political issue of the day may help explain the tone of Hawes's book, which a review in *The Gentleman's Magazine* characterized as filled with 'sourness and rancour'.[64] But disdain for Wesley – as a minister – having the audacity to offer medical advice is also quite evident. This is all the more noticeable because there was little in *Primitive Physic* that merited contemporary criticism. The majority of Wesley's suggested cures were commonplace, taken from standard authorities. He was actually more cautious than most concerning some of the questionable treatments of the time like bleeding and purging. As Deborah Madden has argued, the result is that Hawes's *Examination* became a 'petty, hair-splitting exercise' that only occasionally rose above 'sectarian, political, and even *ad hominem* denunciation of Wesley's text'.[65]

Wesley's initial response to Hawes's publication was a brief letter in *Lloyd's Evening Post* in mid-July, thanking him for publicity that increased the demand for *Primitive Physic*.[66] Hawes replied immediately to this cynical dismissal with his own public letter, which compared Wesley to the 'most mercenary quack that ever disgraced a stage in Moorfields' and ranked him among 'the most base and unworthy of mankind'.[67]

Within a week Wesley published a more serious response to Hawes.[68] He made clear his belief that Hawes was motivated to attack *Primitive Physic* by his strong disagreement with Wesley's *Calm Address*. He rejected the suggestion that he lacked basic medical knowledge, stressing the numerous medical sources he had consulted. Wesley then worked through Hawes's *Examination*, answering several specific criticisms. He ended the letter by thanking Hawes for drawing some problematic prescriptions to his attention and noted that he was preparing a new edition of *Primitive Physic* that addressed these cases.[69]

Hawes's answer to this letter appeared two weeks later.[70] He rejected the suggestion that disagreement with Wesley's political stance motivated him to do the *Examination*. He rebuffed Wesley's assumption that he should have recognized the sources of the remedies, noting that Wesley typically does not cite his sources – in keeping with his 'character as a plagiary'! Hawes contended that Wesley should have responded sooner in correcting the dangerous remedies, charging that the reason he did not call in the earlier unsold copies was fear of financial loss. He closed by suggesting that instead of issuing a revised copy, Wesley should simply cease publishing medical advice.

While the initiating tempest in *The Gazetteer* had not been broadly noticed, Hawes's *Examination* was reviewed in several London journals. Some of the reviews echoed the tone of the book, with one calling for

Wesley to be hanged![71] Others expressed appreciation for the medical insights of Hawes's volume, if sometimes questioning its tone.[72] Most concurred with the *Critical Review* that this case proved the need for respecting professional specialization:

> Had Mr. Wesley prudently restricted himself within the limits of his profession, by elucidating the principles of *primitive religion*, he might have edified his readers much more, without either endangering their temporal welfare, or exposing his own opinions to the imputation of medical ignorance, of which he is so clearly convicted in this examination.[73]

As a formal expression of this sentiment, the recently formed Medical Society of London issued Hawes, the apothecary, public thanks for his efforts to restore 'true medical knowledge'.[74]

Fodder for Public Caricature and Ridicule

In principle, admonitions to restrict himself to his pulpit (in the words of 'Civis') need imply no deprecation of Wesley in his appropriate professional field. But these public criticisms of Wesley's efforts in medical care quickly became fodder not only for challenging his political tracts but also for those who differed with Wesley on theological issues – whether Anglicans wary of his dissenting tendencies or Calvinists scornful of his Arminian and perfectionist stance.

A letter in *The Gazetteer* in early July 1776 by 'Public Applause' was perhaps the first to weave together this threefold attack:

> There has, I doubt not, always been impious divines, seditious quacks, and ignorant and profligate politicians, who have each committed horrid mischiefs in their different professions. But I never till this era found all these enormities united in *one* person, who attempted to poison the soul by religious doctrines, the body individual by quackism, and the body politic by a Jesuitical and daring attempt to vindicate the violent measures of government to tax three millions of unrepresented free-born Englishmen.[75]

This conjoined ridicule was echoed soon after by a satirical broadsheet poem penned by 'A Detester of Hypocrisy' titled *To that Fanatical, Political, Physical Enthusiast, Patriot and Physician, the Reverend Mr. W[esle]y* [reprinted in the Appendix to this chapter].

Such attacks soon became big business. Between December 1777 and early 1779 a series of six booklet-size poetic satires aimed (in varying degrees) at Wesley were published by John Bew, who had just set up the first mass-market publishing concern in London.[76] The anonymous series was almost certainly the work of William Combe, a professional satirist. The chief focus of Combe's satire is Wesley's affirmation of Christian perfection, which Combe considered to be fanatical.[77] Combe attacked the doctrine directly in the first two booklets. He then dedicated the third volley, *Sketches for Tabernacle Frames*, to Richard Hill (Calvinist doctrinal critic), Caleb Evans (political critic), and William Hawes (medical critic) – whom he honoured for having proven that Wesley was 'a *fanatical* preacher, a ministerial scribbler, and a quack doctor'[78] – and used their conjoined authority as the base for satirizing Wesley's teaching and practice in general. In *Fanatical Conversion*, the final and most biting satire, Combe drew a parallel between Wesley's 'quack' medical advice and his 'fanatical' pastoral guidance of the Wesleyan Methodist movement:

> I answer, 'John's priest, wizard, and physician:
> Starv'd bodies with apt nostrums he controuls,
> and with worse physic stupefies their souls.' . . .
> Who causes the disease and sells the cure . . .
> Thus Ambo-dexter like, John raises wealth
> A quack in sickness and a pest in health.[79]

Reactionary Retreat from Formal Medical Care

The growing professional critique and popular satire of his efforts in medical care put Wesley in a bind. Continuing these efforts in public structural forms threatened to undercut the spiritual and theological leadership that he and the lay preachers were providing the movement. So Wesley opted for retreat. When the next edition of the 'Large Minutes' (the official guide for Methodist practice) was released in 1780, it had been carefully pruned of 1) all references to the local 'visitor of the sick', 2) the instruction for lay preachers to visit the sick regularly as they travelled the circuit, and 3) even a suggestion that the lay preachers spend their time between sessions of annual conference in visiting the sick.[80]

These tacit moves to discontinue *public structural* efforts in caring for the sick should not be seen as a decline in Wesley's concern for the sick, or in his expectation that Methodists would embody this concern in their ministry to others. The balance of focus just shifted toward informal and individual expressions of care. Wesley continued to publish *Primitive*

Physic for personal use.[81] Likewise, offering care to the sick remained a highlighted item in the *General Rules* list of expectations for individual Methodists.[82] Indeed, Wesley reinforced this expectation in a sermon published in 1786 that extolled visiting the sick as a 'plain duty' for *all* that are in health.[83]

With these tacit moves Wesley bowed to the emerging specialization that has permeated modern Western cultures. The sub-dividing of professional fields was both a source and the inevitable result of the explosion of knowledge over the last two centuries. While it has had many benefits, it has also tended to foster disciplinary insularity and reductionist approaches to issues. As such, it has threatened the *balance* that characterized Wesley's approach (at its best) to issues of health. As the Methodist experience in North America has particularly illustrated, specialized expertise can spawn populist reaction. One expression of this reaction is to reject human efforts, relying on God alone for healing.[84] Another form rejects only 'professional' medicine, in favour of natural or alternative cures. Modern specialized approaches to issues of health have often undervalued the dynamic connection between physical and spiritual well-being. They have also encouraged a tendency to view health as something bestowed by modern medical intervention, losing sight of the foundational role of life-long practices to promote well-being. Finally, the high cost of specialized medicine limits the access of the poor to adequate care.

Methodists have been shaped by and have struggled with these dynamics over the last two centuries.[85] In their struggle, an increasing number have overcome their inherited embarrassment about – or resulting lack of exposure to – the precedent of their founder.

Reclaiming the Eccentric Parent

Echoes of Hawes's professional disdain and the resulting satirical attacks upon Wesley's efforts in medicine continued to reverberate for some time. When Robert Southey, a prominent British author, published his generally sympathetic biography of Wesley in 1820, he judged the *Primitive Physic* as revealing a 'lamentable want of judgement and perilous rashness'.[86] An essay (apparently) by a physician published on both sides of the Atlantic in 1906 contended that *Primitive Physic* could only strike modern readers as evidence of a hiatus in Wesley's faculties, which was 'natural and inevitable in a theologian of that day, and not unfamiliar even in some of the theological intellects of the present'![87] Similar judgements appear in some historical studies up to the mid-twentieth century.[88]

As a result, many of Wesley's ecclesial descendants view his medical interests as eccentric, if they are aware of them at all.[89]

From Bemused Interest to Rehabilitated Hero

But there also has appeared a growing counter voice to these echoes, rehabilitating this dimension of Wesley's ministry. In 1846, the year after John Stamp had expressed reserve about Wesley's medical advice, Thomas Marriott published an article in the same British Methodist magazine noting that it was the centenary of Wesley's opening a health clinic.[90] While Marriott did not explicitly rebut Stamp, there was an appreciative tone to his survey of Wesley's various efforts in providing medical care. His became the first in a string of publications that have looked with more favour upon the *Primitive Physic* and upon Wesley's medical endeavours more generally (see the Select Bibliography).

The majority of these publications are brief and fall in the vein of surprised/bemused interest on (re)discovering this dimension of Wesley's work. By no means are they all by Methodists or other descendants of the Wesleyan revival. The earliest examples in North America come from the pen of John Plummer, a Quaker physician in Richmond, Indiana. As this suggests, many in this vein come from medical practitioners of various types. Their general tone can be illustrated by the conclusion of a 1902 essay in the *British Medical Journal* about the *Primitive Physic*:

> Such are a few of the quaint ideas and practices dealt within this old book of popular medicine. It is only fair, however, to note the fact that the author's strong common sense guarded him from many of the more absurd and disgusting prescriptions of his day.[91]

Some make this point a bit stronger, contending that 'Wesley's treatment of diseases was at least as reconcilable with common sense as that of the contemporary regular practitioner, much more so in most cases'.[92] A few studies slide over into panegyric, championing Wesley as an exemplary amateur physician.[93]

Increasing Historical Sophistication

The string of publications on Wesley and medicine has been laced with occasional scholarly studies (more frequent in recent years) that explain and evaluate Wesley's general practice and specific prescriptions in their historical context. While noting the limitations and tensions of his efforts, these studies concur in judging *Primitive Physic* as better than most of the popular medical works of the age.[94]

Seeking a Champion of Complementary and Alternative Medicines

Some of the publications in the string are less inclined to portray Wesley as an 'amateur' traditional physician. Often written by practitioners and enthusiasts of complementary and alternative medicine, these studies tout Wesley as the forerunner and champion of their cause.[95] A particular focus in this vein has been Wesley's advocacy of electrical shock therapy.[96] However, some studies of this topic are more concerned with exposition of Wesley's equipment and methods in their historical and political context.[97]

Valuing the Precedent for Integrative Balance in Health Care

A recurrent theme in recent studies is appreciation for the precedent Wesley provides in countering the insular and reductionist tendencies of modern specialization – seeking balanced and integrative models of health and healing.[98] A couple of specific topics within this general theme that have received attention are Wesley on diet[99] and Wesley's mature emphases about the nature and treatment of mental illness.[100]

Reclaiming a Mentor for Holistic Salvation and Mission

In recent studies by Wesley's ecclesial descendants one final characteristic is evident – an interest in Wesley as a resource for overcoming the anaemic 'spiritualized' models of salvation and mission that abound in our present setting. With all deference to John Stamp, they are ready to sit for a time at Wesley's feet as a mentor in both 'divinity' and 'physic', to gain from him a deepened appreciation for God's mission of healing soul and body together and for our call to participate in that mission.[101] One thing they are sure to glean from an engagement with the whole of Wesley's precedent is that this participation needs to include some concrete structural expressions, with a particular concern for the poor.[102]

Notes

1 I have had the fortune of collaborating for several years with James G. Donat in research on Wesley's endeavours in medicine, each of us sharing our findings with the other. It would be hard to recall in this essay every source that was first drawn to my attention by Donat, but there are several – and I am thankful.

2 John S. Stamp, footnote to 'Memoir of the Rev. Charles Atmore', *Wesleyan Methodist Magazine* 68 (1845), p. 10.

3 Randy Maddox, 'John Wesley on Holistic Health and Healing', *Methodist History* 46 (2007), pp. 4–33 (also available online at http://www.divinity.duke.edu/docs/faculty/maddox/wesley/) surveys the dimensions of Wesley's concern for health and healing, summarizing recent scholarship. The present section distils parts of that essay and readers are directed to the original for detailed documentation. They should consult as well Deborah Madden, '"A Cheap, Safe and Natural Medicine": Religion, Medicine and Culture in John Wesley's *Primitive Physic*', *Clio Medica* 83, Amsterdam and New York, Rodopi, 2007, which provides a more extensive exposition.

4 Note his rejection of this explicit suggestion in Letter to 'John Smith' (25 March 1747), *Works*, vol. 26, p. 236.

5 *Farther Appeal to Men of Reason and Religion*, Pt I, §3, *Works*, vol. 11, p. 106.

6 For an elaboration of the various dimensions of Wesley's holistic understanding of salvation, see Randy L. Maddox, 'Celebrating the Whole Wesley', *Methodist History* 43:2 (2005), pp. 74–89 available online at <http://www.divinity.duke.edu/docs/faculty/maddox/wesley>.

7 Letter to Alexander Knox (26 October 1778), in *Letters* (Telford), vol. 6, p. 327.

8 Cf. David Harley, 'John Hart of Northampton and the Calvinist Critique of Priest-Physicians', *Medical History* 42 (1998), pp. 362–86. This is not to say that *all* Calvinist-leaning clergy downplayed the role of offering medical advice, only that those who did downplay this role were more likely to be Calvinist.

9 An excellent 'Arminian' example of emphasizing medical care as part of the pastoral task is Gilbert Burnet, *A Discourse of the Pastoral Care*, London, Richard Chiswell, 1692, pp. 183, 194–201 (a book that Wesley read in October 1729).

10 See *Plain Account of the People Called Methodists*, §XII.2, *Works*, vol. 9, p. 275.

11 *Journal* (7 May 1741), *Works* vol. 19, pp. 193–4.

12 See *Plain Account of the People Called Methodists*, §XI, *Works* vol. 9, pp. 274–5; and 'Minutes' (29 June 1744), Q. 9, in *John Bennet's Copy of the Minutes of the Conferences of 1744, 1745, 1747, and 1748*, London, Charles Kelley, 1896, p. 17. Note also the slight forerunner to this step, in 1743, when Wesley instructed class leaders to visit each member of their class once a week and inform the parish minister of any who were sick; in *The Nature, Design, and General Rules of the United Societies*, §3, *Works* vol. 9, p. 70.

13 See *Nature, Design, and General Rules of the United Societies* (1743), §5, *Works* vol. 9, p. 72.

14 See 'Minutes' (3 August 1745), Q. 3, in *John Bennet's . . . Minutes*, p. 27. Already suggested in 'Minutes' (29 June 1744), Q. 3, A. 12, in *John Bennet's . . . Minutes*, p. 16.

15 'Minutes' (3 August 1745), Q. 13, in *John Bennet's . . . Minutes*, p. 28.

16 Note in this regard that the letter that John and Charles Wesley sent on 25 June 1751 to James Wheatley, a Methodist itinerant who had been caught in sexual impropriety, instructed him to desist not only from preaching but also from practising physic (see *Works* vol. 26, p. 465).

17 *Collection of Receits for the Use of the Poor*, Bristol, Farley, and Newcastle, Gooding, 1745.

18 Methods of calculating changing value vary widely; by one common method, 2 pence in 1745 would be equivalent to about £1.20 today. See <http://www.measuringworth.com/ppoweruk>.

19 *Primitive Physick*, London, Strahan, 1747. On the same model, this would be the equivalent of about £6 today. Note: the title was spelled *Physick* in the earlier editions, being changed to *Physic* with the 20th edn in 1781; I will use consistently the final spelling.

20 See particularly James G. Donat, 'Empirical Medicine in the 18th Century: The Rev. John Wesley's Search for Remedies that Work', *Methodist History* 44 (2006), pp. 216–26, Madden, '"A Cheap, Safe and Natural Medicine"', and Chapter 3, 'Pastor and Physician', by Madden in this volume. The *Primitive Physic* will be included in Vol. 17 of Wesley's *Works* (edited by James Donat), noting the sources for the various prescriptions where these can be established.

21 Cf. *Journal* (4 December 1746), *Works*, vol. 20, p. 150.

22 *Plain Account of the People Called Methodists*, §XII.1–3, *Works*, vol. 9, pp. 275–6. See also Wesley's *Journal* (4 December 1746), *Works* vol. 20, pp. 150–1.

23 Note his desire for a copy of the *Primitive Physic* to be in every 'house' or 'family' in Letter to the Societies at Bristol (1764), *Letters* (Telford), vol. 4, p. 272; Letter to Christopher Hopper (20 November 1769), *Letters* (Telford), vol. 5, p. 161; and Letter to Joseph Taylor (9 Sept. 1782), *Letters* (Telford), vol. 7, p. 139. Cf. 'Large Minutes', Q. 42, in *Works* (Jackson), vol. 8, p. 319.

24 These will all be included in Vol. 17 of Wesley's *Works*. For analysis of the two extracts from Tissot, see Donat, 'The Rev. John Wesley's Extractions from Dr. Tissot: A Methodist *Imprimatur*', *History of Science* 39 (2001), pp. 285–98.

25 The following points are elaborated and documented in Maddox, 'John Wesley on Holistic Health and Healing', pp. 9–27.

26 Chapter 6 in this volume, 'Health of Soul and Health of Body', by Robert Webster develops this point.

27 *Advice with Respect to Health*, Preface, §9, *Works* (Jackson), vol. 14, p. 258.

28 For reflections on both the promise and limitations of Wesley in this regard, see Chapter 4, 'A Necessary Relationship', by Laura Bartels Felleman, Chapter 2, 'A Wesleyan Theology of Environmental Stewardship', by Margaret Flowers, and Chapter 3, 'Pastor and Physician', by Madden in this volume.

29 *Primitive Physic*, Preface, Postscript, §2, *Works* (Jackson), vol. 14, p. 316.

30 For more on this, see Chapter 5 in this volume, 'This Curious and Important Subject', by Linda Schwab.

31 Luke Tyerman, *The Life and Times of the Rev. John Wesley*, New York, Harper, 1872, vol. 1, p. 564.

32 See the summary of recent scholarship, with application to Wesley, in Madden, 'Contemporary Reaction to John Wesley's *Primitive Physic*: Or, the Case of Dr. William Hawes Examined', *Social History of Medicine* 17 (2004), pp. 365–78, esp. pp. 366–7.

33 One of the earliest examples is Tristram Land, *A Letter to the Rev. Mr. Whitefield, Designed to Correct His Mistaken Account of Regeneration*, London, J. Roberts, 1739, p. 5.

34 Cf. W. M. Jacob, *The Clerical Profession in the Long Eighteenth Century, 1680–1840*, New York, Oxford University Press, 2007, pp. 226–7.

35 Nathaniel Lancaster, *Methodism Triumphant*, London, Wilkie et al., 1767, pp. 26, 62.

36 Cf. Lancaster, *Methodism Triumphant*, p. 51; and William Warburton, *The Doctrine of Grace, or The Office and Operations of the Holy Spirit vindicated from the Insults of Infidelity, and the Abuses of Fanaticism*, London, A. Millar, 1763, pp. 138–9.

37 Warburton, *Doctrine of Grace*, pp. 251–2.

38 John William Fletcher, *A Second Check to Antinomianism; occasioned by a Late Narrative*, London, New Chapel, 1771, pp. 22–3.

39 Richard Hill, *A Review of all the Doctrines Taught by the Rev. Mr. John Wesley; Containing a Full and Particular Answer to a Book Entitled 'A Second Check to Antinomianism'*, London, Dilly, 1772, p. 29.

40 Wesley, *Some Remarks on Mr. Hill's 'Review . . .'*, §3, *Works* (Jackson), vol. 10, p. 376.

41 See Richard Hill, *Logica Wesleiensis; or The Farrago Double Distilled. With an Heroic Poem in Praise of Mr. John Wesley*, London, Dilly, 1773, pp. 44–51.

42 For the convenience of those interested, a file collecting full-text copies of the letters and reviews summarized in this and the two subsequent sections of the essay has been posted at <http://www.divinity.duke.edu/wesleyan/texts/index.html>

43 Augustus Montague Toplady, *The Scheme of Christian and Philosophical Necessity Asserted; in opposition to Mr. John Wesley's Tract on that Subject*, London, Vallance & Simmons, 1775, pp. vi–viii.

44 Antidote, 'To the Rev. John Wesley,' *The Gazetteer and New Daily Advertiser* (25 December 1775), p. 1; also printed in the *London Chronicle* (23–26 December 1775), p. 612. The former magazine will hereafter be referred to simply as *The Gazetteer*.

45 John Wesley, 'To the Printer of the Gazetteer (28 Dec. 1775),' *The Gazetteer* (1 January 1776), p. 2; also published in *Lloyd's Evening Post* (29 December 1775–1 January 1776), p. 4.

46 Fly-Flap, 'To the Rev. Mr. Wesley (1 Jan. 1776),' *The Gazetteer* (4 January 1776), p. 2.

47 Civis, 'To the Rev. Mr. Wesley (2 Jan. 1776),' *The Gazetteer* (4 January 1776), pp. 1–2.

48 Antidote, 'To the Rev. Mr. John Wesley,' *The Gazetteer* (10 January 1776), p. 2.

49 A Friend to Truth, 'For the Gazetteer (2 Jan. 1776),' *The Gazetteer* (13 January 1776), p. 2.

50 Alexander Pope, 'Essay on Criticism,' lines 60–61. The Latin proverb is roughly translated 'cobbler, stick to your trade'.

51 Quoted by Wesley in his response that follows; the original has not yet been located.

52 John Wesley, 'To the Editor of *Lloyd's Evening Post*', *Lloyd's Evening Post* (26–29 January 1776), p. 102.

53 Wesley assumed there was a single author behind most of the anonymous letters.

54 XXX, 'To the Printer of the *Gazetteer*', *The Gazetteer* (24 January 1776), pp. 1–2.

55 Antidote, 'To the Rev. John Wesley, A.M.', *The Gazetteer* (25 January 1776), p. 2.

56 John Wesley, 'To the Printer of the *Gazetteer*', *The Gazetteer* (31 January 1776), p. 2; also in *Letters* (Telford), vol. 6, pp. 202–3. Wesley focuses his reply on the letter by XXX; it is unclear if he had seen the last letter by 'Antidote.'

57 William Buchan, *Domestic Medicine*, Edinburgh, Balfour, Auld, & Smellie, 1769. This was the main 'competitor' to *Primitive Physic*, reaching a 10th edn by 1788.

58 A good summary can be found in Donald Henry Kirkham, 'Pamphlet Opposition to the Rise of Methodism' (Duke University PhD thesis, 1973), pp. 290–314.

59 See Caleb Evans, 'To John Wesley', *The Gazetteer* (7 December 1775), p. 2; and Caleb Evans, 'To John Wesley', *The Gazetteer* (23 December 1775), p. 2. The second letter was in the issue immediately preceding Antidote's letter (since the intervening day was a Sunday). John Wesley's reply to Evans's first letter was published in *The Gazetteer* (13 December 1775), p. 1.

60 W. S. (Bristol, 8 January 1776), 'To the Printer of the *Gazetteer*', *The Gazetteer* (20 January 1776), p. 2.

61 See Penelope Hunting, *The Medical Society of London, 1773–2003*, London, Medical Society of London, 2003.

62 *The Gazetteer* (3 February 1776), p. 1.

63 See William Hawes, *An Examination of the Revd. Mr. John Wesley's Primitive Physick*, London, J. Dodsley, 1776, pp. iii–iv.

64 *The Gentleman's Magazine*, 46 (1776), p. 227.

65 Madden, 'Contemporary Reaction to John Wesley's *Primitive Physic*: Or, the Case of Dr. William Hawes Examined', pp. 368, 369. Much of this article is distilled in Madden '"A Cheap, Safe and Natural Medicine"', pp. 129–41.

66 John Wesley, 'To Mr. Hawes, Apothecary and Critic (20 July 1776)', *Lloyd's Evening Post* (19–22 July 1776), p. 79; also in *Letters* (Telford), vol. 6, pp. 225–6.

67 William Hawes, 'To Mr. John Wesley (24 July 1776)', *Lloyd's Evening Post* (24–26 July 1776), p. 95; also printed in *The Gazetteer* (25 July 1776), pp. 1–2. For a similar response, see Talus, 'To the Rev. Mr. John Wesley', *London Chronicle* (3–6 August 1776), p. 127.

68 John Wesley, 'To the Editor (27 July 1776)', *Lloyd's Evening Post* (31 July–2 August 1776), p. 113. A slightly more complete version appeared in *The Gazetteer*

(2 August 1776), p. 2; and *London Chronicle* (1–3 August 1776), p. 117.

69 This 17th edn, published in late 1776, contained a number of deletions and corrections in response to Hawes's critique. Vol. 17 of *Works* will detail the changes.

70 W. Hawes, 'To the Printer', *Lloyd's Evening Post* (7–9 August 1776), p. 140; also printed in *The Gazetteer* (8 August 1776), p. 2.

71 The suggestion of hanging comes at the end of the review in the acerbic *London Review Of English And Foreign Literature* 3 (1776), pp. 412–13. Milder reflections of Hawes's disdain for Wesley are evident in the reviews in *London Magazine: Or, Gentleman's Monthly Intelligencer* 45 (1776), pp. 381–3; and *Monthly Review* 54 (1776), pp. 419–20.

72 Cf. *The Gentleman's Magazine* 46 (1776), pp. 226–7; and *London Chronicle* (25–28 May 1776), p. 1.

73 *Critical Review* 41 (1776), p. 406.

74 Cited in Public Applause, 'To Mr. Hawes, Author of *An Examination of Mr. Wesley's Primitive Physick*', *The Gazetteer* (7 July 1776), pp. 1–2. Hawes apparently was not a member of the Medical Society; however, Dr Thomas Cogan, his partner in 1774 in launching the Society for the Recovery of Persons Apparently Drowned (later the Royal Humane Society), did hold membership.

75 Public Applause, 'To Mr. Hawes, Author of *An Examination of Mr. Wesley's Primitive Physick*', *The Gazetteer* (7 July 1776), p. 1.

76 The booklets were 36–58 pages in length and appeared in the following order: *The Saints: a Satire*, London, J. Bew, 1778 (actually December 1777); *Perfection: a Poetical Epistle calmly addressed to the greatest Hypocrite in England* (1778); *Sketches for Tabernacle-Frames* (1778); *The Love Feast* (1778); *The Temple of Imposture* (1778); and *Fanatical Conversion; or Methodism Displayed. A Satire illustrated and verified by notes from J. Wesley's fanatical Journals* (1779). All are commonly attributed to William Combe (1742–1843).

77 Note that when *The Saints* was issued in a second edition it was retitled *The Fanatic Saints*, London, John Bew, 1778, to show that the author was attacking only folk like Wesley who taught perfection, not 'rational dissenters' (see p. [6]; and same claim in *Sketches*, p. [7]).

78 See the author's note, [Combe], *Sketches*, p. 10. The dedication is on p. [8].

79 [Combe], *Fanatical Conversion*, pp. 28–9.

80 This can be seen most easily in *Minutes of the Methodist Conferences, from the First, held in London, by the Late Rev. John Wesley, A.M., in the Year 1744*, vol. 1, London, John Mason, 1862, where the editions of the Large Minutes are placed in parallel columns. The office of 'visitor of the sick' made it into the Large Minutes only in the form of an instruction for class leaders to inform them of any sick members; this reference, present from the earliest edition through 1770, is missing by 1772, with the larger expectation of class leaders reporting on who is sick disappearing in 1780ff (see pp. 454–5). The charge for the lay preachers to visit the sick is present through 1772, but missing in 1780ff (pp. 552–3). The same applies to the suggestion of visiting the sick during annual conference (pp. 444–5). These changes were drawn to my attention by James Donat.

81 *Primitive Physic* reached a 23rd edn in Britain by 1791, the year of Wesley's death. It continued to be reprinted every 3–4 years up to the middle of the nineteenth century in Britain, though in decreasing sponsorship by the Wesleyan Methodist Church.

82 *General Rules*, §5, *Works*, vol. 9, p. 72, remained unchanged through Wesley's life.

83 Sermon 98, 'On Visiting the Sick', *Works*, vol. 3, pp. 385–97; esp. §4, p. 386.

84 These tensions have been experienced most pointedly in the Holiness and Pentecostal wings of the broad Wesleyan family. Cf. Nancy A. Hardesty, *Faith Cure: Divine Healing in the Holiness and Pentecostal Movements*, Peabody, MA, Hendrickson, 2003; and Kimberly Ervin Alexander, 'Three Hundred Years of Holiness and Healing', *Asbury Theological Journal* 58:2 (2003), pp. 57–77.

85 For reflections on this history see Elmer Brooks Holifield, *Health and Medicine in the Methodist Tradition*, New York, Crossroad, 1986; Harold Y. Vanderpool, 'The Wesleyan Methodist Tradition', in Ronald Numbers and Darrel Amundson eds., *Caring and Curing: Health and Medicine in the Western Religious Traditions*, New York, Macmillan, 1986, pp. 317–53; and (on the British side) Mark Clement, 'Sifting Science: Methodism and Natural Knowledge in Britain, 1815–70', University of Oxford DPhil thesis, 1996, pp. 155–219.

86 Robert Southey, *Life of Wesley; and the Rise and Progress of Methodism*, London, Longman et al., 1820, vol. 2, p. 347.

87 Burton G. Thomas, 'John Wesley on the Art of Healing', *The British Medical Journal* (28 April 1906), pp. 987–88. The published name is probably a pseudonym.

88 E.g., John Harold Plumb, *England in the Eighteenth Century*, Baltimore, Penguin, 1950, p. 96; and Lester S. King, *The Medical World of the Eighteenth Century*, Chicago, University of Chicago Press, 1958, pp. 34–9.

89 See, for example, the description of *Primitive Physic* as 'a strange mix of old wives' tales and recent insights', in John Munsey Turner, *John Wesley: The Evangelical Revival and the Rise of Methodism in England*, Peterborough, Epworth, 2002, pp. 41–2.

90 Thomas Marriott, 'Methodism in Former Days: Medicine and Medical Advice', *Wesleyan Methodist Magazine* 69 (1846), pp. 359–64. Marriott was the minister currently assigned to Wesley's Chapel in London.

91 Anonymous, 'A Medical Tract by John Wesley', *British Medical Journal* (29 March 1902, pp. 799–800), p. 800.

92 William Renwick Riddell, 'Wesley's System of Medicine', *New York Journal of Medicine* 99 (1914), pp. 64–8, p. 68. For quite similar evaluation, see Vaughn Nash, 'The Illustrous Quack', *New Statesman and Nation*, n.s., 1931, vol. 2, pp. 252–3.

93 The most developed example is A. Wesley Hill, *John Wesley Among the Physicians*, London, Epworth, 1958.

94 See especially William C. Cross, 'Wesley and Medicine: *Primitive Physic* and Its Critics', *Wesleyan Methodist Magazine* 137 (1914), pp. 613–18; George Dock, 'The *Primitive Physick* of Rev. John Wesley', *Journal of the American Medical Association* 64 (1915), pp. 629–38; G. S. Rousseau, 'John Wesley's *Primitive Physic* (1747)', *Harvard Library Bulletin* 16 (1968), pp. 242–56; Clifford Wayne Callaway, 'John Wesley's *Primitive Physick*: An Essay in Appreciation', *Proceedings of the Mayo Clinic* 49 (1974), pp. 318–24; S. J. Rogal, 'Pills for the Poor: John Wesley's *Primitive Physick*', *Yale Journal of Biology and Medicine* 51 (1978), pp. 81–90; Eunice Bonow Bardell, '*Primitive Physick*: John Wesley's Receipts', *Pharmacy in History* 21 (1979), pp. 111–21; John Cule, 'The

Rev. John Wesley, M.A. (Oxon.), 1703–1791; "The Naked Empiricist" and Orthodox Medicine', *Journal of the History of Medicine and Allied Sciences* 45 (1990), pp. 41–63; Madden, 'Experience and the Common Interest of Mankind: The Enlightened Empiricism of John Wesley's *Primitive Physic*', *British Journal for Eighteenth-Century Studies* 26 (2003), pp. 41–53; and James G. Donat, 'Empirical Medicine in the 18th Century: The Rev. John Wesley's Search for Remedies that Work', *Methodist History* 44 (2006), pp. 216–26. Madden, '"A Cheap, Safe and Natural Medicine"' is the most extended study in this vein.

95 Early suggestions in this vein appear in Charles E. Dodsley, 'John Wesley as Physician', *Pharmaceutical Journal and Pharmacist* 104 (1920), pp. 26–7 and Hilda M. Coley, 'John Wesley Prescribes for Bodily Ailments', *Bookman* (London) 85 (1934), pp. 446–7. The most forceful recent examples would be J. G. Gadsby, *Rev. John Wesley M.A.: Holistic Healing, Electrotherapy and Complementary Medicine*, Loughborough, Leicestershire, Teamprint, 1996 and Gadsby and Francis Dewhurst, 'John Wesley's Contribution to the Evolution of Alternative and Holistic Medicine', *Epworth Review* 26:1 (1999), pp. 95–104. M. Hughes, 'The Holistic Way: John Wesley's Practical Piety as a Resource for Integrated Healthcare', *Journal of Religion and Health*, forthcoming 2008 and accessible on line at <http://www.springerlink.com/content/yt4h0647165861x5/fulltext.pdf> seeks to integrate this emphasis with traditional medicine.

96 Note the description of Wesley as the 'god-father of electrotherapy', in W. Turrell, 'Three Electrotherapists of the Eighteenth Century: John Wesley, Jean Paul Marat, and James Graham', *Annals of Medical History* 3 (1921), pp. 361–7, p. 367. Other expositions in this vein include Turrell, *John Wesley: Physician and Electrotherapist*, Oxford, Blackwell, 1938; Richard Hunter, 'A Brief Review of the Use of Electricity in Psychiatry with Special Reference to John Wesley', *The British Journal of Physical Medicine* 20:5 (1957), pp. 98–100; Max W. Woodward, 'Wesley's Electric Machine', *Nursing Mirror* 114 (27 July 1962), pp. x, xvi; Dennis Stillings, 'John Wesley: Electrotherapist', *Medical Instrumentation* 8 (1974), p. 66; D. S. H. Cannon, 'John Wesley: A Pioneer in the Use of Electricity in Medicine', *WHS Cumbria Branch Journal* 30 (Autumn 1992), pp. 12–15; and Gadsby, *Rev. John Wesley M.A.: Holistic Healing, Electrotherapy and Complementary Medicine*.

97 E.g., Francis Schiller, 'Reverend Wesley, Doctor Marat, and the Electric Fire', *Clio Medica* 15 (1981), pp. 159–76; Rogal, 'Electricity: John Wesley's "Curious and Important Subject"', *Eighteenth Century Life* 13 (1989), pp. 78–90; Ruth Richardson, 'John Wesley's Ethereal Fire', *The Lancet* 358 (2001), p. 932; and Willem D.Hackmann, *John Wesley and His Electrical Machine*, London, John Wesley's House and The Museum of Methodism, 2003. Paola Bertucci, 'Revealing Sparks: John Wesley and the Religious Utility of Electrical Healing', *British Journal for the History of Science* 39 (2006), pp. 341–62 offers a debatable account of the social agendas that propelled Wesley's interest in public demonstrations of electrical healing. H. Newton Malony, 'John Wesley's *Primitive Physick*: an 18th Century Health Psychology', *Journal of Health Psychology* 1 (1996), pp. 147–59 remains the best overview of Wesley's interest in the healing benefits of electrical shock.

98 See particularly Philip Wesley Ott, 'John Wesley on Mind and Body: Toward an Understanding of Health as Wholeness', *Methodist History* 27 (1989),

pp. 61–72 and Ott, 'John Wesley on Health as Wholeness', *Journal of Religion and Health* 30 (1991), pp. 43–57; Madden, 'Medicine and Moral Reform: The Place of Practical Piety in John Wesley's Art of Physic', *Church History* 73 (2004), pp. 741–5; Maddox, 'John Wesley on Holistic Health and Healing'; and Hughes, 'The Holistic Way: John Wesley's Practical Piety as a Resource for Integrated Healthcare'.

99 William Stroup, 'Meat, Ethics, and the Case of John Wesley', in Regina Hewitt and Pat Rogers eds, *Orthodoxy and Heresy in Eighteenth-Century Society*, Lewisburg, PA, Bucknell University Press, 2002, pp. 267–80; and Charles Wallace, 'Eating and Drinking with John Wesley: The Logic of His Practice', *Bulletin of the John Rylands University Library* 85:2–3 (2003), pp. 137–55.

100 Malony, 'John Wesley's *Primitive Physick*: an 18th Century Health Psychology', Joe Gorman, 'John Wesley and Depression in an Age of Melancholy', *Wesleyan Theological Journal* 34:2 (1999), pp. 196–221; Paul Laffey, 'John Wesley on Insanity', *History of Psychiatry* 12 (2001), pp. 467–79; and Donat, 'John Wesley on the Estimation and Cure of Nervous Disorders', in Harry Whitaker, C. U. M. Smith and Stanley Finger eds, *Brain, Mind and Medicine: Essays in Eighteenth-Century Neuroscience*, New York, Springer-Verlag, 2007, pp. 285–300.

101 See particularly John A. Newton, 'Health and Healing in the Wesleys', *Methodist Recorder* (1988); R. Jeffrey Hiatt, 'John Wesley and Healing: Developing a Wesleyan Missiology', *Asbury Theological Journal* 59 (2004), pp. 89–109; and Maddox, 'John Wesley on Holistic Health and Healing'.

102 Parish nursing programs would be one example. For a more ambitious proposal, in conversation with Wesley, see Leslie Bryan Williams, 'Religious-Based Managed Care: A Wesleyan Paradigm for Reforming Health Care', University of Southern California PhD thesis, 1998.

Select Bibliography
John Wesley and Medicine, 1846–2007

Anderson, Kenneth N. and Richard Dunlap, 'John Wesley: Man of Medicine, Too!', *Together* 8:2 (February 1964), pp. 22–5.

Baragar, C. A., 'John Wesley and Medicine', *Annals of Medical History* 10 (1928), pp. 59–65.

Bardell, Eunice Bonow, '*Primitive Physick*: John Wesley's Receipts', *Pharmacy in History* 21 (1979), pp. 111–21.

Bertucci, Paola, 'Revealing Sparks: John Wesley and the Religious Utility of Electrical Healing', *British Journal for the History of Science* 39 (2006), pp. 341–62.

Bibby, G., 'John Wesley and Vegetarianism', *Methodist Magazine* (May 1958), pp. 221–3.

Bowmer, John C., 'John Wesley – Physician!', *Wesley's Chapel Magazine* (October 1969).

Callaway, Clifford Wayne, 'John Wesley's *Primitive Physick*: An Essay in Appreciation', *Proceedings of the Mayo Clinic* 49 (1974), pp. 318–24.

Cannon, David S. H., 'John Wesley: A Pioneer in the Use of Electricity in

Medicine', *WHS Cumbria Branch Journal* 30 (Autumn 1992), pp. 12–15.

Coley, Hilda M., 'John Wesley Prescribes for Bodily Ailments', *Bookman* (London) 85 (1934), pp. 446–7.

Cone, Thomas E. Jr., 'The Reverend John Wesley as a Pediatrician', *Pediatrics* 61 (1978), p. 416.

Cross, William C., 'Wesley and Medicine: *Primitive Physic* and Its Critics', *Wesleyan Methodist Magazine* 137 (1914), pp. 613–18.

Cule, John, 'The Contribution of John Wesley (1703–1791) to Medical Literature', *XXVIIIth International Congress for History of Medicine 1982, Actes Proceeedings*, Asnières, Editions de médicine pratique, 1983, vol. 1, pp. 328–31.

Cule, John, 'The Rev. John Wesley, M.A. (Oxon.), 1703–1791; "The Naked Empiricist" and Orthodox Medicine', *Journal of the History of Medicine and Allied Sciences* 45 (1990), pp. 41–63.

Dakin, Paul Kingsley, 'John Wesley: Medicine for the Whole Man', *Journal of the Christian Medical Fellowship* 32:4 (October 1986), pp. 18–20; 33:1 (January 1987), pp. 8–11.

Davies, Edward, 'Y Pla Du: gyda rhai sylwadau ar ei ymosodiad ar Gymru', *Cylchgrawn gwyddonol* 17.3 (Spring 1990), pp. 92–7.

Davies, Edward, 'John Wesley a'i Brif Phisigwriaeth', *Y Traethodydd* 147 (1992), pp. 141–7.

Dock, George, 'The *Primitive Physick* of Rev. John Wesley', *Journal of the American Medical Association* 64 (1915), pp. 629–38.

Dodsley, Charles E., 'John Wesley as Physician', *Pharmaceutical Journal and Pharmacist* 104 (1920), pp. 26–7.

Donat, James G., 'The Rev. John Wesley's Extractions from Dr. Tissot: A Methodist *Imprimatur*', *History of Science* 39 (2001), pp. 285–98; French translation: 'Les extraits de Tissot choisis par Wesley: un *imprimatur* Méthodiste', in Vincent Barras and Micheline Louis-Courvoisier eds, *La médecine des Lumières: tout autour de Tissot*, Geneva, Bibliothèque d'histoire des sciences, Chêne-Bourg, Georg, 2001, pp. 261–81.

Donat, James G., 'Empirical Medicine in the 18th Century: The Rev. John Wesley's Search for Remedies that Work', *Methodist History* 44 (2006), pp. 216–26.

Donat, James G., 'John Wesley on the Estimation and Cure of Nervous Disorders', in Harry Whitaker, C. U. M. Smith and Stanley Finger eds, *Brain, Mind and Medicine: Essays in Eighteenth-Century Neuroscience*, New York, Springer-Verlag, 2007, pp. 285–300.

Dunlop, Richard, 'John Wesley: Medical Missionary in the New World', *Today's Health* 42:12 (1964), pp. 20–3, 70–2.

Flachsmeier, Horst Reinhold, 'John Wesley als Sozialhygieniker und Arzt', MD dissertation, Hamburg, 1957.

Foley, Gardner P. H., 'John Wesley's Dental Therapeutics', *Journal of the American Dental Association* 85 (1972), pp. 249–50.

Gadsby, Joseph Gordon, *Rev. John Wesley M.A.: Holistic Healing, Electrotherapy and Complementary Medicine*, Loughborough, Leicestershire, Teamprint, 1996.

Gadsby, Joseph Gordon, 'John Wesley – Whole Person Healer', *Heritage: The*

Journal of the East Midlands Branch of the Wesley Historical Society 5:1 (April 1997), pp. 4–18.

Gadsby, Joseph Gordon and Francis Dewhurst, 'John Wesley's Contribution to the Evolution of Alternative and Holistic Medicine', *Epworth Review* 26:1 (1999), pp. 95–104.

Gallagher, Herbert William, 'John Wesley and the Primitive Physic', *Down Survey: Yearbook of the Down County Museum*, 2000, pp. 46–51.

Gisel, G., 'John Wesley's Tätigkeit und Bedeutung als Arzt', *Schweizer Evangelist* 35 (1928), pp. 190ff. English summary in John G. Tasker, 'John Wesley as Physician: An Appreciation by G. Gisler', *Proceedings of the Wesley Historical Society* 16 (1928), pp. 141–4.

Gorman, Joe, 'John Wesley and Depression in an Age of Melancholy', *Wesleyan Theological Journal* 34:2 (1999), pp. 196–221.

Hackmann, Willem D., *John Wesley and His Electrical Machine*, London, John Wesley's House and The Museum of Methodism, 2003. Incorporated into: 'The Medical Electrical Machines of John Wesley and John Read', in Marco Beretta, Paolo Galluzzi and Carlo Triarico, eds, *Musa Musaei*, Florence, Leo S. Olschki, 2003, pp. 261–77.

Hiatt, R. Jeffrey, 'John Wesley and Healing: Developing a Wesleyan Missiology', *Asbury Theological Journal* 59 (2004), pp. 89–109.

Hill, A. Wesley, 'Was John Wesley a Methodist?', *Proceedings of the Wesley Historical Society* 30 (1955–56), pp. 82–5.

Hill, A. Wesley, *John Wesley Among the Physicians*, London, Epworth, 1958.

Hill, A. Wesley, 'Introduction', in *Primitive Physic by John Wesley*, London, Epworth, 1960, pp. 3–20.

Horby, Peter, '"Medicine to Heal Their Sickness": A Study of the Rev. John Wesley and His Philosophy of Health, Illness and Suffering', Wellcome Institute for the History of Medicine BSc thesis, 1989.

Hughes, Melanie Dobson, 'The Holistic Way: John Wesley's Practical Piety as a Resource for Integrated Healthcare', *Journal of Religion and Health*, forthcoming 2008, accessible on line <http://www.springerlink.com/content/yt4h0647165861x5/fulltext.pdf>.

Hunter, Richard A., 'A Brief Review of the Use of Electricity in Psychiatry with Special Reference to John Wesley', *British Journal of Physical Medicine* 20:5 (1957), pp. 98–100.

Jeffrey, Frederick, 'John Wesley's *Primitive Physick*', *Proceedings of the Wesley Historical Society* 21 (1937), pp. 60–67.

King, Lester S., *The Medical World of the Eighteenth Century*, Chicago, IL, University of Chicago Press, 1958.

Kirkby, William, 'Wesley's *Primitive Physic*', *Pharmaceutical Journal and Pharmacist* (23 April 1932); reprinted in *Proceedings of the Wesley Historical Society* 18 (1932), pp. 149–53.

Kyle, Robert A. and Marc A. Shampo, 'John Wesley', *Journal of the American Medical Association* 240 (1978), p. 2008.

Laffey, Paul, 'John Wesley on Insanity', *History of Psychiatry* 12 (2001), pp. 467–79.

Lichtwardt, Hartman A., 'Ancient Therapy in Persia and in England: Being extracts from *Therapeutics of Joseph*, Herat, 1511 A.D. and from John

Wesley's *Primitive Physick*, London, 1772', *Annals of Medical History* n.s. 6 (1934), pp. 280–84.

McKean, G. R., 'Primitive Physic', *Canadian Magazine* 64 (1925), pp. 238, 256

Madden, Deborah, 'Experience and the Common Interest of Mankind: The Enlightened Empiricism of John Wesley's *Primitive Physic*', *British Journal for Eighteenth-Century Studies* 26 (2003), pp. 41–53.

Madden, Deborah, 'Contemporary Reaction to John Wesley's *Primitive Physic*: Or, the Case of Dr. William Hawes Examined', *Social History of Medicine* 17 (2004), pp. 365–78.

Madden, Deborah, 'Medicine and Moral Reform: The Place of Practical Piety in John Wesley's Art of Physic', *Church History* 73 (2004), pp. 741–58.

Madden, Deborah, 'The Limitation of Human Knowledge: Faith and the Empirical Method in John Wesley's Medical Holism', *History of European Ideas* 32 (2006), pp. 162–72.

Madden, Deborah, '"A Cheap, Safe and Natural Medicine": Religion, Medicine and Culture in John Wesley's *Primitive Physic*', *Clio Medica* 83, Amsterdam and New York, Rodopi, 2007.

Maddocks, Morris, 'Health and Healing in the Ministry of John Wesley', in John Stacey, ed., *John Wesley, Contemporary Perspectives*, London, Epworth, 1988, pp. 138–49.

Maddox, Randy L., 'John Wesley on Holistic Health and Healing', *Methodist History* 46 (2007), pp. 4–33, available online <http://www.divinity.duke.edu/docs/faculty/maddox/wesley>.

Malony, H. Newton, 'John Wesley and the Eighteenth Century Therapeutic Uses of Electricity', *Perspectives on Science and Christian Faith* 47 (1995), pp. 244–54.

Malony, H. Newton, 'John Wesley's *Primitive Physick*: An 18th Century Health Psychology', *Journal of Health Psychology* 1 (1996), pp. 147–59.

Marriott, Thomas, 'Methodism in Former Days: Medicine and Medical Advice', *Wesleyan Methodist Magazine* 69 (1846), pp. 359–64.

'A Medical Tract by John Wesley', *British Medical Journal* (29 March 1902), pp. 799–800.

Meistad, Tore, 'Helbredelse og frelse i wesleyansk teologi og tradiisjon' (Healing and Salvation in Wesleyan Theology and Tradition), in *Studier i Wesleyansk Teologi*, Alta, Norway, Alta Lærerhøgskole, 1994, pp. 179–214.

Menzies, S. W. S., 'Rev. John Wesley, A. M.', *Scalpel and Tongs* 24 (1980), pp. 133–5.

Mitchell, Ben, 'Reverend John Wesley (1703–1791): *Primitive Physic*', *Ethics & Medicine* 15:1 (1999), pp. 2–9.

Nash, Vaughan, 'The Illustrious Quack', *New Statesman and Nation* n.s., 1931, vol. 2, pp. 252–3.

Newton, John A., 'Health and Healing in the Wesleys', *Methodist Recorder* (1988); reprinted in *The Wesleys for Today*, London, Methodist Newspaper Co., 1989, pp. 21–4.

Ott, Philip Wesley, 'John Wesley and the Non-Naturals', *Preventive Medicine* 9 (1980), pp. 578–84.

Ott, Philip Wesley, 'John Wesley on Health: A Word for Sensible Regimen', *Methodist History* 18 (1980), pp. 193–204.

Ott, Philip Wesley, 'John Wesley on Mind and Body: Toward an Understanding of Health as Wholeness', *Methodist History* 27 (1989), pp. 61–72.

Ott, Philip Wesley, 'John Wesley on Health as Wholeness', *Journal of Religion and Health* 30 (1991), pp. 43–57.

Payne, Leonard, '. . . A Doctor in the House?', *Journal of the Royal College of Physicians of London* 19:1 (1985), pp. 55, 58.

Plummer, John T., 'John Wesley', *Nashville Journal of Medicine and Surgery* 13 (1857), pp. 290–7.

Plummer, John T., 'John Wesley's *Primitive Physick*', *Nashville Journal of Medicine and Surgery* 15 (1858), pp. 282–6.

Pye, Jonathan Howard, 'John Wesley's Primitive Physick: "Old Women's Nostrums" or Evidence-based Medicine?', *Bulletin of the Wesley Historical Society, Bristol Branch* 90 (March 2005), pp. 1–18.

Rack, Henry D., 'Doctors, Demons, and Early Methodist Healing', in W.J. Sheils ed., *The Church and Healing*, Oxford: Basil Blackwell, 1982, pp. 137–52.

Richardson, Ruth, 'John Wesley's Ethereal Fire', *The Lancet* 358 (2001), p. 932.

Riddell, William Renwick, 'Wesley's System of Medicine', *New York Journal of Medicine* 99 (1914), pp. 64–8.

Rogal, Samuel J., 'Pills for the Poor: John Wesley's *Primitive Physick*', *Yale Journal of Biology and Medicine* 51 (1978), pp. 81–90.

Rogal, Samuel J., 'Electricity: John Wesley's "Curious and Important Subject"', *Eighteenth Century Life* 13 (1989), pp. 78–90.

Rousseau, George Sebastian, 'John Wesley's *Primitive Physic* (1747)', *Harvard Library Bulletin* 16 (1968), pp. 242–56.

Schiller, Francis, 'Reverend Wesley, Doctor Marat, and the Electric Fire', *Clio Medica* 15 (1981), pp. 159–76.

Scott, J. T., '*Primitive Physic*', *American Journal of Physical Therapy* 6 (1929), pp. 137–40.

Simpson, William C., Jr., 'Pastors, Preachers, and the Healing Arts: The Wesleyan Tradition', *Living Pulpit* 6 (1997), pp. 22–3.

Stewart, David, 'John Wesley, the Physician', *Wesleyan Theological Journal* 4.1 (1969), pp. 27–38.

Stillings, Dennis, 'John Wesley: Electrotherapist', *Medical Instrumentation* 8 (1974), p. 66.

Stillings, Dennis, 'A Survey of the History of Electric Stimulation', *Medical Instrumentation* 9 (1975), pp. 255–9 (256–7 on Wesley).

Storey, Geoffrey O., 'John Wesley (1708–91)', *Journal of Medical Biography* 14 (2006), pp. 218–22.

Stroup, William, 'Meat, Ethics, and the Case of John Wesley', in Regina Hewitt and Pat Rogers eds, *Orthodoxy and Heresy in Eighteenth-Century Society*, Lewisburg, PA, Bucknell University Press, 2002, pp. 267–80.

Sweringen, Hiram Van, 'Rev. John Wesley As a Physician', *Cincinnati Lancet-Clinic* n.s. 46 (1901), p. 238.

Thomas, Burton G., 'John Wesley on the Art of Healing', *The British Medical Journal* (28 April 1906), pp. 987–8; reprinted in *American Physician* (November 1906), pp. 295–8.

Tranter, Julie, 'John Wesley's *Primitive Physic: An Easy and Natural Way of Curing Most Diseases*', *International Journal of Dermatology* 28 (1989), pp. 92–3.

Turrell, Walter John, 'Three Electrotherapists of the Eighteenth Century: John Wesley, Jean Paul Marat, and James Graham', *Annals of Medical History* 3 (1921), pp. 361–7.

Turrell, Walter John, *John Wesley: Physician and Electrotherapist*, Oxford, Blackwell, 1938.

Vanderpool, Harold Y., 'The Wesleyan Methodist Tradition', in Ronald Numbers and Darrel Amundson eds, *Caring and Curing: Health and Medicine in the Western Religious Traditions*, New York, Macmillan, 1986, pp. 317–53.

Wallace, Charles, 'Eating and Drinking with John Wesley: The Logic of His Practice', *Bulletin of the John Rylands University Library* 85:2–3 (2003), pp. 137–55.

Webster, Robert Joseph Jr., 'Chapter 5: Balsamic Virtue: Supernatural Healing in John Wesley', in 'Methodism and the Miraculous: John Wesley's Contribution to the *Historia Miraculorum*', Oxford University PhD thesis, 2006, pp. 241–85.

Weinstein, A. A., 'John Wesley, Physician and Apothecary', *Georgia Review* 10 (1956), pp. 48–54.

'Wesley's Electricity', *Scientific American* 64 (1891), p. 210.

Wilcoxon, Clair D., 'The Whole Man: A Study of John Wesley's Healing Ministry', *Religion in Life* 28 (1959), pp. 580–86.

Woodward, Max W., 'Wesley's Electric Machine', *Nursing Mirror* 114 (27 July 1962), pp. x, xvi.

Appendix

To that Fanatical, Political, Physical
Enthusiast, Patriot, and Physician,
the Reverend Mr. W[esle]y.[1]

As in some country town we often find
The draper, mercer, and the laceman join'd,
So, great monopolist, are found in thee,
Myst'ries more weighty, and in number three.
Hail, holy mountebank! from whose weak stage
Enthusiasm whines, who lately us'd to rage.[2]
Hail, great successor of the frantic mission!

---

[1] [This is a broadsheet, published in 1776 (August or later), with no printer named. At least one copy survives, in the British Library: © British Library Board. All Rights Reserved (shelfmark 1876.e.9.8). The footnotes that follow are original to the broadsheet unless material appears in square brackets.]

[2] Whoever has heard the deceased saint [Whitefield], and his present successor, will easily perceive the contrast between the bellowing vociferations of the squinting professor, and the drawling languor of this lank-hair'd retailer of perdition.

Hail to thee, scurvy, pious politician!
Who stand'st with Satan's fav'rites on a level,
And gratis get'st diploma from the Devil.[3]
Thrice do we hail thee by thy new addition,
Pois'ner in print, and primitive Physician.[4]
How often hast thou fill'd the ears and eyes
Of gaping crowds with horror and surprise?
How oft, with hypocritic frenzy meet,
Snuffled damnation in the publick street?
Each list'ner call'd half devil and half beast;
Nor till thy saintship well was pelted, ceas'd.
O, matchless impudence! and close combin'd
With ignorance, to sport with humankind!
Forever cursed be that fatal day
When first you learnt that trade – to preach and pray.
Fathers and mothers, widows, wives, till death,
May rue the minute when you drew your breath.
How many idle vagrants hast thou made,[5]
Who else had liv'd upon a wholesome trade;
Who now their industry shall use no more,
But to mislead a mob and swell thy store?
For ever cursed be that fatal day
When first in politics you went astray,[6]
When such a wretched fool, so low a thing,
In print presum'd to dictate to his king;
Then many a wretch in peace had slumber'd well,
And only fear'd thy visionary hell.
But doubly cursed be that dreadful day
When to the press thy pamphlet made its way.
That anticlimax, what could make thee tread,

---

[3] For who but the devil could so harden a man's heart that it should permit him to publish and rejoice in the sale of a performance evidently calculated to put a few shillings into the pocket of the diabolical author at the expense of the healths, and perhaps the lives, of his fellow-creatures?

[4] Mr. Hawes has proved, in his very ingenious *Examination of the Primitive Physick* just published, that some of Mr. W's prescriptions would absolutely kill those who were so weak as to make use of them.

[5] [This is a reference to Wesley's itinerating lay preachers.]

[6] The writer alludes to the *Calm Address* and other political matters lately published by Mr. W.

Forsake the heart to tamper with the head?[7]
Art thou so dead to shame, so callous grown
To all disgrace, the brethren's or thy own?
In vain thy predecessor tried to botch
That vile – adventure of the lady's watch.[8]
Given for sale to sooth a widow's woe,
And found within the *holy* man's bureau.
Hast thou so soon forgot the forty pounds
Laid by against th' exciseman went his rounds?
The squinting wretch in vain a husband shunn'd,
And what from Ruth he squeez'd, Tom made refund.
Hast thou so soon forgot thy own reproach,
When late you whin'd and canted for a coach?
All your long service in the faith you told,
And represented you was weak and old;
Strok'd your lank hair, which then more flaccid hung,
And faith and spirit trembled on your tongue;
Trembled for fear thy most audacious talk
Should not prevail, and thou be forc'd to walk.
And wilt thou now, as impudent as base,
Attempt to give the Faculty disgrace;[9]
Men of long practice, eminence, and knowledge,

---

[7] On reflection it does not seem strange that he should prefer the body to the soul, for by his publication he has plainly evinced that where his own temporal interest comes in competition with the life of others, he prefers the former. Had the whole question been confined to others, it is most likely he cares for neither.

[8] This story [about Whitefield] is too well known to need a comment, as also the story of the frail brother who was detected at Bath in a crim. con. [i.e., 'criminal conversation', or adultery; a reference to James Wheatley] and, for the honour of the holy fraternity, ordered to decamp, which he did without beat of drum. The story of the forty pounds, the present apostle's great affection for a chariot, his whinings to obtain it, and the number of disciples he lost by it, are all to public in the neighbourhood of the saints to need further explanation.

[9] Mr. W., in the preface of his *Primitive Physic*, speaks of physicians and apothecaries in the most illiberal and unmanly terms, as such language seemed necessary to promote the sale of his venomous and ignorant pamphlet. But happily Mr. Hawes has opened the eyes of the public, and is the only gentleman of the Faculty that stood forth to support himself and brethren. He has undeniably proved the rashness, folly, and wickedness of this divine empyric, in attempting to impose upon the public the most horrid truth, which he calls a *rational* and *easy* method of curing most diseases. He might have said in some cases also certain, for the operation of some of the prescriptions would have been that never-failing and decisive exhibition called *death*.

Train'd up to physic, members of a college?
Does not thy canting give enough of wealth,
But must thou likewise prey upon our health?
Poison the principles with doctrine vile,
With drams of verdigrease our bowels spoil;[10]
And like the satyr, as in fable told,
From the same breath at once blow hot and cold?[11]
Thank heaven thou shall not, for there still remain
Who can and will thy wicked course restrain.
Art thou in vice, by practice, grown so bold,
To thank opponents that thy poison sold,[12]
So wrapt in av'rice, lost to sober sense,
To sell the peoples lives for eighteen pence?[13]
Thank heav'n thou canst not, while there lives a Hawes,
And learned Pringle stamps him with applause.[14]

A Detester of Hypocrisy

---

[10] One of his vile prescriptions is *a dram or two* of verdigrease; another, *six grains* of opium for a dose. – The writer most earnestly requests every one who has the misfortune to be possessed of Mr. W's book to read Mr. Hawes's answer, as their health, nay even their lives, are much interested in this inquiry. He also submits it to the Faculty, whether it is expedient that an humble address be presented to his Majesty, through the hands of his physicians, setting forth the fatal consequences which may ensue from this pamphlet, and earnestly requesting, as he tenders the lives of his loving subjects, and to deter others from the like offense, that the *Primitive Physic* be publicly burnt by the hands of the common hangman.

[11] Mr. W. prescribes *cold water, hot water, tar water,* and *flint water* for the cholic. – Mr. Hawes says this unaccountable professor prescribes hot and cold remedies in the same breath. See his *Examination*, p. 32.

[12] Mr. W., July 24th, in *Lloyd's Evening Post*, very wickedly addressed Mr. Hawes, thanking him for his publication, as it increased the sale of his pamphlet. Mr Hawes answered this address July 26th in the same paper with that spirit and good sense which does him great honour.

[13] [The revised 17th edn of *Primitive Physick* rose in cost to 18 pence.]

[14] The writer is well assured that Sir John Pringle [President of the Royal Society, and Physician-in-ordinary to the King] has spoke in the highest terms of Mr. Hawes's *Examination of Mr. Wesley's Primitive Physic*. But as the shafts of ridicule have often succeeded beyond more solid opposition, we have endeavoured to attack him from that quarter. There are few misfortunes without some alleviations; let us hope that this publication of Mr. W., replete with evil, will in the end have a contrary effect. Mr. Hawes has checked its course. Let us indulge ourselves in the agreeable expectations, that the many corroborating proofs of the Doctor's possessing a mischievous head and wicked heart may open the eyes of some worthy person now misled by him, to the utter destruction of those three professions he now unwarrantably exercises – politics, quackery, and fanaticism.

2

A Wesleyan Theology of
Environmental Stewardship

MARGARET G. FLOWERS

Introduction

Living conditions in the eighteenth-century English countryside and in cities like London were characterized by an 'impure . . . water supply, non-existent sewage disposal, and atmospheric pollution'.[1] Water was obtained from wells sunk just below the water table, and often were badly polluted; rivers were not necessarily better. Air pollution, a serious problem since before 1285, was caused in large part by the heavy consumption of wood, peat, and high sulphur coal.[2] Yet, 'despite the fact that Londoners complained bitterly about the smog caused by the many coal fires in winter, ecology was not on the theological agenda in Wesley's day.'[3] Such was the setting of John and Charles Wesley, who observed and responded to the conditions of their day, and about this, John Wesley, in particular, left an extensive body of both scientific contributions and theological writings.

Even though focused attention to the environment was not uppermost in Wesley's mind, nevertheless, it was part of the landscape. In this, as in other areas, 'Wesley's greatness lay in his ability to size up the situation of his time accurately and to shape a ministry that was amazingly effective in that situation'.[4] But since the contemporary situation differs so dramatically from the one that pertained to Wesley's time, there is a danger that his teachings might be obsolete – or even part of the problem. For instance, John B. Cobb argued that 'Wesley's theology was formed with little awareness of the full implications of modern science – not at all of post-modern science.'[5] However, since Wesley extended his anthropology – developed to keep in balance both divine grace and human responsibility – to include all creation, he has a valuable contribution to make to contemporary Christian understanding of earth-keeping. For this reason, though anachronistic, it will be helpful to retain a set of modern scientific terms, such as 'science' and 'biology', for analytical purposes when discussing Wesley's ideas on natural history and philosophy.

Currently, there are two communities with an interest in this question: a general scientific community of ecologists and environmental scientists, and a Christian community that might view scientific findings with great scepticism because of the worldviews expressed by some members of the scientific community. The ability to be heard is dependent upon speaking both the language of science and that of theology. Wesley made (or propagated) important 'scientific' contributions in the areas of medicine and what may loosely be termed 'natural history,' which today now also includes the modern discipline of 'environmental science'. Here, Wesley demonstrated an acute appreciation of the importance of observation and verification through experimentation. Additionally, as this chapter will show, Wesley's eschatological views, his advocacy of animal rights and social holiness, as well as his opposition to deism, have profound implications for contemporary issues concerning environmental stewardship.

John Wesley the 'scientist'

It must be stated at the outset that John Wesley was not an experimental 'scientist', but rather a minister of the gospel. He was more an observer than an active participant; he had time only to speculate about the causes of natural events, not the time to conduct detailed experiments. Thus, in analyzing his 'scientific' endeavours, it is not appropriate to judge him with the same standards that we would use today to judge his eighteenth-century scientific contemporaries, such as Joseph Priestley. A note here about the content of Wesley's writing is appropriate. Not all of what he published was entirely from his own pen. He copied and excerpted the works of others (giving appropriate credit), both scientific and theological. While Sara Joan Miles has argued that Wesley's copied material does not necessarily imply his agreement, Wesley's prefaces, intercalated comments, and editing do suggest assent.[6] Indeed, there is precedent for this position. *A Collection of Hymns for the Use of the People Called Methodists* is such an edited work; here, Wesley selected from the vast number of hymns written by Charles Wesley, excised or conflated particular verses, and even substituted specific words.[7] Works published under Wesley's name, as well as those edited by him, will therefore be examined as evidence of Wesley's personal views.

Wesley demonstrated a lifelong interest in science, one that was more intense than that of the average educated English gentleman.[8] He followed its progress and applications, and 'focus[ed] on science to serve his grand purpose of furthering the gospel and helping the sick'.[9] As one nineteenth-century biographer noted, 'natural history was a field in which he walked at every opportunity . . . but he was obliged to view these wonderful works of God in the labours of others; his various and continual employments . . . not permitting him to make experiments and observations.'[10] Despite Wesley's restricted time to pursue his interest in natural history, 'new books on science were devoured by him with almost as much relish as new books on theology . . . he [did not allow] his citizenship in heaven . . . [to] deaden his curiosity concerning the spinning globe on which he was now living'.[11]

John Wesley's scientific endeavours and statements have not received universal approval. Some have noted disapprovingly of Wesley's aversion to mathematics, and his negative attitude toward experimentation and speculative theory. Wesley's attitude towards mathematics was personal, rather than universal; he encouraged others to experiment, even though he did little personally, and he focused on the practical, rather than theoretical aspects of science.[12] In analyzing the 'antiscience' objections to Wesley, J.W. Haas Jr. notes that religious prohibition of scientific activity or of regulating acceptable scientific beliefs results in 'religious antiscience'.[13] Yet Haas did not find this with Wesley. Wesley's enemies were 'deism, atheism, materialism and intellectual pride,' and not 'science' or, what it was generally referred to in the eighteenth century, 'natural philosophy'.[14] Moreover, he was 'unwilling to subscribe to the antiscientific sentiments expressed by leading Tory intellectuals of his day . . . and the typical High-Churchman . . . opposition to everything new and modern'.[15] Wesley is unique, not only because of his fascination with science, but also for his uniquely broad-based and nuanced response to science.[16] An example of this can be seen in his opposition to current views regarding animals, namely, that they were useful, hurtful, or superfluous to humanity.[17] Haas suggests that Wesley's comments on science found in sermons and other writings should be understood in the context of his religious message and evaluated with the perspective of his specifically scientific writings.[18]

Wesley demonstrated numerous characteristics that are the marks of a 'scientific' mind: insatiable intellectual curiosity, keen powers of observation, a passion for making actual experiment the test of truth, an analytical mind, formation of hypotheses, and belief in the universality of natural law.[19] Wesley also demonstrated the important scientific ability to be swayed by new evidence and new perspectives.[20] In his interests and focus, Wesley was not exploring the 'mysteries' of medicine, electricity or natural history, for the sake of pure knowledge. Rather, he was a pragmatic 'applied scientist', who focused on making human life more abundant. We will turn now to his work related to medicine to understand his approach.

Wesley's Interest in Medicine: Nature in the Service of Humanity

Wesley's view of the history of medicine was influenced by his reading of Genesis and the introduction of sickness with Original Sin.[21] Sin came into the world, but the medicines to treat disorders were originally empirically verified; later studies of the human body and other parts of the natural world led to more theoretical and abstruse practices in medicine.[22] Observing the result of prevalent methods within medical practice, Wesley commented, 'the common method of compounding and recompounding medicines, can never be reconciled to Common Sense.'[23] Wesley's goal was a return to the more simple, more easily understandable approach to treatment of illness, and one that was also more affordable: 'to set down cheap, safe, and easy medicines'.[24] An entry in his *Journal* explains his concerns about medical negligence in graphic terms, and also indicates an appreciation of the whole person – mind as well as body, a concept that is recently being rediscovered by the medical profession.[25]

Wesley's goal was a return to experience and experiment, hence his title, *Primitive Physic*. He paid serious attention to 'objections' that were raised, and modified its contents accordingly.[26] In his Preface to the second edition (1755), he omitted medicines that were not easily obtainable and others that were not safe, including opium and quicksilver (mercury).[27] In the 1760 edition, he also added the word 'Tried'.[28] In the same month that *Primitive Physic* appeared, Wesley noted in his *Journal* the success rate of his treatments amongst those who had come for medical assistance.[29] Though written for the poor, *Primitive Physic* was not just for others. Wesley self-medicated treacle for a toothache and 'garlick' applied to the soles of the feet for hoarseness and back pain.[30]

Familiarity with the best medicines available, based on personal observations, was highly valued by Wesley. In his abridgement and republication of Samuel Tissot's *L'Avis au Peuple sur sa Santé* (1762), which was translated and sold in Methodist preaching houses as *Advice with Respect to Health* (1769), Wesley praised the usefulness of this book since it was based on 'sound reason and experience,' though he did not hesitate to criticize treatments he considered to be dubious.[31] Wesley, therefore, did not merely reprint the book, but edited and simplified what he had observed to be wasteful or dangerous cures.[32] This included the overuse of bleeding, a dangerous treatment for most ailments, and here Wesley was one of the most influential critics in this objection.[33] In the introduction to his *Survey of the Wisdom of God in the Creation* (1763), Wesley wrote with amazement and sorrow that transfusions, the beneficial antithesis to bloodletting, were so seldom performed.[34] In view of the modern, professional specialization of medicine, it would be natural to question Wesley's incursions into this field. Yet as recent scholarship has shown, including work undertaken by contributors to this volume, Wesley was 'as qualified as most of the physicians of his time, and more so than many of them'.[35]

Wesley's Interest in Natural History: Demonstration of the Glory of God

While Wesley's contributions to the medical practice of his day demonstrated a compassion for the physical well-being of humanity, his writings in the area of natural history show a concern for matters spiritual: demonstrating God's glory in the creation. These writings, found primarily in his *Journal* and *A Survey of the Wisdom of God in the Creation*, show not only an acute appreciation for detailed and accurate observations of others, but also an ability to make similar observations of his own. The writings from these sources bear most directly on the question of Wesley's value as a 'scientist' for contemporary issues concerning environmental stewardship.

As is evidenced by his *Journal* entries, much of Wesley's life was spent in travel from one ministry location to another. Scattered among the destinations and events that transpired in these locations, there are occasional references to the landscape, often referring to fruitful hills, valleys, woods and green meadows.[36] Wesley also had an eye for the unusual. He noted the aftermath of a flood near Hayfield and included in that day's notations a description from an eyewitness, John Bennet.[37] Attention to the objects of nature was occasionally even necessary for Wesley's ministry activities; a field in Pocklington proposed as a preaching site 'was plentifully furnished with stones – artillery ready at hand for the devil's drunken companions'.[38]

By far, Wesley's most important and extensive scientific work is *A Survey of the Wisdom of God in the Creation*, first published in 1763 in two volumes, but which Wesley expanded to five in the third (1777) edition.[39] In this and subsequent editions, Wesley included an abridgement of

Robert Bonnet's *Contemplation of Nature* (1764) and an extract of Louis Deutens' *Inquiry into the Origin of the Discoveries Attributed to the Moderns* (1766, 1769).[40] These contents were published in numerous English and American editions; about 75 years after its original publication, a three-volume revision by R. Mudie updated the scientific content.[41]

Wesley's goal was to produce a text that was 'plain, clear, and intelligible to one of a tolerable understanding . . . contain[ing] the sum of what is most valuable'.[42] To do this required that Wesley 'retrench, enlarge, or alter every chapter, and almost every section [and add] the choicest discoveries both of our own, and of the foreign societies'.[43] Wesley viewed this compendium of natural philosophy as 'simply and nakedly exprest, in the most clear, easy, and intelligent manner, that the nature of things would allow'.[44] In this work, Wesley noted, 'I endeavour throughout, not to *account for* things; but only to *describe* them. I undertake barely to set down what appears in nature; not the cause of those appearances.'[45] Wesley admitted that the knowledge contained in the *Survey* was far from exhaustive, but did fulfil the purpose of pointing to the creative hand of God.[46]

Schofield characterized this book as 'little more than curiosity as far as science is concerned . . . the best example of Wesley's religious interest in science,' and 'a book to be read for a picture of eighteenth-century popular ideas of science'.[47] It is noteworthy, however, that although there is certainly theological content in the *Survey*, its content and organization are highly scientific and systematic. The *Survey* in its later editions is divided into five parts: 'Of Man,' 'Of Brutes,' 'Of Plants and Fossils,' 'Of Earth, Water, Fire, Air and Meteors,' and 'Of the System of the World, Heavenly Bodies, Properties and Causes of Natural Bodies'.

Wesley's writings obviously refuse tidy classification into modern disciplines, such as taxonomy, ecology, and animal behaviour, to name just a few. The modern study of environmental science is interdisciplinary by its nature, yet Wesley also wanted to see the 'big picture,' the unified whole. While it is difficult to translate much of Wesley's *Survey* into neat categories of inquiry for the twenty-first century, it is, nevertheless, useful to determine Wesley's affinity to scientific experiments, his view of the created world and humanity's responsibility towards it.

Taxonomy, Genetics, and Evolution

What is the number of species currently extant on the planet? There is general consensus, even today, that numerous species and genera, and perhaps even families, remain to be discovered in remote regions, especially in tropical and marine habitats. Wesley sensed this to be true, noting the impossibility of estimating the undiscovered species in each genus, but attempting, as do taxonomists today, to give an accurate estimate of the global populations.[48] In England, with its relatively low species diversity, Wesley was probably not able to gain first-hand knowledge or understanding of species extinction, one of the obvious results of modern environmental degradation. Following the prominent scientists of his day, however, he believed that no new species would be added to the number already present on earth.[49]

For Wesley, the creation was arranged in a 'chain of being', which was uniquely part of God's good creation, though each imperceptibly different.[50] These species were distinct, as Wesley noted in his description of what would later be called the 'common garden experiment' used to distinguish between characteristics that are genetically determined from those that are the result of genetically permitted adaptations to the environment.[51] Despite his belief in the fixity of species, Wesley recognized that change was part of the natural world.[52] He was able to embrace change as integral to the created order, but, contrary to attempts made by some scholars wishing to see his chain of being as a form of proto-Darwinian theory of evolutionary causation, Wesley would not have endorsed any system of thought antipathetic to the theologically orthodox doctrines of Creation, Original Sin or the Atonement.[53] This is most evident in his harsh criticism of the French natural historian George-Louis Leclerc, Count de Buffon.[54]

Natural History

Care of the creation or environmental stewardship requires not only a theoretical knowledge of the number of species, but also presupposes familiarity with their details: their form, function and life cycle (phenology). By including in the *Survey*, as well as his *Journal*, detailed descriptions of a number of plants and animals, both local and foreign, as well as wild species and those domesticated (or otherwise useful to humanity), Wesley documented his own keen powers of observation. Of particular medical interest was a plant (*Cinchona*) from South America – the medicinal properties of which had been discovered during the seventeenth century by Catholic missionaries, hence its nickname, 'Jesuits' Bark'. Wesley noted not only the characteristics of the 'bark' used in European medicine (later identified as quinine) and its fruit used by the indigenous population, but also those parts with little or no medicinal value, as well as its evergreen habit.[55] His observations on animals included information on biogeography, morphology, nutrition, and behaviour. For example, attracted by its size, he included a lengthy discussion of the elephant.[56] Animals of interest were not found only in distant lands. One of Wesley's journal entries includes detailed descriptions of an herbivorous mammal confined to the Tower of London, which he characterized as a 'monster', as well as a pelican, 'one of the most beautiful [birds] in nature.' [57]

Ecology

Ecology is a vast area of modern expertise, encompassing topics such as soil science, hydrology, meteorology, geography, phenology, population, community, eco-system structure, and plant-animal interactions. From the scientist's perspective, 'basic ecology provides a scientific context for evaluating environmental issues'.[58] The ecology of organisms is complex, so a broad, scientific appreciation and understanding is critical to the development of environmental stewardship.

A basic tenet of ecological study is that species distributions are controlled by the environment: temperature, elevation, precipitation, soil structure and composition. From Bonnet's *Contemplation of Nature*, Wesley observed: 'All climates have their productions: all parts of the earth their inhabitants. From the frozen regions of the bear, to the burning sands of the torrid zone, all is animated'.[59] And in the *Survey*, Wesley observed that God 'proportioned the variety of plants in each country, to the exigencies of the inhabitants, and adapted the variety of the soils, to the nature of those plants'.[60] These plants were adapted by physiological and anatomical characteristics to specific climates, with some narrowly restricted, while others were more cosmopolitan. Furthermore, some could serve as food and shelter for other species.[61] Animals, too, both terrestrial and aquatic, were perfectly adapted to their environment. The most dramatic indication of this was those living in rigorous northerly climates, as evidenced by various modifications.[62]

In his publication of the *Survey*, Wesley also demonstrated an understanding of primary/secondary productivity and the energy relations in both terrestrial or marine food chains and webs.[63] Wesley also demonstrated a clear grasp of the processes of forest decomposition and detritivore food chains.[64] He noted the defensive mechanisms of plants against predation and the results of species competition.[65] By various means, the balance of species and number of individuals will reach the carrying capacity of the environment. Wesley recognized this, and noted that competition and predation would result if this carrying capacity were exceeded. He also accurately described 'K-selection' (long lived organisms, producing few offspring with high survival rates) and 'r-selection' (small organisms, with high rate of reproduction),[66] concepts that came into vogue within the ecological community in 1967, nearly two hundred years later.[67]

Wesley understood that the distribution and germination of seeds, necessary steps in the functioning of any ecosystem, was a complex and species-specific process, which sometimes involved structures, such as hooks on the seeds, but all requiring an appropriate micro-environment.[68] Animal predation is required by many plants for seed dispersal, as are the appropriate meteorological conditions.[69] Wesley had an imperfect understanding of the reproductive structure of moss but nevertheless appropriately described its method of dissemination.[70] He thus dispelled a commonplace theory of 'spontaneous generation', which was not conclusively disproved until the work of Louis Pasteur, a century later.[71]

Beyond the study of individual organisms, and their relationship to one another, is Wesley's consideration of the non-living world. With his understanding of the world before Original Sin, Wesley described the earth's mountains, and recognized their importance in the hydrologic cycle, and, ultimately, for the existence of both plants and animals.[72] An aquatic ecosystem that Wesley described was the bog; he not only understood the unique vegetation and character of bogs, but also noted differences between mountain and lowland bogs.[73]

The created world, with its species diversity, interrelationships among individuals, and controlling abiotic environment, is not only complex, but dynamic. The natural process of converting one habitat type to another is termed 'succession'. Primary succession begins with a habitat devoid of organic matter; secondary succession occurs in disturbed habitats where organic matter remains in the environment. In the *Survey*, Wesley provided an excellent description of those early stages of primary xeric succession on rocks.[74] He also identified the more common secondary aquatic succession from marsh to meadow.[75] Although the ecological term had not yet been coined, Wesley described what is now referred to as the 'holocoenotic environment', an environment where all parts, living and non-living, are linked and dependent on one another: 'all the parts of nature therefore were constituted for the assistance of each other, and all undeniably prove the Unity of their Omniscient Creator.'[76]

Animal Behaviour

An aspect of biological science that is intimately linked to ecology, and therefore, to environmental science, is the study of animal behaviour. Indeed, this is absolutely central to the animal rights movement today, which has also found its own niche in some quarters of the contemporary environmental protection movement. As Wesley found from his own observations, some behavioural activities were clearly involved with the survival or reproduction of particular species, though others were not so apparent. For Wesley, this was a lifelong interest; one of his three disputation lectures for the Master's Degree at Oxford concerned animals' 'souls' and their 'reasoning' powers.[77]

Writing before the advent of modern sociobiology, with its distinctions regarding the origins of various behavioural patterns, Wesley attributed all actions of 'brutes' to the powers of reasoning and, in doing so, countered those who took a 'mechanistic' view of animal creation. Noting that reason was a feature common to both humans and 'brutes', Wesley described a dog's strategy to get onto a high table.[78] Apart from these examples of learned behaviour, there were also instances of operant conditioning, and Wesley observed instinctive behaviour in the nest-building activity of birds.[79] He described too the physiological response to lowered temperatures, during which many animals hibernated, or had markedly depressed levels of physical activity, accompanied by drastically lowered respiratory levels.[80]

Altruistic behaviour is often explained in terms of complex reasoning, of which only humans are capable. In other animals, it is less easy to explain and has been the subject of much twentieth-century research. Wesley noted in his *Journal* an example of 'brute' altruism in cats.[81] In addition to this, he commented on the unusual inter-specific behavioural pattern between a Newfoundland dog and old raven.[82] Wesley's fascination with aspects of animal behaviour even extended to conducting simple experiments. He recorded in his *Journal* an attempt to determine whether the fondness for music demonstrated by a lion in Edinburgh was characteristic of other members of that or related species.[83] Later, with this experiment still on his mind, he noted horses gathering around when singing took place during a service: 'is it true then that horses, as well as lions and tigers, have an ear for music?'[84]

God, Humanity, and Creation

The *Survey*, which was not produced as a purely scientific work, but as a natural philosophy, 'treats both of God himself, and of his creatures, visible and invisible . . . with the express purpose of demonstrating the wisdom of God in the creation'.[85] For Wesley, that wisdom did not end with the act of creation, but included his understanding of divine providence, God's continuing care for the created order. Understanding the nature of this continuing care, and humanity's role in it, can serve as the basis for a theology of environmental stewardship.

All parts of the created order show forth the grandeur of God, and these parts are written in such a way that they may be universally understood. There is no part of humanity, no place in the world, where God's character is not evident: in violent or pleasant weather, in the succeeding generations of plants and animals, in the cycle of life and death.[86] Wesley noted that by God's command, the earth brought forth the vast expanse of living creatures, and by his command, the earth continues to preserve them.[87] This preservation accommodates the nutritional requirements of the food chain (he described the autotrophs and primary heterotrophs, prey and predator), while still allowing, through behavioural responses of the heterotrophs, such as grazing mammals, for the plant 'prey' to increase and multiply.[88]

Wesley insisted, in opposition to the deists of his day, that God actively participates in sustaining the creation.[89] It is a creation beyond all our reasoning and understanding because creation is God-centred, not human-centred.[90] It is, therefore, a creation that is sustained by God in all of its complexity, not just those parts that are obviously beneficial to the survival of humanity, but, Wesley noted, 'even the spider, though abhorred by man, is the care of all-sustaining Heaven'.[91]

Wesley made a distinction between those parts of creation that were 'useful' to humanity, and those that were not.[92] He gestured towards the human obligation towards the latter, because 'they are of consequence in the account of their Maker, [they] therefore deserve our regard'.[93] Just as Wesley gave detailed descriptions of animals 'with an aversion to dependence', he was also attentive in the *Survey* to those of 'mild disposition', detailing behavioural characteristics, natural history, and ecology of semi-domesticated animals, such as camel and 'rain-deer'.[94]

Not only are animals useful to humans in various ways, but so too are plants. In addition to cultivated plants, tree species of various kinds that require no human attention for their survival provide useful products for human comfort and survival. For example, Wesley extols various uses of the horse-chestnut for preparation of soap, as well as feed for hogs, poultry, horses and cows, and its multiple uses as forest timber.[95]

Wesley, then, had a nuanced appreciation of the created order: its diversity of species, communities, and environments, with its complexity in ecological relationships. For him:

> All things, even the seemingly insignificant, have their rightful place in the created order and ecological balance. And humanity is endowed with the intellect to comprehend and defend that place . . . Understanding ourselves within the context of the natural world and in relationship to the rest of creation . . . we find our place in *the family of nature*.[96]

In that family of nature, humanity has a God-given obligation, a duty that must be discharged with honour.[97] Just how that duty is discharged with respect to the created order is the very conduct of environmental stewardship.

John Wesley the Theologian

A combination of detailed descriptions and Wesley's glosses in the *Survey* imply that any 'reasonable' person would be compelled to believe in the goodness and wisdom of God the creator. In view of Wesley's explicit view that Spirit, not just reason, was necessary for faith, Maddox has proposed that Wesley's 'apologetic engagement was more modest, namely helping strengthen the religious convictions of his readers (and himself!) by showing how these convictions "make sense" of broadly accepted human knowledge.'[98] Wesley exclaimed:

> Thy works surprise us: the plants and the brutes puzzle and confound our reasonings: we gaze at thy workmanship with sacred amazement: thy ways in the kingdom of nature are untraceable, and thy wonders past finding out.[99]

But while the *Survey* is a substantial and important work of natural philosophy, blending almost seamlessly the descriptions of creation with praise and worship for the Creator, Wesley says little about the nature of desirable human conduct toward the creation. Wesley's more important and extensive life work – that of preacher and theologian – speaks to the ethical demands of a Christian life, not only with respect to the worship of God and service to humanity, but also in humility towards the created world. As in the *Survey*, science and religion are inseparably intertwined in Wesley's sermons; Wesley used eighteenth-century scientific concepts to extend and complement the biblical message as well as difficult theological ideas.[100]

To determine Wesley's contribution toward an ethic of environmental stewardship, it is appropriate first to examine Wesley's view of creation, including the original state of creation, God's role in creation and His continuing role (in opposition to the deists) in sustaining the created order – as well as the human relationship to God and creation. We must then consider his views on the effects of The Fall and the restoration of *imago dei*. Finally, his eschatological views on the new creation and place of animals in the new heaven and new earth will be considered.

The Original State of Creation

What was the state of creation? In his sermon, 'On Divine Providence' (1786) Wesley asserted, 'the Lord saw that every distinct part of the universe was good. But when he saw everything he had made, all in connexion with each other, "behold, it was very good"'.[101] In the introduction to his sermon 'God's Approbation of His Works' (1782), Wesley summarized his vision of the original earth: 'whatever was created was good in its kind; suited to the end for which it was designed; adapted to promote the good of the whole, and the glory of the great Creator . . . every creature was good in its primeval state.'[102] In short, the original state, what Wesley called 'brute creation', was one in which 'the beasts of the field, and all the fowls of the air, were with Adam in paradise [where they were] perfectly happy'.[103] In addition, 'the entire creation was at peace with man, so long as man was at peace with his Creator'.[104]

This was a good creation, one where everything was adapted to promote the perfect whole. Wesley detailed this, envisioning a profoundly beautiful, fruitful and safe land with 'flowers of every hue, shrubs and trees of every kind, every part fertile, and lacking in precipices, chasms, caverns, impassable morasses or deserts of barren sand'.[105] Wesley suggests there is no evidence to suggest that early earth was a flat plain, or that the present-day mountains were by-products of the Flood.[106]

The four elements were perfectly ordered and posed no threat to the created order. Natural geologic disasters, such as earthquakes or volcanoes, for example, were unknown.[107] The water, supplied in felicitous amounts, was never polluted.[108] Meteorological disasters and air pollution were likewise unknown.[109] The original creation, then, contained nothing detrimental to human existence: 'no violent winter, or sultry summer; no extreme, either of heat or cold. No soil was burned up by the solar heat, none uninhabitable through the want of it'.[110] The elements were perfectly ordered in the good creation, but all parts of creation were designed to act as an organized, unified whole. In his sermon 'The Wisdom of God's Counsels' (1784), Wesley noted the goodness, not only of the individual elements of creation, but of the entire biosphere: 'insomuch that each of them, apart from the rest, is good; but all together are very good; all conspiring together, in one connected system, to the glory of God in the happiness of his intelligent creatures'.[111]

God's Role in Creation

This view of God's power and wisdom in the creation was echoed in the *Survey*.[112] Wesley noted that in the good creation there were adaptations – we would now call them genetic adaptations – that would result in phyto-geographic distributions ranging from the endemic to the cosmopolitan. There were vegetables, herbs, tall and stately trees: 'some of these were adapted to particular climates, or particular exposures; while vegetables of more general use were not confined to one country, but would flourish almost in every climate. But among all these there were no weeds, no useless plants.'[113] What did Wesley mean by 'weeds' and 'useless plants'? Organisms not created for human welfare had been created for themselves as further illustrations of God's glory, though these designations must necessarily have come from the post-lapsarian human perspective.[114]

Noting the degree of predation to be found in the post-lapsarian animal kingdom, Wesley envisioned the original creation to have had no need of such behaviour. In the perfection of the original holocoenotic environment, predation was evil, and, therefore, unknown. In fact, in this perfect chain of being, the 'spider was then as harmless as the fly, and did not then lie in wait for blood . . . reptiles of every kind were equally harmless'.[115] Moreover, 'there were no birds or beasts of prey; none that destroyed or molested another',[116] since 'every part was exactly suited to the others, and conducive to the good of the whole'.[117]

A recurrent theme in Wesley's sermons is God's continued care of his creation. Certainly, 'He is the true God, the only Cause, the sole Creator of all things.'[118] But additionally, in his sermon 'Spiritual Worship' (1781), which has been described as containing the 'core of Wesley's views on God's role in nature,' he asserted that God is 'also the supporter of all the things that he has made. He beareth, upholdeth, sustaineth, all created things by the word of his power, by the same powerful word which brought them out of nothing.'[119] This is not a disinterested, general, care, but one that is particular for the needs of each creature, as God directs 'All His power to the advantage of all His creatures,'[120] and as 'he superintend[s] all the parts of this lower world, this "speck of creation," the earth! So that all things are still, as they were at the beginning, "beautiful in their seasons;" and summer and winter, seed-time and harvest, regularly follow each other'. [121] Indeed, each ecological relationship is under God's constant care as he 'preserves them in their several relations, connections, and dependencies, so as to compose one system of beings, to form one entire universe, according to the counsel of his will'.[122]

God's presence is not hidden from view, but is clearly evident. For Wesley, there can be no doubt about God's creating and sustaining action, apparent to those who have the eyes of faith.[123] God, incarnate, who walked on this very planet, is the source and fountain of all life: 'of the lowest species of life, that of *vegetables*; as being the source of all the motion on which vegetation depends . . . of *animals*, the power by which the heart beats, and the circulating juices flow . . . and [of] the *rational* . . . life'.[124]

Opposition to Deism

In his opposition to the 'mechanistic' systems of deist Enlightenment thinkers, Wesley brought God into the picture at every opportunity. As Michael Lodahl remarked,

> While a child of the Enlightenment, Wesley refused to be lured by the Enlightenment ideal of autonomous analytical reason that celebrated the independent individual . . . his doctrine of humanity was too deeply immersed in the early Greek Fathers' fascination with human participation in God to permit any capitulation to Deism.[125]

Wesley, however, was not particularly polemic in his arguments, leading M. Elton Hendricks to conclude that Wesley ignored deism since it was not a prevalent view among the people to whom he ministered.[126] However, as Haas notes, 'while Wesley found few deists in mines or fishing villages, he recognized their force in the intellectual life of the nation. He confronted them in his sermons.'[127]

Whether polemic or not, Wesley's consistent and recurrent assertion (seen with notable frequency in the *Survey*) was that God was everywhere present and continuously acting in the usual, as well as the unusual; 'there is no place empty of God'.[128] He believed that 'God acts everywhere, and therefore is everywhere . . . God acts in heaven, in earth, and under the earth, throughout the whole compass of creation.'[129] This is evident from a *Journal* entry, which describes the effects of a torrential rain storm, accompanied by hail. He concluded, 'how frequent would accidents of this kind be if chance, not God governed the world!'[130] God is not just active in preventing 'accidents' in the world, but is a constant presence in all of the created order.[131] Wesley's view of the immanence of God in all creation is a logical extension of his belief in the immanence of God in all humanity.[132] This contrasted with current enlightened philosophies positing mechanistic machine-like models of the universe.[133] Wesley saw God as being intimately active in both the animate and inanimate world, as 'the only agent in the material world; all matter being essentially dull and inactive, and moving only as it is moved by the finger of God'.[134]

Human Relationship to God and to Creation

Included in the perfect original creation, of course, was the human species, whose 'appointed . . . residence was a garden; not an ivory house,' a species 'made in the image of God'.[135] In his sermon 'The Image of God' (1730), which Wesley never published,[136] the 'image' is defined in terms of possessing 'unerring understanding, an uncorrupt will, and perfect freedom'.[137] Thus, 'God's image upon man consists in knowledge, righteousness, and true holiness'.[138] In addition, '[Humankind] was a creature capable of God; capable of knowing, loving, and obeying his Creator'.[139]

A prerequisite to formulating a theology of environmental stewardship is an understanding of the relationship between humanity and the rest of the created order. The crux here lies in understanding the word 'dominion' in Genesis 1:28. For Wesley, 'as he has the government of the inferior creatures, he is as it were God's representative on earth. Yet his government of himself by the freedom of his will, has in it more of God's image, than his government of the creatures.'[140] Wesley also addressed this point directly in 'The General Deliverance' (1781). Adam was to act as God's deputy, as God's administrator on earth, 'the channel of conveyance between his Creator and the whole brute creation'.[141] Humanity is given the task of mediating God's blessings to the non-human creation.[142]

The difference between humans and the rest of creation is not organic, but relational: 'man is capable of God; the inferior creatures are not. We have no ground to believe that they are, in any degree, capable of knowing, loving, or obeying God. This is . . . the great gulf which they cannot pass over.'[143] This relational difference sets humanity apart from the rest of creation; humanity was created in the image of God, an image capable of knowing, loving, and obeying God, and capable of caring for the rest of creation in the same loving manner that God cares for it.[144]

Wesley's dualism between inanimate (acted upon directly by God) and animate (act as agents dependent on God) is unlike Cartesian dualism, which separates humans from all other created matter, and links animals with the inanimate world.[145] Wesley's dualism also differs from that of Calvin and Reformed theologians, whose view of common grace preserves the world for the sake of the elect only; Wesley's doctrine of prevenient grace is 'the presence of God lavished upon all people, and indeed upon all creation'.[146] Wesley thus affirmed that all members of creation have an inherent worth: 'the Father of All has a tender regard for even his lowest creatures . . . yet I dare not affirm that he has an equal regard for them and for the children of men.'[147] Thus, he stops short of the tenets of modern 'Deep Ecologists' who contend that all living species have *equal* inherent value.[148]

The Effects of the Fall

Wesley's vision of the original creation and of relationships in the created order is, of course, not the world of sensory experience. In 'God's Approbation of his Works' Wesley insisted that the present world is intrinsically different from the created world.[149] Wesley explored this idea, asking, 'if the Creator and Father of every living thing is rich in mercy towards all; if he does not overlook or despise any of the works of his own hands; if he wills even the meanest of them to be happy . . . how is it that misery of all kinds overspreads the face of the earth?'[150] The cause, as Wesley explained, is humanity's misuse of its God-given liberty.[151]

Humanity is not merely a part of the creation that has fallen into brutal behaviours caused by necessity (Wesley 'enjoy[ed] describing the gory details of predation'[152]), but indeed has fallen farther than the rest of creation, inflicting pain and torment without cause. The identification of humanity with nature has been disrupted, while the image of God has been defaced by human corruption and selfishness. This is manifest in human cruelty to animals, a behaviour resting not in the necessity of carnivory, but in free choice, that the 'human shark' directs even to the 'generous horse' and 'faithful dog'.[153]

The nature of the fallen 'human shark' is, indeed, pervasive, touching even those who have given their lives to God's work. In his 'Minutes of Several Conversations' (1791) Wesley recorded advice to his preachers. When posed the question, 'are there any smaller advices relative to preaching, which might be of use to us?' Wesley's response was: 'be merciful to your beast. Not only ride moderately, but see with your own eyes that your horse be rubbed, fed, and bedded.'[154]

Wesley did not specifically address the ecological ramifications of a 'groaning of creation,' but his descriptions of those features that were *not* part of the original good provide many insights. The good creation had 'no horrid precipices, huge chasms, or dreary caverns; with deep, impassable morasses, or deserts of barren sand, no volcanoes, or burning mountains, no putrid lakes, no turbid or stagnating waters, air with no unwholesome vapours, no poisonous exhalations.'[155] We may assume that these were all part of the post-lapsarian landscape. Were the causes of such environmental damage purely the result of natural processes, or were they caused by human activity, such as mining, poor agricultural methods, improper disposal of animal waste, burning of fossil fuels? Certainly, damaged, ugly land, which is useless for agriculture or even dangerous for habitation, is incapable of fulfilling God's purpose of providing for man's pleasure and welfare. As Robert Rakestraw succinctly points out, God did not create pollution.[156]

Restoration of the *Imago Dei*

If the fall of humanity from the image of God had such wide-ranging and disastrous consequences on the creation, including not only humanity, but also other organisms, ecological relationships among species, and even the physical environment, then, logically, restoration would need to reverse this damage. As Wesley explained in the Preface to the second (1741) volume of *Hymns and Sacred Poems* (reprinted in the 1777 edition of *A Plain Account of Christian Perfection*), salvation is 'none other than the image of God fresh stamped on our hearts'.[157] It is the formation of the person as a 'new creation'.

This image of God is threefold: the '*natural image,* a picture of his own immortality; a spiritual being, endued with understanding, freedom of will, and various affections ... [the] *political image,* [as] governor of this lower world having "dominion over the fishes of the sea, and over all the earth" ... [and the] *moral image* ... "righteousness and true holiness"'.[158] As a result of the Fall, the natural image was retained, and a portion of the political image, 'but the moral image of God is lost and defaced'.[159] Bartels has commented that Wesley did not specifically mention the renewal of a political image.[160] Yet since the new birth involves a change that 'is wrought in the whole soul,' and the moral image consists of the 'right state of . . . intellectual powers, and in love, which is true holiness,' it is not unreasonable to suggest that in Wesley's mind, the entire image of God – natural and political, as well as moral – was capable of renewal.[161]

There is certainly a cosmic nature of the new creation, but it was focused for Wesley on the renewal of individual persons in the *imago dei* after the pattern of the early Eastern Fathers: cosmic redemption is inseparable from the salvation of humanity. This involves an actual transformation – a re-creation.[162] As Wesley described it in *The Scripture Way of Salvation* (1758), salvation involved 'a *real* as well as a *relative* change'.[163] The restored image, then, is marked by a change in 'humility, a knowledge of ourselves, a just sense of our condition, . . . the understanding thus enlightened by humility immediately directs us to reform our will by charity'.[164] In short, the restoration of the *imago dei* is the restored human relation with God, and this, in turn, is manifested in 'love of our neighbour; of every soul which God hath made,' and in obedience of heart and life.[165]

Wesleyan Christian perfection or entire sanctification represents a critical point in the continuum of sanctification – the restoration of the *imago dei* that begins with the new birth. Christian perfection is 'loving God with all our heart, mind, soul, and strength . . . [so] that all the thoughts, words, and actions are governed by pure love'.[166] Wesley envisioned it as 'a renewal of heart, not only in part, but in the whole image of God,' with the person 'inwardly and outwardly devoted to God; all devoted in heart and life'.[167] Wesley's characterization of sanctification as the 'renewal of the image of God' described both the personal and social dimensions of Christian life.[168] Since entire sanctification is identified with the restoration of God's image, this, in turn, brings us into right relationships, with all their complexity, with other created beings.[169]

For Wesley, this restoration begins with God's grace and is expressed in heart and hands. In his sermon 'On Working out our own Salvation' (1785) he explained that 'we are to observe that great and important truth which ought never be put out of remembrance: "It is God that worketh in us both to will and to do of his good pleasure."'[170] He then filled in the details of what this looks like. Those renewed 'labour to serve their Master that is in heaven; that is, First, with the utmost earnestness of spirit, with all possible care and caution; and Secondly, with the utmost diligence, speed, punctuality, and exactness'.[171] The impetus for doing good pleasure with utmost diligence, speed, punctuality, and exactness is the example set by God himself: 'first, God works; therefore you *can* work: secondly, God works, therefore you *must* work . . . God worketh in you; therefore, you must work: You must be "workers together with him."'[172]

In Wesley's view, it would follow, then, that in the restoration of the *imago dei*, humanity is returned to the position of dominion over the earth as God's deputy in the care of creation. This is closely connected with love of neighbour, including neighbours of the future for whom we must work to make the world habitable. Since God's compassion is for all he has made, love of neighbour, by extension, should not be limited to humans.[173] There is a close connection between the restoration of the political image and the moral image; sanctification is critical to the renewal of responsibility. Theodore Runyan concludes: 'without this, the discipline and self-sacrifice required to turn around the ecological crisis lie beyond human capability'.[174]

Eschatology

What one believes and expects about the future and, specifically, the 'end times' has profound implications for care of God's creation in the present. An eschatology that envisions the earth to ultimately end in a fireball, and which views every natural disaster as evidence of an imminent end, will be unlikely to emphasize the importance of caring for the present environment. Indeed, 'traditional ways of thinking about eschatology tend to undercut [the] necessity for creaturely agency and responsibility . . . if the world is to be transformed by divine love labouring in and through us, then it is obvious that the world requires a viable future'.[175]

For Wesley a post-millennial view was important.[176] His was also a realized eschatology, relying heavily on Johann Albrecht Bengel's interpretation of the Book of Revelation, with a mild acceptance of the Puritan emphasis on judgement.[177] Thus, in sermons and *Journal* entries, John Wesley interpreted the meaning of present natural events and disasters, such as earthquakes, and looked forward to the meaning of the new creation and place of animals or other life forms in a new heaven and earth.

John Wesley's Interpretation of Natural Events

Earthquakes were among the dramatic natural occurrences that caught Wesley's notice. In *Journal* entries for 1750, Wesley noted the effects of two London earthquakes for that year.[178] His description was terse, as was his analysis: 'today God gave the people of London a second warning'.[179] He also related accounts of other British earthquakes in 1757 and 1763 as well as the results of an unusual flood, the cause of which Wesley attributed to an earthquake.[180]

Wesley wished to make his own personal observations. In a *Journal* entry for 1755, and also in his 'Serious Thoughts on the late Earthquake in Lisbon' (1755) he described the events of a localized earthquake. He also proposed theories, based on the four 'elements', which speculated about the physical cause of destruction. The ultimate cause was 'God, who arose to shake terribly the earth; who purposely chose such a place where there is so great a concourse of nobility and gentry every year.'[181] In 1773, he observed the geologic upheaval and flooding in the aftermath of an earthquake, remarking, 'such a scene of desolation I never saw. Will none tremble when God thus terribly shakes the earth?'[182]

Wesley's accounts of earthquakes consist mainly of his own observations, though he also pondered their meaning and ultimate cause. It is clear that Wesley had no illusions about the destructive forces involved and the magnitude of damage done, both in terms of changes to the landscape, as well as human cost. Here too, Wesley was consistent in his view that God is no distant creator, but remains actively involved in the events of his creation; earthquakes, however, were not a sign of God's ultimate judgement on the earth, but rather a warning, a call to repentance.

This view is also evident in Charles Wesley's sermon 'The Cause and Cure of Earthquakes' (1750), which John included in his collection of *Sermons on Several Occasions* (1760).[183] Charles's two volumes of *Hymns Occasioned by the Earthquake (1750)* – with additions prompted by the disastrous Lisbon earthquake of 1755 – and *Hymns for the Year 1756, Particularly for the Fast-Day, February 6* relied heavily on the apocalyptic imagery of Revelation; the message was that the end of the world was at hand, and, through the mechanism of earthquakes, God would bring about the new creation.[184] The early sermons, letters and hymns written by Charles seem to have held a strongly pre-millennial view.[185] This contrasted to the post-millennial view held by John.[186] In his early years John may have shared Charles's pre-millennial leanings, but the mature theologian who selected and edited hymns in the 1780 *Collection of Hymns for the Use of the People Called Methodists* emphasized the new heaven and earth, rather than examining the process by which it came about.[187]

The New Creation

The new creation, the new work of God in the world, has both individual and global results. There is a 'carefully articulated, well nuanced, multi-valent conception of the new creation that repeatedly surfaces' in Wesley's writings.[188] Analyzing 2 Corinthians 5:17, 'therefore, if any man be in Christ, he is a new creature: old things are passed away; behold, all things are become new', Wesley noted the magnitude of this change: 'only the power that makes a world can make a Christian'.[189] The Christian 'has new life, new senses, new faculties, new affections, new appetites, new ideas and conceptions . . . God, men, the whole creation, heaven, earth, and all therein, appear in a new light, and stand related to him in a new manner, since he was created anew in Christ Jesus.'[190] The new creation is the 'very real transformation in the creature and the world which salvation brings about'.[191]

Not only was the individual made new through regeneration and sanctification, but the world would be made new as well. Maddox remarks that 'Wesley's functional understanding of the nature of salvation . . . ran counter to assumptions about eschatology that had reigned for some time in the church . . . most Christians by Wesley's day . . . assum[ed] that our final state is "heaven above"'.[192]

In his sermon 'The New Creation' (1785) Wesley envisioned a delivered and perfected world, returned to an existence reminiscent of that time before the Fall, as described in 'God's Approbation of his Works'. But how would this come about? Wesley postulated, 'destruction is not deliverance: therefore whatsoever is destroyed, or ceases to be, is not delivered at all. Will, then, *any part of the creation be destroyed? Into the glorious liberty* – The excellent state wherein they were created.'[193] Yet he admitted that 'our knowledge of the great truth which is delivered to us in these words, is exceedingly short and imperfect . . . this is a point of mere revelation, beyond the reach of all our natural faculties'.[194]

In the new creation, there would be no more danger from heavenly bodies.[195] Meteors will be non-existent, the destructive forces of atmospheric disturbances, such as hurricanes, will be eliminated, and there would be no more air pollution or 'poisonous damps'.[196] Nor will there be water pollution in the new creation, for 'water . . . will be, in every part of the world, clear and limpid; pure from all unpleasant, or unhealthful mixtures'.[197] Geologically and topographically, the earth will again become safe and beautiful.[198] Damaging thermal extremes would be eliminated.[199]

The resulting earth would be a return to the beauty and productivity of the Garden of Eden, concurrent with the elimination of natural evil, so that all organisms, from plants to animals, lived in harmony.[200] The warped condition of humanity caused by the Fall would now glimpse the goodness of an entirely new creation and, in Wesley's view, plants' physical and chemical defences against predation would no longer be required, because predation itself would cease.[201] All of creation, degraded as a result of the Fall, would share in the final salvation of the new creation, the new earth.

Wesley clearly viewed the new earth of Revelation 21 as work in progress: work that had already begun, rather than work belonging to a distant and unknowable future. In the conclusion of his sermon 'The General Spread of the Gospel' (1783) he wrote: 'all unprejudiced persons may see with their eyes, that He is already renewing the face of the earth'.[202] What is the responsibility of humanity toward this new creation? In his sermon 'The Good Steward' (1758) Wesley considered those things that God had entrusted to us, and for which we would be judged, our soul, body, worldly goods and talents, which were to be used 'as our Master's goods, and according to the particular directions which he has given us in his word'.[203] And since creation was put under the 'dominion' of humanity, it, too, must be cared for according to God's intentions. The logical extension of this meant that private property did not exist; everything is held in trust for the creator.[204]

The Place of Animals and Other Life Forms in the New Heaven and New Earth

A theology of environmental stewardship or care of creation must necessarily hold the non-human parts of creation in high regard: as inherently *worth* stewardship and care. This requires, certainly, theological reflection, but also a deep scientific appreciation and understanding: form and function of the natural world, its biotic and abiotic components, as well as the complex interactions within, between and among these components.

Wesley showed not only a life-long interest in science, but also a fascination with animals. One of his Oxford Master's orations in 1727 was entitled *De Anima Brutorum*, which was concerned with animals' 'souls' and reasoning powers.[205] Unfortunately, this has not survived, so we are unable to see the long-term development of Wesley's thought on this topic. However, given this interest, it is not surprising that Wesley 'became convinced that the range of animals would be present in this renewed creation'.[206] Arguing against the prevalent mechanistic view, Wesley asserted that the existence of animal pain placed the 'brutes' closer to humans than to plant life in the chain of being. Pain sensation was also a dividing line in discerning 'cruelty'.[207]

For Wesley, animal pain was a significant theological problem. Wesley 'had long doubted the adequacy of a theodicy that justified God's goodness in permitting the possibility of the Fall by noting that God would eventually restore things to their pre-fallen condition'.[208] In *God's Love to Fallen Man* (1782) Wesley wrote 'that, by the fall of Adam, mankind in general have gained a capacity, First, of being more holy and more happy on earth, and, Secondly, of being more happy in heaven, than otherwise they could have been!'[209] Wesley insisted that 'God's mercy is over *all* his works,' and this increased holiness, thus happiness, should not be restricted to the human species, but extend also to all of the created order. Therefore, 'in Wesley's view, a truly loving God would only permit the present evil in the world if an *even better* outcome might be achieved by allowing this possibility than without it. On these terms, he believed that God would not just restore fallen creation to its original state, God would recreate it with greater capacities and blessings than it had at first.'[210] In the new creation, all brutes, as well as humans, would be saved and 'Wesley seems to know an indecent number of details': 'the whole brute creation will then, undoubtedly, be restored, not only to the vigour, strength, and swiftness which they had at their creation, but to a far higher degree of each than they ever enjoyed'.[211]

Wesley suggested that God had 'a tender regard for even his lowest creatures, and that in consequence of this he will make them large amends for all they suffer while under their present bondage.'[212] He might not only increase the 'the vigour, strength, and swiftness' of animals, but compensate them for the pain and suffering inflicted by fallen humanity, by raising animals to the level of created humanity, with its ability to relate to God, to make them: 'capable of God; capable of knowing and loving and enjoying the Author of their being'.[213]

Wesley affirmed that all parts of the new creation, like the present creation, were of inherent value, both the 'useful' and those that did not seem so. It is not for us to judge God's design of the new creation any more than the old.[214] Even though God's ultimate design may be unknown and unknowable, Wesley urged that we must take seriously what we *do* know, what has been revealed to us through Scripture.[215]

If, therefore, God's mercy is over *all* his works, expressed in the care for birds and beasts, as well as for humans, and if both man and beast will be saved, then there are practical implications. This knowledge 'may soften our hearts towards the meaner creatures, knowing that the Lord careth for them . . . and enlarge our hearts towards those poor creatures'.[216] Those rejecting their place as image-bearers and vicegerents of God will sink in the 'chain of being' to the level of an animal, specifically to that of a post-lapsarian animal. However, since Wesley envisioned the possibility that animals of the new heaven and earth would be 'capable of God,' any human-beings rejecting God's role, by implication, would be condemning themselves as lower in the chain than animals.[217] Maintaining these ranks meant affirming God's mercy over *all* his works, over *every* aspect of creation; that the human is a living image-bearer of God, to care for that very creation as a steward who carries out the explicit will of his master. From this, Wesley 'draws an ethical conclusion from an eschatological expectation,' a forerunner for the theologies of hope and liberation.[218]

Wesley's was a 'realized eschatology' in which the 'now' merged with the 'not yet' through obedience to God. The coming of the Lord would bring an end to sorrow and suffering for the animals as well as humanity. But this general deliverance is not just something for an unknown future; it was for the here and now. Perhaps, prompted by the words of an anonymous letter that Wesley received, he gave practical advice to children, outlining their proper behaviour, not only towards siblings, but also to 'brute creation' – birds, snakes, toads, and even flies.[219] This might well have influenced his sermon 'On the Education of Children' (1783).[220] Even children needed to exercise a stewardship of creation, which was rooted in God and his demonstrated love for humanity through Christ. Love for God would extend to love of neighbour, even the non-human neighbour. This required diligent parental teaching from the earliest years.[221]

Wesley might, then, be considered a forerunner of the present-day animal rights movement. His 'cherished peculiar views on animals had an enduring influence on English attitudes and an unexpected effect on the way that anatomical research was carried out in the early nineteenth century'.[222] Opposition to vivisection, animal mutilation, and blood sports was bolstered by Wesley's sermons, which continue to influence contemporary animal rights activists.[223] What would have been the limits of Wesley's support of 'animal rights'? In analysing the implications of Wesley's reaction to experimental blood transfusions, Rakestraw postulated that Wesley would embrace any use of technology that enhanced love of God and humanity.[224]

It is also appropriate to speculate about his views on the preservation of wilderness habitats. Although he did not address the issue of wilderness conservation, when examining the *Survey* we are left in no doubt that Wesley had a very deep understanding and appreciation of the natural environment.[225] His was not, however, a blanket adulation for anything natural. He recorded his impressions of Mount Eagle, which he termed 'one of the greatest natural wonders in Ireland'. He reported that 'the top [was] a grassy plain . . . waste and uncultivated [and] . . . not very pleasing'. What he did not indicate, if, indeed, he knew himself, was whether the summit was 'waste and uncultivated' from exposure to cold and wind, or from overgrazing. When reading the *Journal* entries, it becomes apparent that Wesley saw great beauty in cultivated lands. For example, he admired Lord Tullamore's gardens, including the 'groves, little meadows, kitchen gardens, plots of flowers, and little orchards'.[226]

Wesley had no difficulty with cultivation and domestication, and even used the work of husbandry as a metaphor for spiritual life.[227] His 'main ethical applications regarding plants concern the wise use and development of those herbs, grains, vegetables and fruits suitable for human nutrition and healing, and the avoidance of whatever contributes to the debilitation of men and women'.[228] Indeed, 'plants and herbs . . . were made to be food for man'.[229] Thus, 'whatever enhances such love of God and humanity would be heartily embraced and promoted by him'.[230]

John Wesley's Ecotheology

To suggest that Wesley had a well-developed ecotheology, theology of creation care, or environmental ethics, even for the eighteenth century, is to make claims on his writings that are too ambitious. But to claim that the absence of such a systematic treatment indicates a lack of knowledge or concern is equally false. Wesley was a scientifically-informed theologian who wrote throughout his life on moral matters pertaining to the treatment of non-human creation. This he did through the lens of scientific knowledge of the natural world. The natural world, for Wesley, was one to be appreciated for its intrinsic value, as well as its value for human life and health. Plants, for example, could provide treatments or cures for human ailments.

Wesley's natural philosophy shows a detailed appreciation of both the biotic and abiotic components of the natural world in all their diversity and in the intricacies of their dynamic interrelationships. As it did not remain static, but underwent several revisions by Wesley's own hand, this would seem to indicate that the subject was not a closed matter. In fact, natural philosophy and science were subjects of continued interest and importance for him. Scientific consideration of the natural world, then, was an ongoing and long-standing commitment, which informed many of Wesley's sermons.

Wesley's theology of the environment is connected to his view of God's relationship to humanity and the non-human world. Wesley took a long view of creation, one that might be termed 'post-millennial'. Natural disasters such as earthquakes were sent as God's warning to sinful humanity, not as signs of the imminent destruction of his created order. Thus, the original state of creation was 'good'; the state of his 'new creation' would be a return to this original state of goodness. How would this come about? For Wesley, the key was in the restoration of *imago dei*, the moral, political, and natural image of God, in which humanity was created. Pure love of God and love of neighbour (human and non-human) would be manifested in the humane treatment of animals. Humanity's role as God's steward over the non-human creation would be restored and modelled on God's own constant, loving care for his creation.

The Contemporary Context

Although contemporary authors such as Ian Barbour and John Polkinghorne have strongly suggested that science and religion (including Christianity) need not be in an antagonistic relationship, influential voices of the past, such as Andrew Dickson White, continue to shape this relationship as 'science *vs* religion'.[231] The title of his two-volume book, *A History of the Warfare of Science with Theology in Christendom* (1896), with its military metaphor, reveals that 'White viewed the early centuries of the Christian era as an unmitigated disaster for science.'[232] According to White, the 'tyranny' of scriptural authority and 'theological views of science . . . forced mankind away from the truth, and . . . caused Christendom to stumble for centuries into abysses of error and sorrow'.[233] For White, 'the normal development of the physical sciences [was arrested] for over fifteen hundred years'.[234]

In a 1967 paper entitled 'The Historical Roots of our Ecological Crisis', published in the prestigious journal *Science*, medieval historian Lynn White, Jr. set the context, as well as the tone, of contemporary debates between Christian churches and environmental scientists. He concluded that medieval, Renaissance and Enlightenment advances in science were brought about primarily for religious reasons; that the Christian view of humanity, which dominated nature, eliminated attitudinal barriers against damaging or exploiting the environment. Therefore, the resultant environmental damage caused by the 'marriage' of science and technology could be placed squarely at the door of Christianity in its orthodox form, which, he says, 'bears a huge burden of guilt' and is antithetical to environmental health.[235] In the scientific community, White's 'complaint against Christianity' continues to be the starting point – at least for some authors – in the academic search for causes of the current ecological crisis. In the intervening years, White's article has been reprinted in a variety of books and on internet sites, extensively excerpted and critically revised.[236] Indeed, it has not simply sparked a controversial scholarly debate, but has achieved 'cult status within the environmental movement'.[237] It has become 'a cornerstone in the environmental studies literature' and continues to be quoted in college textbooks.[238]

Within the Christian community, reaction to White has been mixed. Some Christian writers, such as Jürgen Moltmann, Sallie McFague and Douglas John Hall, agree that the Christian church should bear some of the guilt for the environment's deterioration.[239] There is also evidence of apathy, disbelief and strident opposition to an alliance with environmentalists, who might be proponents of liberalism and socialism (particularly opposed by the 'Wise Use Movement') or of worldviews shaped by New Age, Gaia, and 'Deep Ecology'.[240]

The charges of 'science *vs* Christianity' and 'environment *vs* Christianity', signalled by Andrew Dickson White and Lynn White, Jr. respectively, have therefore set the 'rules of engagement', both within the scientific community, as well as the church. Moreover, these 'sides' have, in recent years, become even more polarized. Charges of anti-environmentalism have been levelled against conservative evangelical Christians.[241] This is due, in part, to the fact that within some of the more evangelical quarters of the Christian community 'science' and 'environment' are synonymous with atheistic materialism.[242] Here, there are claims that 'left-tilting environmentalism' does little but taint the Christian environmental movement with a 'perhaps-unconscious pagan nature'.[243] Historically, the debate was not always so. In his important and much-quoted work, H. Paul Santmire describes the opposing theologies of nature that have existed since the time of the early church.[244] As David C. Lindberg and Ronald L. Numbers point out in their incisive analysis and critique of Andrew Dickson White's *History,* with the '"Galileo affair" . . . it was not a matter of Christianity waging war on science. All of the participants called themselves Christians.'[245] This is no less true in the 'modern' era. Both Andrew Dickson White and Lynn White, Jr. have also referred to themselves as Christians.[246]

Within the Christian community, dissension concerning the necessity and extent of environmental stewardship continues. Part of the reason for this is an in-built suspicion of the scientific community in general and ecologists in particular:

> far too often ecology is considered a fringe issue by Christians. Ecologists are conceived as scraggly-haired bearded extremists wearing blue jeans and corduroy jackets or media moguls spouting New Age ideology. Ecology is seldom preached from evangelical pulpits or discussed in Sunday school classes.[247]

Even vocal advocates of the 'Wise Use Movement' admit there are severe environmental problems, such as air and water pollution, deforestation, desertification, and loss of agricultural soils, but maintain that these problems are mainly located in 'developing countries and in present and former communist countries'.[248] Others suggest paying due attention to creation, based on philosophical views about the relationship between God, humanity, and the non-human creation.[249] Based on these differences, evangelicals, especially, continue to 'square off' over the issue of global climate change, some urging immediate attention to greenhouse emissions, which are projected to cause increased human suffering. Others, however, discount the projections, claiming, additionally, that reduction of greenhouse gases would cripple the US economy to such an extent that the worldwide impact would be more devastating than that projected to be caused by global warming.[250]

The result has been that 'evangelicals have often neglected or positively denied Christian responsibility to address ecological issues'.[251] Despite the scientific consensus of climatologists and oceanographers, and the formal statements supporting their findings, many conservative Christians, especially those with a dispensationalist eschatology (and these are far from being a 'lingering voice' from a minor Christian community), have joined forces with others from the world of politics, commerce, and media to discuss the severity (or reality?) of global warming.[252] There seems to be general consensus here that humanity belongs together with the rest of creation in the Genesis garden; differences lie in the vision of exactly what we should be doing there.[253]

Wesley and the Contemporary Context

For Christians, the need and responsibility for care of creation would seem to be a *sine qua non*. There is a strong biblical warrant (from both the Old and New Testaments) for the practices of God-honouring environmental stewardship. Calvin B. DeWitt, while enumerating stumbling blocks and pitfalls to environmental stewardship, has summarized the biblical principles for such action.[254] Steven Bouma-Prediger has discussed at length the traits of character that are *'central* to creation care'.[255] Christians must give serious attention to the ethical demands of the gospel because they understand themselves to be 'living within the very shadow of eternity. Such obedience flows from love to God.'[256]

There are pragmatic reasons for environmental stewardship as well. Witt, for instance, has pointed out that Christian camp and retreat centres have been constructed in places where there is great natural beauty, for these environments have the power to open a person to the inspiration of God.[257] Where the environment is degraded, natural beauty has been compromised.

But the responsibility as stewards of creation demands more than motivation or the right model of a created order: 'it demands a thorough involvement in understanding the physics, chemistry and biology of environmental interactions so that we can be creative in our responsibility, combining concern for our environment with concern for the needs of human beings on earth.'[258] Lodahl noted that 'contemporary Western evangelicalism, including the Wesleyan-Holiness movement, has not followed Wesley's example'. Furthermore, an under-appreciation of the doctrines of creation and divine immanence has caused a drift from theism to deism, as evidenced in the suspicion surrounding Christian ecological awareness. He concludes, 'a renewed appreciation for the theology of creation in Wesley might serve well both Wesleyanism and Western societies.'[259]

What remains, overall, is the public debate within the Christian community concerning environmental stewardship and the public discomfort felt by many Christians concerning science and the recommendations espoused by the scientific community. The question may be fairly asked: is there a model in the Christian tradition that combines a respect for and knowledge of environmental science with serious theological reflection on the place of humanity within God's works of creation? I would propose that John Wesley represents just such a model.

Wesley was obviously well educated and widely read, but expected this to be the mark of all Christians, beginning first with field preachers. In a

Journal entry he noted, 'at ten (and so every morning) I met with the preachers that were in town and read over with them the *Survey of the Wisdom of God in the Creation*.'[260] Concern over the accessibility of this work prompted Wesley to include selected passages in issues of the *Arminian Magazine*.[261]

Moreover, Wesley prescribed a course of 'academic' learning for the Kingswood School, which he characterized as equal or superior to that obtainable at Oxford or Cambridge; the curriculum included over a period of four years, the Bible in original languages, his *Explanatory Notes*, the *Survey*, *Christian Library* and various mathematical, philosophical and literary works.[262] Such education was not only for schoolboys. In a letter 'To Miss L——,' Wesley advocated that 'to know God, in order to enjoy him in time and in eternity' and to 'have knowledge enough for any reasonable Christian,' would mean a four or five year course of study, which would include natural philosophy (beginning with the *Survey*, but extending this to include works of other authors).[263]

Wesley viewed the creation as worthy of care. His was not a stewardship based solely on utility to the human species, but on the intrinsic value of all creation in the eyes of God. Thus, he held a balanced position between the modern-day 'Deep Ecologists' and those who currently make up the 'Wise Use Movement.' Even though Wesley welcomed 'improved' parts of the landscape, he understood this as 'dominion' and not 'domination'. Wesley's position on human responsibility towards the creation, like so many of his theological doctrines, is not worked out systematically.[264] One of the great strengths of Wesley's view of creation care lies in the fact that he himself was something of a 'Renaissance man', someone who had more than a passing familiarity with a wide range of topics. *A Survey of the Wisdom of God in the Creation* underwent several revisions in his lifetime. Wesley's *Survey* is, however, much more than a natural philosophy that can only be viewed exclusively for its purpose of demonstrating the goodness and wisdom of the Creator.[265] It is a profoundly thorough and accurate scientific document. Indeed, James A. Nash notes that Wesley 'had an enormous interest in and a good understanding of ecological process for his time'.[266] In the *Survey* Wesley reflected that trend in Anglican theology which aspired to bridge, but not obliterate differences between theology, philosophy and science.[267] An important result of the publication of his *Survey* was that Wesley's followers 'were assured that the subject matter of science was worthy of interest'.[268] Wesley, therefore, serves as a model for modern Christians to 'keep abreast of the latest findings of careful science, read with open minds the newest works of authenticated authorities, [and] make the scientists our friends'.[269]

Wesley was also a product of his time. It has been argued that he did not select the 'best' science of his time.[270] Yet this is anachronistic; arguably, it is significant that he delved into the world of science at all. It must be remembered that the 'best' science also included the work of Carl Linnaeus, some of whose work subsequently proved 'incorrect' as new discoveries in biology were made, but whose system of binomial nomenclature remains the *lingua franca* of biological systematics. Work in genetics by Gregor Mendel, as well as observations made by Charles Darwin and Alfred Wallace in the field of evolution, would not occur until more than fifty years after Wesley's death.

Wesley's science, or at least his theological interpretation of the natural world, can also be a stumbling block to acceptance of a Wesleyan approach to environmental stewardship. We know that the universe is not made of four elements, but of over one hundred. And Wesley's view of Eden's perfection flies in the face of modern scientific interpretations of the world; there is no geological evidence of a world devoid of predation as, for example, in the scenario posited by Wesley in 'The General Deliverance'. Contemporary science tells us that creation has always been a 'groaning creation'. However, destructive natural events and 'natural hazards' in this 'groaning creation' are frequently caused by human ignorance and/or arrogance in the development of naturally disturbed areas accompanied by efforts to forcibly control or alter the natural system.[271] One must, therefore, read Wesley in the context of his age and extrapolate, as he did, that which is applicable. What Wesley believed about cosmology, geologic history or biological phenomena 'does not bind his followers to the same knowledge or to religious inductions made from that knowledge. On the other hand, though, to know what use he made of science and his attitude to scientific inquiry may be . . . interesting and immensely profitable.'[272]

It is worthy of note that the majority of Wesley's sermonic material touching on aspects of environmental stewardship was published in his later years – from 1780 to 1788.[273] This, then, would indicate Wesley's thinking as a mature man and, as such, is appropriate material to present a 'finalized' picture of his position. Creation is worthy of care because every species has intrinsic value. God's immanent presence and care of his creation is to be mirrored in the actions of the human species, which he has set as stewards. The Wesleyan doctrines of prevenient grace, God as holy love, entire sanctification in this life, and witness of the Holy Spirit, offer an important theological contribution to these issues.[274]

In this sense, Wesley serves as a bridge between the scientific and theological. He was an ecologist, but 'a different kind of ecologist who [was] trying to place ecological reflection in the context of the history of sin, the divine–human reconciliation and the eschatological vision of general deliverance'.[275] Maddox notes that 'Wesley's basic theological perspective is conducive to an ecological ethic' because it offers a 'theology that joins a strong doctrine of grace with an equally strong place for *responsible human willing*'.[276] Can Wesley serve as a model for ecological and theological reflection in the twenty-first century? One of the strengths of Wesleyan theology, including his environmental holism, is that it was an ecumenical project, being informed by Puritan, Anglican, Moravian, Lutheran, Pietist, Roman Catholic and Eastern Orthodoxy.[277] Yet to be used as a practical model will require a change of heart and mind, even amongst Wesley's closest theological descendants.

Notes

1 Edward Royle, *Modern Britain: A Social History 1750–1985*, London, Edward Arnold/Hodder & Stoughton, 1987, p. 24.

2 N. J. G. Pounds, *The Culture of the English People: Iron Age to the Industrial Revolution*, Cambridge, Cambridge University Press, 1994, pp. 369–71; Bjorn Lomborg, 'Take a Deep Breath . . . Air Quality is Getting Better', *Guardian Unlimited*, Wednesday, 15 August 2001, <www. guardian.co.uk/print/0,3858,4239182–110970,00.html>.

3 Theodore Runyan, *The New Creation: John Wesley's Theology Today*, Nashville, Abingdon Press, 1998, p. 200.

4 John B. Cobb, Jr., *Grace & Responsibility: A Wesleyan Theology for Today*, Nashville, Abingdon Press, 1995, p. 7.

5 Cobb, *Grace & Responsibility*, p. 7.

6 Sara Joan Miles, 'From Being to Becoming: Science and Theology in the Eighteenth Century', *Perspectives on Science and Christian Faith* 43 (December 1991), pp. 215–23, p. 222.

7 Oliver A. Beckerlegge, 'John Wesley as Hymn-book Editor', in Franz Hildebrandt and Oliver A. Beckerlegge, eds, *Works*, vol. 7, p. 56.

8 Robert Schofield, 'John Wesley and Science in 18th Century England', *Isis* 44 (1953), pp. 331–40, p. 331.

9 J. W. Haas, Jr., 'John Wesley's Vision of Science in the Service of Christ', *Perspectives on Science and Christian Faith* 47 (December 1995), pp. 234–43, p. 235.

10 John Whitehead, *Life of John Wesley with Life of Charles Wesley*, 2 vols, Philadelphia, William E. Stockton, 1845, vol. 2, p. 286.

11 William C. S. Pellowe, 'Wesley's Use of Science', *Methodist Review* 110 (May 1927), pp. 294–403, pp. 394–5.

12 Schofield, 'John Wesley and Science', p. 338.

13 Haas, 'John Wesley's Views on Science and Christianity: An Examination of the Charge of Antiscience', *Church History* 63:3 (September 1994), pp. 378–92, p. 386.

14 Haas, 'John Wesley's Vision of Science in the Service of Christ', p. 236.

15 Haas, 'John Wesley's Vision of Science in the Service of Christ', p. 242.

16 Haas, 'Eighteenth Century Evangelical Responses to Science: John Wesley's Enduring Legacy', *Science and Christian Belief* 6:2 (1994), pp. 83–102, pp. 84, 100.

17 Andrew Dickson White, *A History of the Warfare of Science with Theology in Christendom*, 2 vols, New York, D. Appleton, 1897, vol. 1, p. 30.

18 Haas, 'John Wesley's Views on Science and Christianity', pp. 387, 391.

19 Frank W. Collier, *John Wesley Among the Scientists*, New York, Abingdon Press, 1928, pp. 134–5.

20 John Wesley, *The Journal of the Rev. John Wesley, A.M.*, 21 July 1758, Standard Edition, ed. Nehemiah Curnock, 8 vols, London, Epworth Press, 1909–16, vol. 4, p. 279; Wesley, *Journal*, 12 November 1767, vol. 5, p. 238.

21 John Wesley, *Primitive Physic: or, An Easy and Natural Method of Curing Most Diseases*, 24th ed., London, G. Paramore, 1792, p. iii.

22 Wesley, *Primitive Physic*, p. vi.

23 Wesley, *Primitive Physic*, p. x.

24 Wesley, *Primitive Physic*, p. xv.

25 Wesley, *Journal*, 12 May 1759, vol. 4, p. 313.

26 Wesley, *Primitive Physic*, p. xviii.

27 Wesley, *Primitive Physic*, p. xv.

28 Wesley, *Primitive Physic*, p. xvii.

29 Wesley, *Journal*, 6 June 1747, vol. 3, p. 301.

30 Wesley, *Journal*, 30 August 1757, vol. 4, p. 233; *Journal*, 14 September 1780, vol. 6, p. 294.

31 John Wesley, *The Family Physician; or Advice with Respect to Health, Including Directions for the Prevention and Cure of Acute Diseases. Extracted from Dr. Tissot*, 6th ed., London, G. Whitfield, 1797, pp. 3ff.

32 Wesley, *The Family Physician*, p. 7.

33 A. Wesley Hill, *John Wesley Among the Physicians*, London, Epworth Press, 1958, p. 16.

34 John Wesley, *A Survey of the Wisdom of God in the Creation or A Compendium of Natural Philosophy containing an Abridgment of that Beautiful Work, "The Contemplation of Nature," by Mr. Robert Bonnet, of Geneva also An Extract from Mr. Deuten's Inquiry into the Origin of the 'Discoveries Attributed to the Ancients'*, § Intro. 10, 2 vols, Philadelphia, Jonathan Pounder, 1816, vol. I, p. xiv; John Wesley, 'The Gradual Improvement of Natural Philosophy', *The Works of John Wesley*, 14 vols, London, Wesleyan Methodist Book Room, 1872. Reprint, Grand Rapids, Baker Books, 2002, vol. 13, p. 484. Hereafter abbreviated as WJW.

35 David Stewart, 'John Wesley, the Physician', *Wesleyan Theological Journal* 4:1 (Spring, 1969), pp. 27–38, p. 37; See also J. Cule, 'The Rev. John Wesley, M.A. (Oxon.), 1703–1791: "The Naked Empiricist" and Orthodox Medicine', *The Journal of the History of Medicine*, 45 (1990), pp. 41–63; Randy L. Maddox, 'John Wesley on Holistic Health and Healing', *Methodist History* 46:1 (2007), pp. 1–33; Deborah Madden, '"A Cheap, Safe and Natural Medicine": Religion, Medicine and Culture in John Wesley's *Primitive Physic*', *Clio Medica* 83, Amsterdam and New York, Rodopi, 2007.

36 Wesley, *Journal*, 3 June 1790, vol. 8, p. 68.

37 Wesley, *Journal*, 29 August 1748, vol. 3, p. 375.

38 Wesley, *Journal*, 25 April 1752, vol. 4, p. 22.

39 The *Survey* was an abstraction of John Buddoeus' *Elementa Philosophiae Practicae et Theoreticae* (1703) and notes from John Ray's *Wisdom of God in the Creation* (1691), William Derham's *Physico and Astro-theology* (1713), Bernard Niewentyt's *Religious Philosopher* (1715), and Cotton Mather's *Christian Philosopher* (1721); for a useful examination of some of the philosophical under-pinnings and sources that informed the *Survey*, see Randy Maddox, 'Anticipating the New Creation: Wesleyan Foundations for Holistic Mission', *Asbury Journal* 62:1 (2007), pp. 49–66.

40 Originally published in 1766, English translation (used by Wesley) 1769. The complete title of this work, *An Inquiry into the Origins of the Discoveries Attributed to the Moderns: Wherein it is Demonstrated, that our Most Celebrated Philosophers have, for the Most Part, Taken What they Advance from the Ancients; and that Many Important Truths in Religion were Known to the Pagan Sages*, was included on the title page of the Survey in the 1816 and 1823 American editions, and abbreviated to *Inquiry into the Origin of the 'Discoveries Attributed to the Ancients'*. In these editions, the author of this work was recorded as 'Mr. Deuten'.

41 John Wesley and Robert Mudie, *A Compendium of Natural Philosophy Being A Survey of the Wisdom of God in the Creation*, 3 vols, London, Thomas Tegg and Son, 1836.

42 Wesley, *A Survey of the Wisdom of God*, §Preface, vol. 1, p. v.

43 Wesley, *A Survey of the Wisdom of God*, §Preface, vol. 1, p. v.

44 Wesley, *A Survey of the Wisdom of God*, §Preface, vol. 1, p. iv.

45 Wesley, *A Survey of the Wisdom of God*, §Preface, vol. 1, p. v.

46 Wesley, *A Survey of the Wisdom of God*, §III.II.7, vol. 1, p. 361.

47 Schofield, 'John Wesley and Science', pp. 336–7.

48 Wesley, *A Survey of the Wisdom of God*, §II.VI.1, vol. 1, p. 298.

49 Wesley, *A Survey of the Wisdom of God*, §II.VI.9, vol. 1, p. 306.

50 Wesley, *A Survey of the Wisdom of God*, §V.III.10, vol. 2, p. 185.

51 Wesley, *A Survey of the Wisdom of God*, §III.II.8.III, vol. 2, pp. 374–5.

52 Wesley, *A Survey of the Wisdom of God; Contemplation*, §V.10, vol. 2, p. 226.

53 Not withstanding the attempts of twentieth-century scholars, such as Collier (pp. 148ff) to force Wesley's observation of the 'chain of being' into the mould of evolutionary causation.

54 Wesley, 'Remarks on Count de Buffon's "Natural History"' (1782), *WJW*, vol. 13, p. 452.

55 Wesley, *A Survey of the Wisdom of God*, §III.II.1, vol. 1, p. 347.

56 Wesley, *A Survey of the Wisdom of God*, §II.I.10, vol. 1, pp. 128–30.

57 Wesley, *Journal*, 16 September 1790, vol. 8, p. 95.

58 Neil A. Campbell, *Biology*, 4th edn, Menlo Park, Benjamin/Cummings Publishing Co., 1996, p. 1062.

59 Wesley, *A Survey of the Wisdom of God; Contemplation*, §V.8, vol. 2, pp. 225ff.

60 Wesley, *A Survey of the Wisdom of God*, §II.VI.9, vol. 1, p. 306.

61 Wesley, *A Survey of the Wisdom of God*, §III.II.7, vol. 1, pp. 364–465.

62 Wesley, *A Survey of the Wisdom of God*, §II.VI.5, vol. 1, pp. 302–3.

63 Wesley, *A Survey of the Wisdom of God*, §III.II.6, vol. 1, pp. 359ff, §III.II.8.IV, vol. 1, pp. 375ff, §III.II.8.IV, vol. 1, pp. 375ff.

64 Wesley, *A Survey of the Wisdom of God*, §III.II.7, vol. 1, p. 366.

65 Wesley, *A Survey of the Wisdom of God*, §III.II.7, vol. 1, p. 365.

66 Wesley, *A Survey of the Wisdom of God*, §II.VI.7, vol. 1, p. 304.

67 R. H. MacArthur and E. O. Wilson, *The Theory of Island Biogeography*, Princeton, Princeton University Press, 1967.

68 Wesley, *A Survey of the Wisdom of God*, §III.I.19, vol. 1, p. 330.

69 Wesley, *A Survey of the Wisdom of God*, §III.I.19, vol. 1, p. 334.

70 Following the work of Carl Linnaeus, Wesley believed the spores of mosses to be seeds. He was correct, however, in understanding that the plants propagated by these structures.

71 Wesley, *A Survey of the Wisdom of God*, §III.II.6, vol. 1, p. 359.

72 Wesley, *A Survey of the Wisdom of God*, §IV.I.4, vol. 1, pp. 414–15.

73 Wesley, *A Survey of the Wisdom of God*, §IV.I.15, vol. 1, p. 466.

74 Wesley, *A Survey of the Wisdom of God*, §III.II.7, vol. 1, p. 366.

75 Wesley, *A Survey of the Wisdom of God*, §IV.III.10, vol. 2, pp. 184–5.

76 Wesley, *A Survey of the Wisdom of God*, §III.II.7, vol. 1, p. 368.

77 Robert V. Rakestraw, 'The Contribution of John Wesley Toward an Ethic of Nature,' *The Drew Gateway* 56 (1986), pp. 14–25, p. 19; Runyan, *The New Creation*, p. 203.

78 Wesley would later expand on this in his sermon, 'The General Deliverance.' (1781); Wesley, *A Survey of the Wisdom of God*, §II.VI.3, vol. 1, pp. 300–301.

79 Wesley, *A Survey of the Wisdom of God*, §II.VI.6, vol. 1, pp. 303–4.

80 Wesley, *A Survey of the Wisdom of God*, §II.VI.4, vol. 1, p. 302.

81 Wesley, *Journal*, 31 March 1788, vol. 7, p. 371.

82 Wesley, *Journal*, 5 April 1790, vol. 8, pp. 57–8.

83 Wesley, *Journal*, 31 December 1764, vol. 5, p. 104.

84 Wesley, *Journal*, 3 July 1769, vol. 5, p. 326.

85 Wesley, *A Survey of the Wisdom of God*, Introduction, vol. 1, p. xii.

86 Wesley, *A Survey of the Wisdom of God*, §II.VI.9, vol. 1, p. 308.

87 Wesley, *A Survey of the Wisdom of God*, §III.II.8.III, vol. 1, p. 373.

88 Wesley, *A Survey of the Wisdom of God*, §III.II.7, vol. 1, p. 365.

89 Wesley, *A Survey of the Wisdom of God*, §III.II.8.II, vol. 1, p. 372.

90 Wesley, *A Survey of the Wisdom of God*, §III.II.7, vol. 1, p. 369.

91 Wesley, *A Survey of the Wisdom of God*, §II.VI.10, vol. 1, p. 310.

92 Wesley, *A Survey of the Wisdom of God*, §II.VI.9, vol. 1, p. 306.

93 Wesley, *A Survey of the Wisdom of God*, §III.II.7, vol. 1, p. 368.

94 Wesley, *A Survey of the Wisdom of God*, §II.I.10, vol. 1, p. 133, §II.I.10, vol. 1, p. 139.

95 Wesley, *A Survey of the Wisdom of God*, §III.I.1, vol. 1, p. 344, §IV.I.14, vol. 1, pp. 448ff.

96 Runyan, *The New Creation*, pp. 201–2.

97 Wesley, *A Survey of the Wisdom of God*, §III.II.8.V, vol. 1, p. 382.

98 Randy L. Maddox, '"Vital Orthodoxy": A Wesleyan Dynamic for 21st-Century Christianity', *Methodist History* 42:1 (October 2003), pp. 3–19, p. 15.

99 Wesley, *Survey of the Wisdom of God*, vol. 1, p. 380; Maddox also cites a lengthy and explicit passage to this effect, which was included in the conclusion of the 5th (London) edition of the *Survey*, but deleted from the first (1810) and second (1816) American editions; see Maddox, 'Vital Orthodoxy', p. 16.

100 Haas, 'Eighteenth Century Evangelical Responses', p. 93.

101 Wesley, 'On Divine Providence' (1786), Sermon 67, §8, *WJW*, vol. 6, pp. 313–25.

102 Wesley, 'God's Approbation of His Works' (1782), Sermon 56, §I.2, *WJW*, vol. 6, pp. 206–7.

103 Wesley, 'The General Deliverance' (1781), Sermon 60, §I.1, *WJW*, vol. 6, p. 424.

104 Wesley, *Primitive Physic*, p. iii.

105 Wesley, 'God's Approbation', §I.2, *WJW*, vol. 6, p. 207.

106 Wesley, 'God's Approbation', §I.2, *WJW*, vol. 6, p. 208.

107 Wesley, 'God's Approbation', §I.3, *WJW*, vol. 6, p. 208.

108 Wesley, 'God's Approbation', §I.4, *WJW*, vol. 6, pp. 208ff.

109 Wesley, 'God's Approbation', §I.5, *WJW*, vol. 6, p. 209.

110 Wesley, 'God's Approbation', §I.6, *WJW*, vol. 6, p. 209.

111 Wesley, 'The Wisdom of God's Counsels' (1784), Sermon 68, §2, *WJW*, vol. 6, p. 325.

112 Wesley, *A Survey of the Wisdom of God*, §III.II.8.I, vol. 1, p. 371.

113 Wesley, 'God's Approbation', §I.9, *WJW*, vol. 6, pp. 210–11.

114 Wesley, *A Survey of the Wisdom of God*, §III.II.7, vol. 1, p. 368.

115 Wesley, 'God's Approbation', §I.12, *WJW*, vol. 6, p. 212.

116 Wesley, 'God's Approbation', §I.13, *WJW*, vol. 6, pp. 212–13.

117 Wesley, 'God's Approbation', §I.14, *WJW*, vol. 6, p. 213.

118 Wesley, 'Spiritual Worship' (1780), Sermon 77, §I.2, *WJW*, vol. 6, p. 426.

119 Haas, 'John Wesley's Vision of Science in the Service of Christ', p. 240; Wesley, 'Spiritual Worship', §I.3, *WJW*, vol. 6, p. 426.

120 Wesley, 'To Dr. Conyers Middleton' (4 January 1739) §VI.I.12, *WJW*, vol. 10, p. 70.

121 Wesley, 'The Wisdom of God's Counsels', §3, *WJW*, vol. 6, p. 326.

122 Wesley, 'Spiritual Worship', §I.4, *WJW*, vol. 6, p. 426.

123 Wesley, 'Upon our Lord's Sermon on the Mount, Discourse III' (1739), Sermon 23, §I.6, *WJW*, vol. 5, p. 281.

124 Wesley, 'Spiritual Worship', §II.3, *WJW*, vol. 6, pp. 429–30.

125 Michael Lodahl, 'The Cosmological Basis for Wesley's "Gradualism"', *Wesleyan Theological Journal* 36 (Spring 2001), pp. 17–32, p. 22.

126 M. Elton Hendricks, 'John Wesley and Natural Theology', *Wesleyan Theological Journal* 18:2 (Fall 1983), pp. 7–17, p. 8.

127 Haas, 'John Wesley's Vision of Science in the Service of Christ', p. 238.

128 Wesley, 'The Imperfection of Human Knowledge' (1784), Sermon 69, §I.1, *WJW*, vol. 6, p. 338.

129 Wesley, 'On the Omnipresence of God' (1788), Sermon 111, §II.1, *WJW*, vol. 7, p. 240.

130 Wesley, *Journal*, 17 March 1756, vol. 4, p. 152.

131 Wesley, 'Upon our Lord's Sermon on the Mount III', §I.11, *WJW*, vol. 5, p. 283.

132 Michael Lodahl, *God of Nature and of Grace: Reading the World in a Wesleyan Way*, Nashville, Kingswood Books/Abingdon Press, 2003, p. 194.

133 Cobb, *Grace & Responsibility*, p. 51.

134 Wesley, 'Upon our Lord's Sermon on the Mount, Discourse VI' (1740), Sermon 26, §III.7, *WJW*, vol. 5, p. 335.

135 Wesley, *Explanatory Notes on the Old Testament*, Genesis 2:8–15, <http://wesley.nnu.edu/john_wesley/notes/index.htm>.

136 Albert C. Outler and Richard P Heitzenrater, eds, *John Wesley's Sermons: An Anthology*, Nashville, Abingdon, 1991, p. 13.

137 Wesley, 'The Image of God' (1730), §I.4, in *John Wesley's Sermons: An Anthology*, p. 16.

138 Wesley, *Explanatory Notes on the Old Testament*, Genesis 1:26–8.

139 Wesley, 'The General Deliverance', §I.2, *WJW*, vol. 6, p. 243.

140 Wesley, *Explanatory Notes upon the Old Testament*, Genesis 1:28.

141 Wesley, 'The General Deliverance', §I.3, *WJW*, vol. 6, pp. 243–4.

142 James A. Nash, *Loving Nature: Ecological Integrity and Christian Responsibility*, Nashville, Abingdon Press, 1991, p. 103.

143 Wesley, 'The General Deliverance', §I.5 *WJW*, vol. 6, p. 244.

144 Wesley, 'The General Deliverance', §1 *WJW*, vol. 6, p. 241.

145 Cobb, *Grace and Responsibility*, p. 52.

146 Lodahl, *God of Nature and of Grace*, pp. 194–5.

147 Wesley, 'The General Deliverance, §III.5, *WJW*, vol. 6, p. 250.

148 Lodahl, *God of Nature and of Grace*, p. 197.

149 Wesley, 'God's Approbation', §II.1, *WJW*, vol. 6, p. 213.

150 Wesley, 'The General Deliverance', §2 *WJW*, vol. 6, p. 242.

151 Wesley, 'God's Approbation', §II.3, *WJW*, vol. 6, pp. 214–15.

152 Nash, *Loving Nature*, p. 127.

153 Wesley, 'The General Deliverance', §II.6 *WJW*, vol. 6, pp. 247–8.

154 Wesley, 'Minutes of Several Conversations between the Rev. Mr. Wesley and others from the year 1744 to the year 1789', *WJW*, vol. 8, pp. 317–18.

155 Wesley, 'God's Approbation', §I.2–5, *WJW*, vol. 6, pp. 207–9.

156 Rakestraw, 'Contribution of John Wesley', p. 18.

157 Wesley, 'A Plain Account of Christian Perfection' (1777), §13, *WJW*, vol. 11, p. 378.

158 Wesley, 'The New Birth' (1743), Sermon 45, §I.1, *WJW*, vol. 6, p. 66.

159 Wesley, 'The Doctrine of Original Sin' (1757), §4.5.2. *WJW*, vol. 9, pp. 410–11.

160 Laura A. Bartels, 'The Political Image as the Basis for Wesleyan Ethics', *Quarterly Review* 23:3 (Fall 2003), pp. 294–301, pp. 296–7.

161 Wesley, 'The New Birth', §II.5, *WJW*, vol. 6, p. 71; 'The Doctrine of Original Sin'. §2.2, *WJW*, vol. 9, p. 316.

162 Runyan, 'The New Creation', p. 7.

163 Wesley, 'The Scripture Way of Salvation' (1758), Sermon 43, §I.4, *WJW*, vol. 6, p. 45.

164 Wesley, 'The Image of God', §III.1–III.2, *John Wesley's Sermons*, p. 19.

165 Wesley, 'Marks of the New Birth' (1741), Sermon 18, §III.3, *WJW*, vol. 5, p. 219; 'The Marks of the New Birth', §III.5, *WJW*, vol. 5, p. 220.

166 Wesley, *A Plain Account of Christian Perfection*, §18, *WJW*, vol. 11, p. 394.

167 Wesley, *A Plain Account of Christian Perfection*, §15 (6), *WJW*, vol. 11, 385. This was reprinted from the Preface of the third volume of *Hymns and Sacred Poems*, 1742; 'A Plain Account of Christian Perfection', §28, *WJW*, vol. 11, p. 444.

168 Runyan, 'The New Creation', p. 19.

169 Lodahl, *God of Nature and of Grace*, p. 204.

170 Wesley, 'On Working out our own Salvation' (1785), Sermon 85, §I.1, vol. 6, p. 508.

171 Wesley, 'On Working out our own Salvation', §II.3, *WJW*, vol. 6, p. 510.

172 Wesley, 'On Working out our own Salvation', §III.2. III.7, *WJW*, vol. 6, pp. 511, 513.

173 Lodahl, *God of Nature and of Grace*, p. 205.

174 Runyan, *The New Creation*, p. 205.

175 Lodahl, *God of Nature and of Grace*, pp. 191–2.

176 Jerry L. Mercer, 'The Destiny of Man in John Wesley's Eschatology', *Wesleyan Theological Journal* 2 (Spring 1968), pp. 56–65, p. 60.

177 Mercer, 'The Destiny of Man', p. 57.

178 Wesley, *Journal*, 8 February 1750, vol. 3, p. 453; *Journal*, 8 March 1750, vol. 3, pp. 456–7.

179 Wesley, *Journal*, 8 March 1750, vol. 3, p. 456.

180 Wesley, *Journal*, 18 May 1757, vol. 4, pp. 211–12; 2 November 1763, vol. 5, pp. 39–40; 7 December 1771, vol. 5, pp. 439–40.

181 Wesley, *Journal*, 2 June 1755, vol. 4, pp. 119–20; Wesley, 'Serious Thoughts Occasioned by The Late Earthquake at Lisbon' (1755), *WJW*, vol. 11, p. 5.

182 Wesley, *Journal*, 5 July 1773, vol. 5, p. 517.

183 Charles Wesley, 'The Cause and Cure of Earthquakes' (1750), Sermon 129, §I, *WJW*, vol. 7, p. 387.

184 Margaret G. Flowers, Wayne G. McCown, and Douglas R. Cullum, '18th Century Earthquakes and Apocalyptic Expectations: The Hymns of Charles Wesley', *Methodist History* 42:4 (July 2004), pp. 222–35, pp. 227ff.

185 Kenneth G. C. Newport, 'Premillennialism in the Early Writing of Charles Wesley', *Wesleyan Theological Journal* 32 (Spring 1997), pp. 85–106, pp. 87ff.

186 Newport, 'Premillennialism', p. 106; for a treatment on millennial views, see Randy Maddox, 'Nurturing the New Creation: Reflections on a Wesleyan Trajectory', in M. Douglas Meeks, ed., *Wesleyan Perspectives on the New Creation*, Nashville, Kingswood, 2004, pp. 34–43.

187 Flowers et al., '18th Century Earthquakes', p. 231.

188 Kenneth Collins, 'The New Creation as a Multivalent Theme in John Wesley's Theology', *Wesleyan Theological Journal* 36 (Spring 2001), p. 77.

189 Wesley, *Explanatory Notes on the New Testament*, 2 Corinthians 5:17, <http://wesley.nnu.edu/john_wesley/notes/index.htm>.

190 Wesley, *Explanatory Notes on the New Testament*, 2 Corinthians 5:17.

191 Runyan, 'The New Creation', p. 6.

192 Maddox, '"Celebrating the Whole Wesley": A Legacy for Contemporary Wesleyans', *Methodist History* 43:2 (January 2005), pp. 74–89, p. 84.

193 Wesley, *Explanatory Notes on the New Testament*, Romans 8:21.

194 Wesley, 'The New Creation' (1785), Sermon 64, §2, *WJW*, vol. 6, p. 289.

195 Wesley, 'The New Creation', §8, *WJW*, vol. 6, p. 290; [cf. 'God's Approbation of His Works', §10].

196 Wesley, 'The New Creation', §11, *WJW*, vol. 6, pp. 291–2; [cf. 'God's Approbation of His Works', §I.5].

197 Wesley, 'The New Creation', §12, *WJW*, vol. 6, p. 292; [cf. 'God's Approbation of His Works', §I.4].

198 Wesley, 'The New Creation', §15, *WJW*, vol. 6, p. 294; [cf. 'God's Approbation of His Works', §I.3].

199 Wesley, 'The New Creation', §14, *WJW*, vol. 6, p. 293; [cf. 'God's Approbation of His Works', §I.6].

200 Wesley, 'The New Creation', §16, *WJW*, vol. 6, p. 294; [cf. 'God's Approbation of His Works', §I.9].

201 Wesley, 'The New Creation', §17, *WJW*, vol. 6, pp. 294–5; [cf. 'God's Approbation of His Works', §I.12].

202 Wesley, 'The General Spread of the Gospel' (1783), Sermon 63, §27, *WJW*, vol. 6, p. 288.

203 Wesley, 'The Good Steward' (1758), Sermon 51, §I.1, *WJW*, vol. 6, p. 137.

204 Runyan, *The New Creation*, p. 206.

205 Haas, 'Eighteenth Century Evangelical Responses', p. 97; Maddox, '"Celebrating the Whole Wesley,"' p. 86.

206 Maddox, '"Celebrating the Whole Wesley"', p. 86.

207 Wesley, *A Survey of the Wisdom of God*, §II.VI.3, vol. 1, p. 301.

208 Maddox, '"Celebrating the Whole Wesley"', p. 87.

209 Wesley, 'God's Love to Fallen Man' (1782), Sermon 59, §4, *WJW*, vol. 6, p. 233.

210 Maddox, '"Celebrating the Whole Wesley,"' p. 87.

211 Nash, *Loving Nature*, p. 128; Wesley, 'The General Deliverance', §III.3, *WJW*, vol. 6, p. 249.

212 Wesley, 'The General Deliverance', §III.5, *WJW*, , vol. 6, p. 250.

213 Wesley, 'The General Deliverance', §III.6, *WJW*, vol. 6, p. 250.

214 Wesley, 'The General Deliverance', §III.7, *WJW*, vol. 6, pp. 250–1.

215 Wesley, 'The General Deliverance', §III.8, *WJW*, vol. 6, p. 251.

216 Wesley, 'The General Deliverance', §III.10, *WJW*, vol. 6, pp. 251–2.

217 Wesley, 'The General Deliverance', §III.12, *WJW*, vol. 6, p. 252.

218 Nash, *Loving Nature*, p. 129.

219 Wesley, *Journal*, 15 July 1756, vol. 4, p. 176. Included in this letter were the explicit words, 'If tenderness, mercy and compassion to the brute creatures were impressed upon the infant breast, and conducted into action according to its little power, would it not be confirmed in the human heart? . . . Does not experience show the sad effects of a contrary education?'

220 Wesley, 'On the Education of Children' (1783), Sermon 95, §25 *WJW*, vol. 7, p. 98.

221 Wesley, 'On the Education of Children', §14, *WJW*, vol. 7, p. 91.

222 R. Southey, *Life of Wesley*, 2 vols, New York, Harper, 1847, vol. 2, p. 88.

223 Haas, 'Eighteenth Century Evangelical Responses', p. 98.

224 Rakestraw, 'Contribution of John Wesley', p. 21.

225 Randy Maddox, 'Anticipating the New Creation', pp. 62–3.

226 Wesley, *Journal*, 24 May 1762, vol. 4, p. 504i, *Journal*, 16 July 1756, vol. 4, p. 175.

227 John Wesley, ed., 'Husbandry Spiritualized or, the Heavenly Use of Earthly Things', by John Flavel, in *A Christian Library: Consisting of Extracts from and Abridgements of the Choicest Pieces of Practical Divinity Which Have Been Published in the English Tongue*. 2nd ed., vol. 27, pp. 135–279, <http://wesley.nnu.edu/john_wesley/christian_library/vol27/index.htm>.

228 Rakestraw, 'Contribution of John Wesley', p. 19.

229 Wesley, *Explanatory Notes on the Old Testament*, Genesis 2:4–7.

230 Rakestraw, 'Contribution of John Wesley', p. 21.

231 Ian Barbour, *Where Science Meets Religion: Enemies, Strangers, or Partners?*, San Francisco, HarperSanFrancisco, 2000, pp. 2ff; see also John Polkinghorne, *Science and Theology: An Introduction*, London, SPCK, 1998.

232 David C. Lindberg and Ronald L. Numbers, 'Beyond War and Peace: A Reappraisal of the Encounter between Christianity and Science', *Perspectives on Science and Christian Faith* 39:3 (1987), pp. 140–9, p. 141.

233 Andrew Dickson White, *A History of the Warfare of Science with Theology in Christendom*, 2 vols, New York, D. Appleton, 1896, vol. 1, p. 325.

234 White, *A History of the Warfare*, vol. 1, p. 375.

235 Lynn White, Jr., 'The Historical Roots of Our Ecological Crisis', *Science* 155 (1967), pp. 1203–7, pp. 1206–7.

236 Ben A. Minteer and Robert E. Manning, 'An Appraisal of the Critique of Anthropocentrism and Three Lesser Known Themes in Lynn White's "The Historical roots of our Ecologic Crisis"', *Organization and Environment* 18 (2005), pp. 163–76, p. 163.

237 Maddox, 'Anticipating the New Creation', *Asbury Journal*, p. 51; Alister McGrath, *The Reenchantment of Nature: The Denial of Religion and the Ecological Crisis*, New York, Doubleday/Galilee, 2003, p. xv.

238 Minteer and Manning, 'An Appraisal', p. 163.

239 Nash, *Loving Nature*, pp. 72ff.

240 See Richard H. Bube, 'Do Biblical Models Need to be Replaced In Order to Deal Effectively with Environmental Issues?', *Perspectives on Science and Christian Faith* 47 (June 1994), pp. 90–7, pp. 93ff.

241 Rick Flood, 'Speak Truth to Power: Thoughts on a Bold Strategy for Conservation Biologists', *Conservation Biology* 19:2 (April 2005), p. 293; David W. Orr, 'Armageddon Versus Extinction', *Conservation Biology* 19:2 (April 2005), pp. 290–2.

242 Mark Bergen, 'Love thy neighbor, love the neighborhood', *World* 20:30 (6 August 2005), pp. 22–3, p. 23; Richard T. Wright, 'Tearing Down the Green: Environmental Backlash in the Evangelical Sub-Culture', *Perspectives on Science and Christian Faith* 47 (June 1955), pp. 80–91, p. 80; see also E. Calvin Beisner, *Where Garden Meets Wilderness*, Grand Rapids, Eerdmans, 1997.

243 Kevin Phillips, 'Theocrats and Theocons', *The Nation* 282 (1 May 2006), pp. 18–23, p. 21.

244 H. Paul Santmire, *The Travail of Nature: The Ambiguous Ecological Promise of Christian Theology*, Minneapolis, Fortress Press, 1985, pp. 9, 94–5, 122.

245 David C. Lindberg and Ronald L. Numbers, 'Beyond War and Peace', p. 44.

246 White, *History of the Warfare*, p. vii; Lynn White, 'Historical Roots', p. 1206.

247 Mark Stanton and Dennis Guernsey, 'Christians' Ecological Responsibility: A Theological Introduction and Challenge', *Perspectives on Science and Christian Faith* 45 (March 1993), pp. 2–7, p. 2.

248 E. Calvin Beisner, 'Issues and Evidence, not *ad Hominem*, Should Characterize Environmental Debate; A Response to Richard Wright', *Perspectives on Science and Christian Faith* 47 (December 1995), pp. 285–7, p. 285.

249 Jim Ball, 'The Use of Ecology in the Evangelical Protestant Response to the Ecological Crisis', *Perspectives in Science and Christian Faith* 50 (March 1998), pp. 32–40, p. 33.

250 Mark Bergen, 'Red Light, Green Light: Global Warming Initiative Highlights Evangelical Gridlock', *World* 21:8 (25 February 2006), p. 29.

251 Howard Snyder, 'Salvation Means Creation Healed: Creation, Cross, Kingdom, and Mission', *Asbury Journal* 62:1 (2007), pp. 9–47, p. 9.

252 In Great Britain, the John Ray Initiative (www.jri.org.uk); in the US, the Evangelical Environmental Network (www.creationcare.org/resources/declaration.php); Maddox, 'Anticipating the New Creation', p. 50; Snyder, 'Salvation Means Creation Healed', p. 25.

253 Maddox, 'Anticipating the New Creation', p. 56.

254 Calvin B. DeWitt, 'Creation Environmental Stewardship: Preparing the Way for Action', *Perspectives on Science and Christian Faith* 46 (June 1994), pp. 80–9.

255 Steven Bouma-Prediger, 'Creation Care and Character: The Nature and Necessity of the Ecological Virtues', *Perspectives on Science and Christian Faith* 50 (March 1998), pp. 6–21.

256 Mercer, 'The Destiny of Man', p. 64.

257 Kevin Witt, 'Biblical and Theological Foundations for Nature and Environmental Care', <www.gbod.org/camping/earth.html>.

258 Bube, 'Biblical Models', p. 97.

259 Lodahl, 'The Cosmological Basis', p. 23.

260 Wesley, *Journal*, 8 November 1764, vol. 5, p. 101.

261 Wesley, 'List of Works Revised Abridged from Various Authors, by the Rev. John Wesley, M.A. XCVII. The Arminian Magazine: Consisting of Extracts of Original Treatises on Universal Redemption. Fourteen Volumes. 8vo., 1778–1791.' Preface to vol. 4. §8, *WJW*, vol. 14, pp. 288–9.

262 Wesley, 'A Short Account of The School in Kingswood, Near Bristol' (1768), §6, *WJW*, vol. 13, pp. 287–9.

263 Wesley, 'Letter CCXX. – TO *Miss L*—— ', *WJW*, vol. 12, pp. 260–2; 'To Margaret Lewen, June 1764', *Letters* (Telford), vol. 4, pp. 247–9.

264 Haas, 'John Wesley's Vision of Science in the Service of Christ', p. 234.

265 Laura Bartels Felleman, 'John Wesley's *Survey of the Wisdom of God in the Creation*: A Methodological Inquiry', *Perspectives on Science and Christian Faith* 58:1 (March 2006), pp. 68–73, p. 71.

266 Nash, *Loving Nature*, p. 127.

267 Haas, 'John Wesley's Views of Science and Christianity', p. 386.

268 Schofield, 'Wesley and Science', p. 338.

269 Pellowe, 'Wesley's Use of Science', p. 403.

270 Schofield, 'Wesley and Science', p. 337.

271 Keith Miller, 'Natural Hazards: Challenges to the Creation Mandate of Dominion?', *Perspectives on Science and Christian Faith* 53:3 (September 2001), p. 185.

272 Pellowe, 'Wesley's Use of Science', p. 394.

273 Timothy L. Smith, 'Chronological List of John Wesley's Sermons and Doctrinal Essays', *Wesleyan Theological Journal* 17:2 (Fall 1982), pp. 88–110: 'The Image of God', 1730; 'Sermon on the Mount III', 1739; 'Sermon on the Mount VI', 1740; 'Marks of the New Birth', 1741; 'The New Birth', 1743; 'Scripture Way of Salvation', 'The Good Steward', 1758; 'Spiritual Worship', 1780; 'The General Deliverance', 1781; 'God's Approbation of His Works', 'God's Love to Fallen Man', 1782; 'On the Education of Children', 'The General Spread of the Gospel', 1783; 'On the Imperfection of Human Knowledge', 'The Wisdom of God's Counsels', 1784; 'On Working Out Our Own Salvation', 'The New Creation', 1785; 'On Divine Providence', 1786; 'On the Omnipresence of God', 1788.

274 Lodahl, *God of Nature and of Grace*, pp. 192–3.

275 Thomas C. Oden, *John Wesley's Scriptural Christianity: A Plain Exposition of His Teaching on Christian Doctrine*, Grand Rapids, Zondervan, 1994, pp. 129–30.

276 Maddox, *Responsible Grace: John Wesley's Practical Theology*, Nashville, Abingdon/Kingswood, 1994, p. 247.

277 Runyan, 'The New Creation', p. 6.

3

Pastor and Physician:
John Wesley's Cures for Consumption

DEBORAH MADDEN

We study health, and we deliberate upon our meats, and drink, and air, and exercise, and we hew and we polish every stone that goes to that building; and so our health is a long and regular work: but in a minute a cannon batters all, overthrows all, demolishes all; a sickness unprevented for all our diligence, unsuspected for all our curiosity; nay undeserved if we consider only disorder, summons us, seizes us, possesses us, destroys us in an instant.

John Donne, *Devotions Upon Emergent Occasions* (1623)[1]

Introduction: Consumption – the Dreaded Disease

No one died of 'consumption' after 1882, when the German medical scientist, Robert Koch, discovered that the micro-organism, tubercle bacillus, or *mycobacterium tuberculosis*, was the cause of this most feared of all early-modern diseases – though 'tuberculosis' remains a leading cause of global morbidity and mortality.[2] 'Consumption', or what the Greeks referred to as 'phthisis', which, roughly translated, means 'wasting' or 'decaying', dominated the minds of our ancestors. Apart from the bubonic plague, it was one of the most dreaded illnesses, claiming millions of lives. Hippocrates identified the fatal consequences of 'phthisis' in its late stages and advised his students against treating it – dead patients damaged the reputations of burgeoning physicians. The way that this 'dangerous and frightful' condition corroded and literally consumed a patient's flesh, causing 'putrid' decay and, finally, death, can be seen in Sir Richard Blackmore's *A Treatise of Consumptions* (1724) – Blackmore had served as one of King William's physicians-in-ordinary and was a much esteemed medical authority:

Nocturnal sweats, and great thirst, as well as purulent expectoration, are symptoms that discover a confirmed consumption . . . in this confirmed state of the distemper there is generally a great dejection of appetite, and a nauseous loathing of foods, with dead sickness of stomach, frequent vomitings, which are sometimes caused by excess of green choler, like verdigrease, or juice of leeks, that is often ejected, to free the stomach of its burden; and sometimes excited by a long and vehement fit of coughing, that nature employs to pump and ease the lungs.[3]

Symptoms for consumption included a 'rapid' or 'hard' pulse, chest pain, rasping cough, discoloured urine and catarrh, vomiting or coughing up blood, a fever appended with an unquenchable thirst, swollen legs or feet, the last of which, so physicians believed, indicated that death was fast approaching. According to Blackmore, the essential and distinguishing character of a 'confirmed consumption' was a 'wasting of the body, by reason of an ulcerated state of the lungs', attended with a 'hectick fever' and cough that discharged 'purulent matter'.[4] Eighteenth-century medics attributed consumption to innumerable causes, including hereditary factors, excessive eating and drinking, internal 'distempers', intense study, violent religious or sexual 'passions' and immorality. A stagnant, stale, damp or malodorous atmosphere, including any extreme changes in atmospheric conditions, was also blamed for causing the disease.

In his medical manual, *Primitive Physic* (1747), John Wesley listed more remedies for '*A Consumption*' than any other disease, which is suggestive, perhaps, of both its serious and ubiquitous nature.[5] Wesley's *Journal*, as well as letters written to relatives, friends and Methodist ministers, depict with moving tenderness many occasions where he is advising, assisting or comforting consumptive patients. This can be seen in a journal entry, written for 8 May 1777:

I went to Yarn. There I found a lovely young woman in the last stage of a consumption; but such a one as I never read of, nor heard any physician speak of, but Dr. Wilson. The seat of the ulcers is not the lungs, but the windpipe. I never knew it cured . . . this young woman died in a few weeks.[6]

When writing on 16 August 1767 to the prominent female Methodist preacher, Mary Bosanquet, Wesley made the following observation about their mutual friend, Sarah Ryan, who, suffering from a recent bout of consumption, made an unexpected recovery:

Undoubtedly she was (and so was I) in the third stage of a consumption. And physicians have long since agreed that this is not curable by any natural means. But what signifies this in the sight of God? As,

'When obedient nature knows His will,

A fly, a grapestone, or an hair can kill';

So, when it is His will to restore life or strength, any means shall be effectual. But we are slow of heart to believe that He is still the uncontrolled, Almighty Lord of health and earth and heaven.[7]

Like John Donne, Wesley was acutely aware of the brevity of earthly existence, which, depending on 'His will', could be destroyed in an instant by 'a fly, a grapestone, or an hair', despite our best efforts to preserve and lengthen life. The 'third' stage of consumption, in which the patient experienced a severe deterioration, usually signalled the steady march towards death.[8] During this stage, emaciation was extreme, and patients repeatedly vomited infected, bloody sputum, symptomatic of ulcerated, tubercular lesions in the lungs, which made every breath taken both acrid and painful.[9] As Wesley remarks, survival rates for those in this stage were vanishingly rare and physicians usually only advised palliative care. Classic cases of 'pulmonary consumption' were chronic and intermittent; this, combined with the fact that consumptive patients were always mentally alert until the very end, sometimes fostered false hope and stories of miraculous remissions, shortly before they suffered terrible relapses.[10] Yet Wesley was not alone, or merely deluded, in his belief that chronic consumption could sometimes be cured, and this was widely recognized during the period, even amongst medically qualified practitioners.[11]

The sentiments expressed in Wesley's letter to Mary Bosanquet encapsulate perfectly the theological underpinnings of his holistic approach to 'health and earth and heaven'. As an Anglican minister, his first duty to the Church involved providing spiritual counsel to its flock, though part of this Christian ministry also included dispensing physic to those who desperately needed it, which is why he wrote *Primitive Physic* in 1747. In the Preface to this manual, Wesley makes clear his Augustinian belief in the *dis-ease* of original sin, a necessary condition of pain and suffering that man had endured since his fall from grace, but does not spiritualize physical illness itself – the remedies listed are, in fact, based on contemporary medicine and operate within the parameters of 'orthodox' medical practice.[12] That Wesley believed in God's ability to completely restore health, both physically and spiritually, is evident in his letter to Mary Bosanquet, but also in many other letters, journal entries and commentaries that appear in the *Arminian Magazine*. For him this preternatural element was the framework into which everything else in the world fitted. Wesley saw these different modes of existence, the temporal and spiritual, converging, not in disease itself, but in the patient's experience of illness. On this, Wesley was heavily influenced by the pietist physician George Cheyne, who believed that the mind, body and soul were separate, but inextricably linked categories. Laura Bartels Felleman and Robert Webster have shown how Wesley regarded the convergence of these categories as a powerful intersection between visible and invisible realms of existence.[13] Like Cheyne, Wesley was dissatisfied with a purely Lockean definition of the human faculties, which rendered man devoid of a spiritual 'sense' of an immaterial 'reality'.[14] Yet this spiritual sense was kept in perfect balance with an empirical approach to rational knowledge. This can be detected in the letters written to John Valton, a leading Methodist minister, who received from Wesley valuable spiritual guidance, health advice and cures for consumption.

Valton, a cradle Catholic who had converted to Methodism via Anglicanism in 1764, became one of Wesley's foremost itinerant ministers, though, owing to repeated bouts of consumptive ill health, he increasingly needed to intermit from preaching, before finally withdrawing from public lay-ministering altogether. Contemporary critics of Methodism were quick to note the turbulent, emotional and spiritual effusions of its adherents, who were scornfully dubbed 'enthusiasts', and Valton certainly seemed to confirm some of the suspicions exemplified in these caricatures. Religious 'enthusiasm', it was argued, mistook 'fancies' for divine inspiration; these fantasies were not spiritual in basis, but prompted, instead, by chemical imbalances or 'obstructions' in the body. Physicians, in fact, thought that particular physical illnesses or conditions, including those associated with consumption, could potentially induce psychological states susceptible to religious 'enthusiasm' and melancholia. Cheyne summarized this best in his *Essay of Health and Long Life* (1724):

> There is a kind of *melancholy*, which is called *religious*, because 'tis conversant about matters of religion; although, often, the persons so distempered have little *solid piety*. And this is merely a *bodily disease*, produced by an ill *habit* or *constitution*, wherein the *nervous system* is broken and disordered, and the *juices* are become *viscid* and *glewy*.[15]

By the time Cheyne was writing his *Essay*, Robert Burton's *Anatomy of Melancholy* (1621), in which the term 'religious melancholy' was first coined, had entered into mainstream medical discourse. Established

Anglican churchmen, who associated 'religious melancholy' and 'enthusiasm' with Puritanism or other forms of Nonconformist dissent, agreed with medical orthodoxy in regarding visions, revelations, inspired prophets, religious despair, or 'extraordinary' operations of the Holy Spirit as pathological symptoms of illness rather than authentic spiritual experiences – the root cause being an 'ill *habit*' or 'defect' of the mind.[16] This madness, or what Jon Mee has called 'dangerous enthusiasm', needed to be repressed because it threatened to raise the spectre of Puritanical 'fanaticism' in the form of theological schism and political turmoil, a potent reminder of England's darkest chapter in recent history.[17]

Valton's diaries and testimonies reveal protracted episodes of deep spiritual anguish, emotional crisis and suicidal despair, which usually went hand-in-hand with very poor physical health.[18] Those antipathetic to Methodism would have dismissed Valton's spiritual agonies as 'religious melancholia', though, contrary to Cheyne's general observation, the depth of his conviction and piety was beyond reproach. Sceptical observers, who detected 'enthusiasm' when Methodism was displayed, sought to discredit its followers by conflating religious despair with disease and, as Michael MacDonald points out, this emotionalism was thought to be a treatable medical condition rather than a spiritual state.[19] The distortions of polemical discourse here should not imply that Valton's experiences were purely symptomatic of melancholy or depression. To label them as such, MacDonald argues, ignores the 'particular cognitive content of religious despair, which was an overwhelming sense of rejection or guilt, and helplessness *with respect to God*'.[20] Certainly, Wesley recognized this and demonstrated an unerring ability to distinguish between spiritual malaise and physical disorders, including mental health problems like lunacy or depression.[21] Spiritual 'lowness' might not, in fact, be spiritual in essence, but relate instead to other diseases, fatigue or poverty. On the other hand, as Randy L. Maddox has suggested, Wesley also believed that 'milder' forms of emotional stress could be 'authentic responses to spiritual realities', which was God's way of indicating to an individual that they were not living as he would like them to be.[22]

Wesley invited Valton, along with several other 'eminent Methodist preachers', to note down and publish their spiritual experiences by way of inspiring others. Spiritual autobiographies provided graphic, but edifying, depictions of the emotional and physical trials that individuals underwent when they embraced a holy, disciplined life. Here, MacDonald notes, authors tended to be of humble social status, so that their personal stories could elicit sympathy and provide a source of piety to others.[23] Valton's testimony is important because it depicts an archetypal journey of Protestant Christian struggle, in which the protagonist fends off satanic temptation, as well as the worst symptoms of man's other ancient, implacable enemy: consumption. Valton, in fact, regarded each new bout of consumption as yet another 'sore trial' or tribulation, through which Satan was testing his faith and commitment.[24] Yet, like Wesley, he clearly distinguished between spiritual malaise and the deep unhappiness produced by his ever-declining physical health:

> My constitution was ruined, chiefly by the unwholesome air of the place where I lived. The physician told me that sitting at a desk would not do for me. Another eminent man told me that I was murdering myself. Riding was proposed to me as the most promising expedient to protract my life, and perhaps the only one.[25]

Wesley's response to Valton's letters are interesting for their mix of commonsense practical advice, which is combined with a firm, though understated, belief in supernatural forces. In this letter, written on 13 October 1784, Wesley also extols the healing efficacy of prayer:

> My Dear Brother,
>   Dr Davison's advice was good. I desire you would not offer to preach within these four weeks. I was suspended for near four months; but good is the will of the Lord. I suppose nettle tea is the best bracer in the world; and next that, elixir of vitriol (ten drops in a glass of water at ten or eleven in the morning). I am inclined to think that temptation is purely preternatural. I was strongly assaulted by it toward the close of my fever, when I could hardly set a foot to the ground. Many years ago I told you the case of Mr Colley, who was just in your case. He married and died. And do we not know
>   'All the promises are sure
>   To preserving prayer?'[26]

The experience of illness could sometimes, though not always, produce a 'preternatural' effect in the form of doubt, uncertainty and temptation; when head and breast were 'sorely afflicted', it rendered a patient's mind weak, his or her spirits low, thereby opening the door to Satan's tempting and seductive charms. This was precisely why Wesley insisted that he and other Methodists regularly visit and attend to the sick, but especially those in hospitals: when a patient's body was weighed down with illness, Methodists needed to protect and take care of their souls.

To avoid the sort of spiritual 'assault' that Wesley, himself, had been subjected to after a fit of fever, it was imperative to preserve health and remedy diseases quickly, safely and effectively. Wesley's practical advice to Valton thus includes asking him to take a break from the exerting demands of preaching: to rest his mind, body and spirit. Next, he is offered medicines that can act as 'bracers', nettle tea and elixir of vitriol, the latter of which was recommended amongst a range of other remedies in *Primitive Physic*. 'Bracing' medicine was required to 'constrict' the body's 'lax fibres', 'solids' or 'nerves' and, as we shall see later in this chapter, these prescriptions fully conformed to eighteenth-century medical thinking. Finally, there is Wesley's cautionary reminder about the fate of 'Mr Colley', who, like Valton, had also been prone to repeated bouts of consumption, though in this case, the condition rapidly deteriorated shortly after 'Mr Colley's' wedding – Benjamin Colley was from Yorkshire and joined the Methodists in 1761. Wesley had already issued this salutary warning to Valton in 1773:

My Dear Brother,
    When Dr Monkley attended that good man Mr Colley in his consumptive disorder, he said one day, 'I can't imagine how it is none of my medicines have any effect'. After pausing, he asked one standing by, 'is this gentleman lately married?' On her answering, 'About four months since', he replied, 'then he is a dead man'.
    Finding Sam Levick in Dublin of a consumptive habit, having been married some months, I advised him to leave his wife there and ride with me around the kingdom. But she persuaded him to remain with her; in consequence of which in a few months more she buried him.
    Humanly speaking, this would be the case with *you* if you married during your present state of health. I think you ought at all events to take a journey of a thousand miles first.[27]

Valton's health in 1773 had 'suffered greatly' as a result of the 'unwholesome air of Purfleet', where he was then living, but also because of the 'incessant labours' and hardships of his itinerant life.[28] Wesley was adamant that marriage would exacerbate Valton's condition, just as it had for Benjamin Colley. On this he concurs with 'Dr Monkley', who represents current Georgian medical thinking, though neither referred directly to the root cause of this deterioration. Their underlying assumption, however, is that sexual activity, particularly when conducted in the honeymoon phase of marriage, was ruinous to the health of anyone suffering from consumption. Valton was strongly advised therefore to resist marriage and persuaded instead to take the restorative expedient of exercise on horseback.

Valton had harboured ideas of marriage and finding a suitable companion for a long time, but took Wesley's advice to heart for many more years to come. Eventually, it was John Fletcher who encouraged Valton to enter into the blissful union of matrimony. Fletcher, an Anglican clergyman and fellow traveller of Methodism, had been an early supporter of the Wesleys, though, due to his own health considerations, was reluctant to take on a leading role in the movement. His marriage to Mary Bosanquet took place in 1781, and together they shared an evangelical ministry, which brought Fletcher a great deal of security and happiness. Fletcher's recommendation was simple: Valton should follow his example and find a suitable companion who could nurse him through the infirmities of life. He even had the very woman in mind, a 'Mrs Purnell', and, following Fletcher's advice, Valton duly married Judith Purnell in 1786.[29] On hearing the news of their happy nuptials, Wesley anxiously prescribed a mixture of regimen, medicine and prayer by way of safeguarding Valton from further trials of ill health, insisting too that he would consult the physician, John Whitehead:

My Dear Brother,

When I was quite worn down, it pleased God to make *my* marriage a means of restoring my health and strength. I trust yours will have the same effect upon you; though not by natural but divine efficacy. But this cannot be, unless you intermit preaching. I therefore positively require you, for a month from the date of this, not to preach more than twice a week; and if you preach less, I will not blame you. But you should at all hazards ride an hour every day, wrapping yourself up very close. Take care not to lodge in too close a room and not to draw your curtains. For medicine I should chiefly recommend stewed prunes, and either beef tea or a small cup of *fresh churned* buttermilk four times a day. Let my dear friend Sister Valton make note of this . . . that grace and peace be multiplied upon you both is the prayer of

Your affectionate friend and brother.[30]

The 'cooling regimen' advocated here by Wesley in the form of fresh air, exercise and draughts of '*churned* buttermilk' will be examined later in its Georgian medical context. Undoubtedly, though, as is evidenced by his correspondence with Valton, one of Wesley's greatest gifts was an ability to take a pragmatic approach – to put his theological and medical knowledge to 'useful effect' – which meant that he judged each case on an individual basis, switching between the role of pastor and physician as the need arose.

In this sense, Philip W. Ott suggests, Wesley consistently underscored the interdependence of mind, body and soul.[31] This he did to protect and preserve the supernatural basis of revealed religion, whilst maintaining intellectual credibility when using physic to mitigate the worst excesses of fleshly pain. By contrast, Wesley's role as minister and pastor ensured that he could offer spiritual consolation and balm for the soul to those facing a lingering, painful death. Robert Webster points out that Wesley and his followers saw themselves fitting into an *ars moriendi* tradition, which attempted to value the experience of a good death. Methodists, he says, were not 'ultimately overcome by the terror of death but were triumphant with their confidence in the assurance that God's presence was a living reality in their hearts'.[32] The experience of consumption was deeply embedded in Wesley's heart, as he had almost died from the 'dreaded disease' in 1753, though, typically, he used this experience or 'living reality' to help others by incorporating into later editions of *Primitive Physic* the treatment prescribed by his own physician, Dr John Fothergill, a leading and fashionable physician. Consumption was an ever-present danger and, as well as providing a range of cheap remedies for its cure in *Primitive Physic*, Wesley was eager to give much needed medical advice by post to family, friends and followers.

In a recent study outlining the significance of Wesley's medical work, I have identified the ways in which his treatments reveal several points of contact with contemporary methods, but also some interesting differences, which can testify to the quality of his critical engagement with other established medics.[33] Wesley was not a 'professionally' trained physician, but *Primitive Physic* contains a detailed knowledge of 'orthodox' medicine and its practice, including those 'Faculty' members from the Royal College of Physicians. Many of the treatments listed in *Primitive Physic* can be traced back to authoritative, 'professional' and enlightened practitioners, such as Thomas Sydenham, Richard Blackmore, John Radcliffe, Richard Mead, Herman Boerhaave, George Cheyne, Thomas Dover, John Huxham, Samuel Tissot, Jeremiah Wainewright and William Buchan.[34] Extensive use was made of Cheyne's *Essay of Health and Long Life* (1724) and *Natural Method of Curing Most Diseases* (1742).[35] The Swiss professor of medicine, Samuel Tissot, influenced Wesley's medical writing greatly; *L'Avis au Peuple sur sa Sante* (1765) went to nine editions throughout Europe and sprang from a concern about depopulation in Switzerland.[36] It was written so that country clergymen could mediate important medical advice to a much wider audience.[37] Wesley did not obtain any of the remedies for the first edition of *Primitive Physic* from Tissot, but integrated the doctor's findings into subsequent later editions. He also anonymously produced an abridged version of *L'Avis* in 1769, which was entitled *Advice with Respect to Health* (1769). Tissot's text was abridged into a 'penny pamphlet' and rewritten to make allowances for English constitutions, which he thought were generally 'less robust' than those of the Swiss.[38]

The remedies he adopted and applied when treating the deathly distress of consumption are, perhaps, the best example of Wesley's engagement with the Georgian medical scene and demonstrate that his concern for spiritual health did not prevent him from providing empirically grounded medical assistance to those who most needed it. His pragmatic approach to the disease of consumption and other consumptive disorders, as well as his Christian compassion towards patients suffering from these conditions, provides an extremely useful heuristic device for a fuller understanding of his enlightened medical holism. By placing John Wesley's cures for consumption into a much larger historical framework of developments in disease definition, medical practices and experienced illness, this chapter will show that his ability to treat patients on an individual basis, in their own context, was premised on an ancient or 'primitive' empiricist standard in physic, which is the desideratum now being sought in modern medicine as it grapples with the alarming numbers dying of the 'dreaded disease', tuberculosis, in developing countries.

Consumption: Disease Definition, Causal Factors and Patient Power

The prevalence of consumption in the eighteenth and nineteenth centuries, which appeared to be polymorphous in nature, was reflected in the mutable vocabulary and definitions used to describe other 'consumptive' conditions, such as 'ancient enemy', 'wasting disease', 'Pott's disease', 'lupus vulgaris', 'white plague', 'crude tubercles', 'Tabes mesenterica', 'scrofula' and 'King's Evil' – the latter term arose out of a medieval belief that being touched by a newly crowned monarch would, in fact, cure this otherwise chronic disease. That Wesley treated 'King's Evil' and 'scrofula' as separate categories of the disease in *Primitive Physic* reflects eighteenth-century medical thinking, which made a distinction between this and 'pulmonary consumption'.[39] Wesley assumes his readers will understand that the remedies listed under '*A Consumption*' refer to pulmonary consumption. The 'King's Evil', he observes in an appended footnote, appears first by 'the thickness of the lips; or a stubborn humour in the eyes; then come hard swellings in the neck chiefly: then running sores'.[40] 'Consumptive' illnesses, which could be linked to several other lingering or wasting conditions, might – though not necessarily – result in cases of pulmonary consumption. Buchan believed that other diseases could bring on pulmonary consumption by 'vitiating' the body's 'humours'. The conditions that were potentially accountable for this, he argued, included scurvy, asthma, smallpox, measles and venereal disease. He also thought that 'consumptive' illnesses, like King's Evil and scrofula, could lead to pulmonary consumption and in this his views differed from those propounded by Blackmore, who urged physicians to make a clear distinction between 'consumption' and 'consumptive'.[41]

Classic cases of pulmonary consumption denoted ulcerated tubercles in the lungs, though the term 'consumption', like that of 'wasting disease', was frequently used interchangeably by patients and medical practitioners when attempting to describe different chronic or lingering illnesses. The preliminary phase of pulmonary consumption featured a variety of symptoms that were typical of the common cold or fever; even spitting up blood was not necessarily indicative of ulcerated lungs. Moreover, eighteenth-century physicians often thought that bronchial tubes and lungs were simply inflamed and therefore treatable.[42] Without recourse to modern medical and technological techniques which could determine conclusively whether a patient had ulcerated lungs, such as the X-ray or invasive surgery, eighteenth-century physicians were forced to rely on their sense perceptions and a purely empirical approach when making their diagnosis. An example of this can be seen in the very simple and useful, though obviously imperfect, method of 'tapping' on the chest of a consumptive patient; here, a physician attempted to discern, through its sound, whether the underlying pathological processes indicated a state of ulceration in the lungs.[43] The title of Blackmore's *A Treatise of Consumptions and Other Distempers Belonging to the Breast and Lungs* thus gestures towards the multitudinous nature of consumptive illnesses.[44] Yet, importantly, Blackmore is keen to mark out the difference between pulmonary consumption and other consumptive distempers:

A consumption, or loss of flesh, may likewise be occasioned by internal ulcers either in the bladder, the guts, or kidneys; or by external running sores, or sinuous fistulas, whole secret caves and winding burrows empty themselves by copious discharges. But no wasting of the fleshy parts, proceeding from the various causes hitherto described, while the lungs are found un-ulcerated, is the consumption treated of in this dissertation; for though the patient may from other causes be exceedingly emaciated, and appear as a ghastly skeleton, covered only with dry skin, yet nothing but the ruin and destruction of the lungs denominates a consumption in the strictest sense of the word, in which I here use it; and no other idea is it the subject of this discourse.[45]

The correct medical definition of a consumption properly understood, as far as Blackmore was concerned, should only ever involve that which was pulmonary.

We have noted already the innumerable contributory causal factors for consumption listed by eighteenth-century medics, including stagnant, stale, damp or malodorous atmospheres. Damp and malodorous living conditions were nearly always associated with the poor, and poverty was thought to be a key factor. Mental and physical fatigue were also important factors and here consumption was clearly demarcated along socio-economic lines; the labouring poor were burdened by the physical demands of their work, while scholars, clergymen and others who engaged in intense periods of study were prone to 'nervous consumption', 'scrofula' and 'King's Evil' because of mental fatigue, a sedentary lifestyle and lack of exercise and fresh air. It was noted that miners, ironworkers and plumbers were particularly susceptible to consumptive illnesses due to the noxious fumes from metals or minerals that they inhaled. In *Primitive Physic* Wesley makes the following suggestion to this group of skilled workers:

174. Smelters of metals, plumbers &c. may be in a good measure preserved from the poisonous fumes that surround them, by breathing through cloth of flannel mufflers twice or thrice doubled, dipt in a solution of sea salt, or salt of tartar, and then dried. These mufflers might also be of great use in similar cases.[46]

Thomas Beddoes, an eminent and leading physician, pointed to the frequency of respiratory consumptive disorders amongst individuals who were exposed to dust, such as stonecutters, millers, weavers, flax dressers and cotton workers – many of whom were also confined to hot, overcrowded working conditions, which aggravated the condition.[47]

Consumption in the early-modern period was therefore Janus-faced; it infected patients for very different socio-economic reasons. Its cultural significance was also Janus-faced, cleft between images peddled in popular imaginative works of fictional drama and those sober accounts given in medical volumes by physicians. The connection between creative genius and consumptive illness became a useful dramatic trope in popular works of literature during the eighteenth century; we need only think of John Keats, who, on coughing up a drop of consumptive blood one cold February evening in 1820, recognized its colour as the 'arterial blood' carrying his 'death-warrant'. This was later recalled by his friend, John Arbuthnot Brown:

> Before his head was on the pillow he coughed and I heard him say – 'This is blood'. I approached him and saw that he was examining a stain on the sheet. 'Bring me a candle, Brown, and let me see this blood'. After I handed him the candle and he examined the blood he looked up into my face with a calmness of countenance that I can never forget and said: 'This is arterial blood: I cannot be deceived by its colour. It is my death warrant'.[48]

One year later the disease had, indeed, claimed Keats's life. This certainty was doubtless informed by his years as a medical student, though both Keats's mother and brother had already died of consumption.[49] Keats's observation about his own 'death warrant', however, was symbolic of something that could be positively valorized; part of the patient's strategy to reclaim consumption as a tool for self-fashioning – a self-image which was actually at odds with the terminology of medical pathology.[50] It found cultural expression in an idea that assumed gifted writers or poets, those with natural creative genius, should suffer for the sake of their art: that creative genius came at a price, but it was a price worth paying.

Clark Lawlor and Akihito Suzuki have seen how consumption presents an interesting paradox in the cultural meaning of disease during the eighteenth century; although it was a major killer, its romantic allure was repeatedly enunciated by contemporaries.[51] The 'aestheticization' of consumption, they suggest, allowed it to function pre-eminently as a disease of the 'Self', formulated as a 'powerful cultural device of self-fashioning'.[52] Patients sought to find something positive in their experience of consumption, despite the fact that dying from this debilitating disease was a distinct possibility. Such sentiments were epitomized in numerous deathbed scenes, either in novels or operas, which involved consumptive patients dying gracefully, pining away, in a calm and dignified manner. Here, consumption was imaged and represented as a disease without symptoms, inoculated, it seemed, from the harsh realities of dying consumptives. Lawlor and Suzuki explain this apparent contradiction: 'people in the eighteenth century found a mild, civilized, and individualized death in consumption', which marked them out as special among the countless dead.[53] In her now oft-cited classic text, *Illness as Metaphor* (1979), Susan Sontag contrasts the different metaphors associated with two deadly diseases: cancer and consumption. Whilst cancer denoted unremittingly bleak and negative cultural values, consumption implied those most desired: beauty, creativity, genius, refined aesthetic taste and heightened sensibility.[54] Positive aesthetics focused mainly on the young, who were portrayed as particularly fragile, delicate and slender. With their vitality seriously compromised, Guenter B. Risse has seen how sufferers displayed the 'hectic glow' created by pale skin, sparkling eyes, erotic red lips and rosy cheeks, all of which became highly desirable physical attributes: consumption, he says, became extolled as a process of ethereal transformation, a triumph of soul over flesh. When death finally extinguished the vital flame, 'the end was quite civilized: painless, slow and peaceful'.[55]

These cultural values made a virtue out of orthodox medical opinion, which did not glamorize consumption and, from a long list of probable causal factors, suggested that it was predominantly a self-inflicted disease, borne out of excessive drinking, passion, sensuality and sexual immorality. Physicians attending those dying of consumption knew all too well that patients faced a protracted and distinctly unglamorous death. On this, Roy Porter has seen how Beddoes's bleak description of consumption, combined with his rather revolting remedies for its cure, such as animal odours, formed part of a sustained attack against the aestheticized culture of pleasure that was growing out of this disease.[56] Beddoes's critique was not informed by the moral, 'primitivist', ideals that galvanized physicians like Cheyne and Buchan, but by what he regarded as a frivolous fashion, which refined the biological realities of disease and body out of existence.[57] This was particularly true, Beddoes believed, of female consumptive patients. Here, the disease was completely self-inflicted – women deliberately made themselves susceptible by wearing clothing that exposed their upper bodies, whilst attempting to achieve new cultural standards of slimness, through starvation diets, laced with tea and coffee, which 'relaxed' their naturally delicate 'fibres'.[58]

By the last quadrant of the eighteenth century, consumerism dovetailed with an economically astute medical service industry. In this socio-economic milieu, physicians themselves were keen to exploit profits gained from commercializing and glamorizing consumption, which was fast becoming a desirable fashion accessory. This was most noticeable in the area of regimen and self-medication amongst those moving in 'polite' circles, where fashionable physicians instructed wealthy clients to visit newly established health resorts or spa towns, both at home and abroad;

here patients could more easily consult resident doctors who specialized in their condition. These resorts were explicitly catering for those rich who aspired 'no less to cultural distinction than to health'.[59]

Moralists, pietists and evangelicals, on the other hand, conjured up images of deathly distress when describing how patients' bodies over-heated as they were gradually consumed from within by the disease. Susan Juster argues that consumption was the 'archetypal' disease for eighteenth-century evangelicals:

> In physiological terms, consumption is the inverse of sanctification: blood leaks into and clogs the lungs, contaminating, rather than purg-ing the body . . . as they slid into what they feared was a 'consumptive' state, evangelicals felt their bodily and spiritual powers leached away . . . itinerant preachers feared at one time or another that they were dying of the disease, a fear that, for some, became a reality.[60]

The following passage from Valton shows that bodily weakness was, indeed, a 'sore clog' to his spirit, though he also tries to fight the condition and hopes to remain Christ's true servant until the very end. In this sense, Valton's hope, both in terms of a cure for his physical weakness, but also that of spiritual sanctification and salvation, was thoroughly Wesleyan; it eschewed that Calvinist doctrine of predestination, which, in its rejection of Christian perfection, diminished the importance of physical health and wellbeing:

> I still find my whole soul in the work. But my spirits are far too active for my body. My constitution is very weak, and, like Saul's armour to David, is a sore clog to my spirit. I hope to live and die in the cause of my adorable Redeemer and his beloved people.[61]

As consumption heated up the economic sphere, Juster notes, the disease whose name it shared grew to dominate health concerns among physi-cians and laity alike.[62] It is for this reason, she observes, that cultural and social historians like to point to the tangled etymological roots of the term 'consumption', which in Britain denoted both an emerging capitalist economy and overcrowded unsanitary living conditions.[63] Britain's increasing decadence was bitterly criticized by moralist medical men like Cheyne, Buchan and Wesley, who also detested the commercial interest that was creeping into medicine and sought to improve the living condi-tions of those most susceptible to the disease – namely, the labouring poor. By contrast, symptoms of self-indulgent, wealthy, urban living were all too evident in excessive eating, drinking, indolence, and vice, which gave rise to innumerable nervous and consumptive disorders. Porter summarizes the argument best:

> Provoked by the very obvious rise in wasting diseases in an increasingly commercial society, people were forced to reflect upon the resonances between the active verb 'consuming' – an act of incorporation – and the intransitive 'consuming' or being 'consumed' – the condition of wasting. Consuming was always producing waste. The traditional world – the world of the humours, of Christian asceticism, of the rural, bucolic economy – saw the disease of consumption as a disease of excess.[64]

In *Primitive Physic*, Wesley, like Cheyne, utilized a traditional, 'primitive', empirical model of medicine, which was combined with a moderate Anglican approach to asceticism, though underpinned by Christian theological ideas relating to holism (wholeness) and Christian perfection. His was primarily a practical manual intended for the labouring poor, yet Wesley, like Cheyne and Buchan, could not resist making moral judgements about the times in which he lived. When treating consumption, however, Wesley managed to transcend the two very different perspectives that were counterposed: romantic allure or medical horror. He offered patients a less gloomy prognosis than his established medical counterparts, remaining cautiously optimistic, whilst also staying in touch with biological realities. Taking a realistic stance necessarily meant fully embracing the possibility of death and Webster sees how most deathbed stories and narratives related by Methodists emphasized the importance of a dying saint annunciating their parting testimony, which witnessed to the pure goodness of God. The art of holy dying, a seamless and God-given shift that relinquished patients from the temporal ravages of their suffering, thereby releasing them into an eternal, blissful state of perfection, was central to these narratives.[65] Wesley's Christian compassion and his belief in the afterlife did not mean that he became overly sentimental, romantic or dramatic about those suffering and dying from consumption. Pragmatism and hope – hope in this and the afterlife – combined with his strong faith in God, permitted him to resist framing consumption in the language of 'medical horror and visceral disgust' when practising physic.[66]

The socio-economic and cultural centrality of consumption in eighteenth- and nineteenth-century Europe obscures the fact that this condition invaded entire swathes of illness, colonizing or disguising allied diseases, and even changing the perception of those with very dissimilar symptoms. Evidence of this can be seen in an observation made by Fothergill to the Medical Society about the perceived prevalence of consumption in eighteenth-century London:

> In this city the weekly bills are supposed to exhibit a tolerably exact account of those who die of the respective diseases mentioned in that list. But I am informed that the article of consumptions includes generally all those who die of any lingering disease, and are much emaciated; by which the list is vastly enlarged beyond what ought to be . . . foreigners imagining that this disease is much more frequent amongst us, than in reality.[67]

The mutable nature of its symptoms, which invaded other illnesses, combined with the plurality of causal factors, contributed to its cultural dominance in the eighteenth century. The complexity of causal factors was outlined by Buchan in the opening passages to his chapter 'Of Consumptions', which is contained in *Domestic Medicine*. Like Cheyne, he argued that the English were particularly vulnerable to consumption for the following reasons:

> Consumptions prevail more in England than in any part of the world, owing perhaps to the great use of animal food and strong liquors, the greater application to sedentary employments, and the great quantity of pit-coal which is there burnt; to which we may add the perpetual changes in atmosphere, or variableness of the weather.[68]

Damp conditions, as well as wearing damp clothes, contributed to consumptive disorders, which, when combined with a diet of 'sharp', aromatic, or rich animal food, might 'inflame' the blood, thereby producing lethal consequences. Other medical conditions with more clearly defined symptoms, such as the 'fever', 'obstructed perspiration', menstrual 'flux', and haemorrhoids, were also possible sources of contagion. Frequently it was the case that causal factors were imbued with a strong moral component; many eighteenth-century practitioners, including Blackmore, Cheyne, Tissot and Buchan, argued that venereal disease, sexual 'immorality', masturbation, and violent sexual passions, were responsible for the prolific nature of consumption and other consumptive illnesses.[69] This is encapsulated in the following extract from *Domestic Medicine*:

> Frequent and excessive debaucheries, late watching and drinking of strong liquors, which generally go together, can hardly fail to destroy

the lungs. Hence the *bon companion* often falls a sacrifice to this disease.[70]

'Passions' hurried the blood and disordered a patient's 'animal spirits', thereby heating and worsening any consumptive condition, whilst ejaculation defrauded the body of vital fluid.

Two competing explanations for the cause of consumption co-existed: heredity and contagion. Proponents of hereditary disease pointed to the observation that consumptive cases often clustered among members of the same family. Those espousing theories about contagion countered this by suggesting that infectious clusters formed because family members living under the same roof passed the disease around.[71] Most physicians argued that consumption was hereditary and thus incurable. Blackmore thought this to be the case and offered his reader palliative care to reduce the severity of symptoms.[72] Buchan stated that the disease was owing to an 'hereditary taint; in which case it is generally incurable'.[73] Medicines would seldom produce a cure and, therefore, he argues in *Domestic Medicine*, one needed to be aware of its causes and take preventative measures by following a sensible regimen.[74] Freely confessing to following the example of Cheyne and Tissot, the whole thrust of Buchan's manual is designed to empower patients to prevent diseases like consumption through regimen and, if they did become sick, to self-medicate safely: disease was man's enemy, but to be warned of an approaching adversary – to know and understand this threat – would fend off any possible danger. It was always within the patient's power to play an active role in their own recovery, rather than relying exclusively upon the physician.

Wesley's medical manual fitted into this climate of education or enlightened self-improvement and *Primitive Physic* formed part of a new-found confidence that, with expert clinical guidance, every man could potentially 'heal thyself'. Involvement with the poor increased Wesley's awareness of their desperate need for urgent medical treatment, which had to be cheap, safe and accessible, particularly for those who could not afford to call a physician or apothecary. In a letter to his friend, Vincent Perronet, the Vicar of Shoreham, Kent, he explained how he had decided to 'prepare and give physick' out of sheer necessity. He wrote this in 1746 and later that same year Wesley opened Dispensaries in London and Bristol.[75] In 1747 *Primitive Physic* was produced from a list of 'receipts', arranged in alphabetical order, which were drawn from Wesley's own medical experience, as well as those of other Methodist ministers. These 'receipts', in conjunction with heavy emphasis on following an exact regimen, were used to guide Methodists when visiting the sick.[76]

After 1747, *Primitive Physic*, along with Wesley's *Sermons* and *Appeals to Men of Reason and Religion*, entered into the canon of 'valuable books' to be widely disseminated. Ministers and preachers had a responsibility to provide their circuit with the most up-to-date edition of *Primitive Physic*, which was also available 'at all the Methodist Preaching-Houses in Town and Country'.[77] Ministers needed to put this knowledge to 'useful effect' by implementing the principles set down in the manual, as well as sending Wesley information about their experiences when practising physic. Despite having to contend with serious health problems of his own, John Valton used *Primitive Physic* and its underlying principles to practise medicine among the poor:

I began to study and practise physic for the good of the poor, hoping thereby to have access to sickbeds, and be instrumental to the good of their souls. I procured an electrical machine, learnt to bleed, and laid in a large assortment of medicines. The Lord most wonderfully prospered my undertaking. The deaf, the halt, the withered, and many others diseased, received a cure under my hands.[78]

Wesley, in fact, wrote to Valton the day after completing and dating a postscript to the twentieth edition of *Primitive Physic*. This latest edition, dated 20 April 1780, was sent to Valton with the following instructions: 'interleave one of the *Primitive Physicks*, and insert into it as many *cheap and simple medicines as you please*'.[79] Preachers were encouraged to use their own tried and tested remedies, which were often inserted into the next edition of Wesley's manual.

Through 'regimen', or a disciplined approach to diet and exercise, the poor could avoid serious illnesses. A healthy regimen ensured due moderation of the six 'non-naturals' – air, diet, sleep, exercise, 'the passions', 'evacuations' – and prevented a patient's blood from becoming 'sizy', 'viscous' or, more worryingly, 'obstructed'. 'Sizy', 'viscous' or 'obstructed' blood hampered its complete and healthy circulation around the tubes, vessels and channels that made up a human body, which could potentially cause serious disease and illness. In the Preface to *Primitive Physic* Wesley extrapolates from Cheyne's *Essay* to provide some 'simple rules' to preserve health, which included maintaining a healthy diet, getting the right amount of sleep, exercise and fresh air, as well as keeping 'the passions' and 'evacuations' in check.[80] Eighteenth-century physicians believed that cold bathing and exercise, but especially horseback riding, would 'contract', 'constrict' and toughen the body's 'fibres', thereby attenuating the 'fluid' brought on by consumption and evacuating the 'viscous matter' or catarrh lodged in the lungs.[81] The clinical imperative to promote horseback riding had been strongly advocated by Sydenham, who insisted that it was especially good for treating 'phthisis'.[82] This recommendation was fully endorsed by John Locke, a colleague, friend and admirer of Sydenham, who described how this physician cured his nephew of consumption – Locke's father and brother had already died of consumption, whilst he himself suffered from the condition all his life:

> Ye Doctor sent him into ye Country on Horseback (tho he was soe weak yt he could hardly walk) & ordered him to ride six or seven miles ye first day (which he did) & to encrease dayly his journey as he shd be able, until he had rid one hundred and fifty miles: when he had travelld half ye way his Diarrhoea (sic) stopt & at last he came to ye end of his journey & was pretty well (at least somewhat better) & he has a good appetite: but when he had staid at his Sister's house some four or five days his Diarrhoea came on again; the Doctor had ordered him not to stay above two days at most; for if they stay above two days before they are recovered this spoils all again; & therefore he betook him self to his riding again, and in four days he came up to London perfectly cured.[83]

Following Sydenham's directives, most Georgian physicians warmly recommended horseback riding as part of a healthy regimen, but especially when treating consumption. In *Primitive Physic* Wesley extracted and simplified this knowledge by way of encouraging individuals to be proactive in their physical wellbeing.

Wesley conducted his medical activity as a lay practitioner, but in common with other pietistic physicians, he believed that the careful mediation of medical knowledge could empower the poor to take care of their own health. Buchan, in fact, argued that very often patients had more expertise and knowledge than they realized:

> Physicians generally trifle a long time with medicines, before they come to know how to use them. Many peasants at present know better how to use some of the most important articles in *materia medica*, than physicians did a century ago.[84]

Taking individual responsibility for one's own health precluded the need to levy large sums of money required to pay medical fees, whilst removing the dangerous influence of unscrupulous practitioners keen to exploit the commercial opportunities produced by a market that was becoming increasingly patient-led. *Primitive Physic* was Wesley's way of ensuring that the labouring poor had a physician in their home – one that could be called upon at any time, but one who would not charge exorbitant fees or peddle dangerous nostrums and chemical compounds.

Like Buchan, Wesley endorsed the sanguine principles underlying preventive strategies set down by Cheyne and, later, Tissot, though he took this optimism one step further in *Primitive Physic*; he did not think that consumption, or other chronic conditions, such as gout, could be attributed solely to hereditary factors and, crucially, he differed too in his belief that consumption could be cured. This refusal to believe that even the most entrenched disease was incurable, combined with his remedies set down in *Primitive Physic*, defied those who assumed that consumption represented an irrevocable death sentence.[85] Wesley's assurances on this score were not merely deluded; hope, he argued, could strengthen mind and body against even the most inveterate condition – whether it was physical, psychological or spiritual. In *Primitive Physic* Wesley sought to offer hope to those suffering from a severely intractable disease. He believed that providing hope to patients was a powerful aid to physical recovery in itself and hence his insistence that all should engage in prayer for spiritual and emotional nourishment.

It was commonly acknowledged amongst eighteenth-century physicians that melancholy sped up and increased the symptoms of consumption. Both Cheyne and Buchan argued that the patient's mind needed to be kept 'easy' and 'cheerful' for this very reason.[86] Healing was central to Wesley's theology but hope and an enlightened optimism regarding the advances made in science and medicine were pivotal to his medical practice. Wesley's belief in the materially effective power of hope never threatened to compromise the integrity of his empirically and rationally grounded medicines in *Primitive Physic*. Nor did this optimism spring from what Wesley would have regarded as the superficial and self-serving values of Shaftsburian enlightened thinking, which was merely simpleminded in its worldly happiness. Wesley's optimism sprang, instead, from a deeply held belief in the vocation of practical piety, which developed out of a theologically holistic view of nature and healing inspired by Primitive Christianity.

'The True Dignity of Medicine'

Wesley's interest in the spiritual and physical health of the labouring poor stemmed from an Anglican devotion to practical piety and a passionate belief in the special role specifically assigned to Christian healers. The

Church of England placed heavy emphasis upon the value of clerical healing and dispensed medical licences for its ministers to practise physic,
particularly in remote areas where access to treatment was scarce.[87] His
charitable initiatives in health and welfare were underpinned and
informed by his own distinctive theological and spiritual holistic ideals of
Primitive Christianity, that golden age of the apostolic era, but a casuist
concern for practical, medical works as part of a larger programme of
Christian duty was certainly not unique in this period.[88] Many physicians
and enlightened experimenters carried out their work for the 'benefit of
mankind', whilst acknowledging this as part of that tripartite duty to
God, neighbour and oneself. In the Preface to his *Treatise* Blackmore
urges 'men of fortune and leisure, especially the clergy' to acquire the
medical knowledge needed to direct those poor living in remote areas
'where no physician can be had' for 'the benefit of the people and their
own honour'.[89] This attitude amongst medical practitioners ran parallel
with but also contributed to a steady rise in literacy levels amongst the
labouring poor in England and across Europe. A profusion of health,
hygiene and regimen-related literature sprang from a utopian hope that
widespread education might improve the health of community and
nation.

The God-given duty of physicians wanting to encourage patient power
was to propagate safe and 'useful' scientific or medical information in
English rather than Latin, whilst divesting this knowledge of fashionably
speculative philosophical theories – so-called 'Faculty' physicians, members of the Royal College, usually liked to protect their status and prestige
by publishing medical works in Latin, replete with theoretically inclined
technical jargon. Like religion, Blackmore argued, medicine needed to be
transparent and accessible to all of mankind – released from scholastic
darkness and Papal mystery:

> It is an indelible reproach on the clergy of the Church of *Rome*, that
> they deny to the people the knowledge of the Christian religion, which,
> however, they oblige them to profess; and instead of opening the Book
> of Life, and instructing them in their Articles of Faith, compel them to
> take their Creed upon content; cruel injustice! And all others are culpa-
> ble in proportion, who lock up any beneficial knowledge in their own
> breasts, as misers do money in their coffers.[90]

Christian duty and justice in this context involved publishing 'books of
physic' in English by way of improving and benefiting Britain as a whole.
Had not the ancients themselves written in their own native tongue

without betraying the dignity of the medical profession? In this, Blackmore exclaimed, many modern European physicians followed that example set down by the ancients and published medical works in vernacular French, German and Italian.[91]

The true dignity of medicine lay, not in technical phrases or obscure jargon, but in the beauty and wisdom wrought by pure light and transparency: only 'deformity and turpitude' refused to remove the veil of mystery for fear of being exposed.[92] Wesley also railed against this tendency in his Preface to *Primitive Physic*, where his rhetoric is sharply focused against 'Faculty' physicians who, concerned with 'profit' and 'honour', deliberately designed to keep the 'bulk of mankind at a distance'. This they did to prevent ordinary people from prying into 'the mysteries of the profession':

> To this end, they increased those difficulties by design, which began in a manner by accident. They filled their writings with abundance of technical terms, utterly unintelligible to plain men. They affected to deliver their rules, and to reason upon them, in an abstruse and philosophical manner . . . those who understood only, how to restore the sick to health, they branded with the name of Empirics.[93]

Wesley sought to remind 'Faculty' members of the ancient and efficacious standard in physic, which could 'restore the sick to health'. This standard was the tested empirical method of trial and experience. Medicine, Buchan observed, was founded in nature and should therefore be consistent with human reason and 'common sense'. This was the first principle of medicine and, in fact, the 'ancient physicians' had carried out their duties in the manner of 'nurses'. If men had been more attentive to this principle, and less concerned with chasing 'secret remedies', then physic would be considerably improved, rather than it being an object of ridicule. Buchan wrote his medical manual, he argued, to show that not all physicians sought deliberately to conceal their art.[94] If more physicians wrote according to light and transparency, Blackmore insisted, medicine could civilize English society.[95] The ancient physicians acquired their knowledge, virtue and success in medicine through trial and experience. They were called 'empiricks' because of the experimental nature of their art, though Blackmore notes in his day that the term was associated with medical 'quack' and religious mountebank. Hence Wesley's empirical approach to medicine was frequently dismissed and lampooned by critics for its alleged 'quackery'. This 'quackery' posed as much danger to mind, body and soul as the 'superstitious' proclivities and religiously inspired 'enthusiasm' peddled by emotionally over-wrought Methodists.

116

Blackmore understood that the original or 'primitive' role of an 'empirick' denoted a physician who recognized the virtue of simple, readily available remedies, using plants, metals and minerals through repeated trials – moreover, a doctor who specifically avoided entering into the secret, hidden world of 'causes', which, despite the many ornamental novelties of learned 'chymists' or 'modern mathematical physicians', nevertheless remained obscured from view. Such 'tedious' systems merely distracted physicians from the main purpose of their special calling.[96] Wesley, like Blackmore, did not denounce and condemn medical theoretical knowledge *per se*. In common with Blackmore, but also Buchan and Tissot, Wesley esteemed and revered a practical, critical intelligence, which engaged with contemporary medical debates, as opposed to demonstrating a superficial learning that was unserviceable to mankind. The caricatures made by Blackmore and Wesley about the Georgian medical scene were intended for maximum rhetorical effect and, for this reason, they are only partially true. The effect of Wesley's rhetoric, directed in his Preface towards 'Faculty' physicians, is suggestive of someone antipathetic to 'orthodox' medicine and its practitioners, though, as I have shown elsewhere, this lack of respect was more apparent than real and, when required, he also demonstrated sufficient deference to 'professional' physicians.[97] Despite Wesley's complaints to the contrary, the empirical tradition continued to dominate medical practice in eighteenth-century England. Certainly, a steady percolation of New Science discoveries and its attendant terminology made dramatic changes to the intellectual landscape in terms of theorizing about disease in a medically or scientifically precise language. Yet the general tool-kit deployed by eighteenth-century doctors continued to draw on empirically tested methods, which relied on a body of knowledge inherited from antiquity.[98] Georgian medics may have conceptualized disease in terms of iatrochemical, corpuscularian or mechanical theories, but needed recourse to a classical corpus of medical writings, which paid due attention to the 'non-naturals' when treating ill patients, as well as instructing them in the virtues of regimen for the purpose of preventing poor health. In this respect, Wesley himself was a man of his age; he, too, utilized the language of corpuscularian and mechanical concepts to frame his own arguments in medical writings and even sermons.[99]

The English empiricist tradition in natural philosophy, which took root during the seventeenth century amidst political, religious and social turmoil by way of reaching consensus in medical science, had deliberately turned trial, error and perseverance into a positive methodological virtue to which all enlightened Christians should aspire; in Greek the word for 'trial' – and 'tribulation' – is *peirasmos*, from which the term 'empiric' is derived. Proponents of this approach believed that gradual insights and probable knowledge could build up an accurate, though not complete, picture of man, nature and the environment. But first, one had to concede to the limitation of human knowledge, particularly when compared to that of the Creator, so that any insights or revelations granted through God's grace were glimpsed only through a glass darkly after much trial and tribulation. It is easy to see how this tradition in natural philosophy and medicine would have appealed to Wesley, particularly when its theological correlate, namely that of Christian struggle in the world for holiness and perfection, was such a central feature of his preaching. When conducting medical duties Wesley thus drew from this empiricist tradition, which had already included exponents like Sydenham, Locke and Robert Boyle, among many others, who believed that physic and the natural sciences should be based upon experience – hence experimental philosophy – as opposed to theoretical or metaphysical speculation.[100]

Wesley's 'easy and natural method', in tandem with his 'plain speech', was a deliberate move to balance rhetorically the confusion of contemporary medical practice with the simplicity and singularity of an empirical philosophy that derived from God's sovereign power. In 1771 Wesley reminds Valton of the importance of simplicity as a guiding principle when practising medicine:

> My Dear Brother,
>   Many of our brethren have begun to assist their neighbours on the principles of the *Primitive Physick*. At first they prescribed only *simple* things, and God gave a blessing to their labours. But they seldom continued as they began; they grew more and more *complex* in their prescriptions. Beware of this; keep to the simple scheme. One thing will almost always do better than two.[101]

There was always an inherent temptation to eschew simplicity in favour of complexity and practitioners needed to guard against this tendency. Wesley was aware of the dangers involved when taking fashionable, but lethal, compounds and nostrums. For this reason he was antipathetic to the overuse of so-called 'Herculean' medicines – opium, bark, steel and mercury – which were restricted in his manual. Wesley's antipathy to the 'bark' (Peruvian or Jesuits' Bark) ran contrary to prevailing wisdom – its anti-malarial qualities were noted, later identified as quinine, and it was used to treat 'agues' and other fevers. Wesley's doubt about its efficacy was informed by his own extreme (allergic) reaction he had suffered when taking powdered bark for an ague. He was convinced that this medicine had brought on a consumption. Wesley had no objection to bark being taken as a decoction, but worried about the varying quality and quantity of 'powdered' bark, which was often adulterated by unscrupulous apothecaries, and thus warned others against taking it.[102] In January 1784 he thus tells Valton, who had just been prescribed 'powdered wood' by 'Dr Davison', that many have perished by swallowing large quantities of this medicine: 'beware of this, and you may live and do good'.[103]

Simplicity and singularity of method, which also respected the healing power of nature provided by God, could defeat the irreducible, multi-valent phenomena of disease, which had plagued man since the Fall. Written in the vernacular, *Primitive Physic* is based, so Wesley tells his reader in the Preface, on nothing but experience and common sense – his own, or that pertaining to other trusted physicians, friends and followers. Throughout the main body of its receipts there are repeated instances of remedies that have been 'tried' and tested in this way, as seen clearly in those remedies he listed for '*A Consumption*':

177. *Cold bathing* has cured many deep consumptions: tried.
178. One in a deep consumption was advised to drink nothing but *water*, and eat nothing but *water-gruel*, without salt or sugar. In three months time he was perfectly well.
179. Take no food but new *butter-milk*, churned in a bottle; and *white bread* – I have known this successful.
180. Or, use as common drink, *spring-water* and *new milk*, each a quart: and *sugar candy* two ounces.
181. Or, boil two handfuls of *sorrel* in a pint of whey. Strain it, and drink a glass thrice a day: tried.
182. Or, turn a pint of skimmed milk, with half a pint of small beer. Boil in whey about twenty *ivy-leaves*, and two or three sprigs of *hyssop*. Drink half over night, the rest in the morning. Do this, if needful, for two months daily – this has cured in a desperate case: tried.
183. Or, take a *cow-heel* from the tripe-house ready drest, two quarts of *new milk*, two ounces of *hartshorn shavings*, two ounces of *isinglass*, a quarter of a pound of *sugar-candy*, and a race of ginger. Put all these in a pot: and set them in an oven after the bread is drawn. Let it continue there till the oven is near cold: and let the patient live on this – I have known this cure a deep consumption more than once.
184. Or, every morning cut up a little turf of fresh earth, and lying

down, breathe into the hole for a quarter of an hour – I have known a deep consumption cured thus.

185. 'Mr *Masters*, of *Evesham*, was so far gone in a consumption, that he could not stand alone. I advised him to lose six ounces of blood every day for a fortnight, if he lived so long: and then every other day: then every third day: then every fifth day, for the same time. In three months he was well' – (Dr Dover). Tried.

186. Or, throw *frankincense* on burning coals, and receive the smoke daily through a proper tube into the lungs: tried.

187. Or, take in for a quarter of an hour, morning and evening, the steam of *white rosin* and *bees-wax*, boiling on a hot fire-shovel. This has cured one who was in the third stage of a consumption.

188. Or, the steam of sweet *spirit of vitriol* dropt into warm water.

189. Or, take morning and evening, a tea-spoonful of *white rosin* powdered and mixt with *honey*. This cured one in less than a month, who was very near death.

190. Or, drink thrice a day two spoonfuls of juice of *water-cresses*. This has cured a deep consumption.

191. In the last stage, *suck a healthy woman* daily. This cured my father.

For diet, use *milk* and *apples*, or *water-gruel* made with fine flour. Drink *cyder-whey*, *barley-water* sharpened with *lemon-juice* or *apple-water*.

So long as the tickling cough continues, chew well and swallow a mouthful or two, of biscuit or crust of bread, twice a day. If you cannot swallow it, spit it out. This will always shorten the fit, and would often prevent a consumption. See Extract from Dr. *Tissot*, page 33.[104]

The 'tried' and tested remedy offered reassurance to patients and there are numerous examples here of Wesley easing anxieties with phrases like 'this has cured a deep consumption' and 'I have known this successful'. Furthermore, the reader is given a range of different 'tried' and tested remedies to choose from and, like many eighteenth-century physicians, Wesley believed that what worked for one person may not work for another. He points this out in the Preface, though there are also other important considerations to bear in mind, such as cost and accessibility:

15. As to the manner of using the medicines here set down, I should advise, as soon as you know your distemper, (which is very easy, unless in a complication of disorders, and then you would do well to apply to a physician that fears God:) *First*, use the first of the remedies for that

disease which occurs in the ensuing collection: (unless some other of them be safer to be had, and then it may do just as well). *Secondly*, after a competent time, if it takes no effect, use the second, and third, and so on. I have purposely set down (in most cases) several remedies for each disorder; not only because all are not equally easy to be procured at all times, and in all places: but likewise because the medicine that cures one man, will not always cure another of the same distemper. Nor will it cure the same man at all times. Therefore it was necessary to have a variety.[105]

When treating pulmonary consumption, physicians sought to remove the 'crudities' and 'impure humours' that had built up in the patient's lungs. For this, a patient needed to swallow or inhale medicines that would evacuate the infected catarrh and we can see from those listed above that many of Wesley's remedies were designed to do precisely this. One of Blackmore's less palatable treatments for removing infected, consumptive phlegm, consisted of drinking a 'horse-dung' infusion.[106] Utilizing animal odours for treating consumption was also advocated by Beddoes, who believed that butchers were free from consumptive disorders because they absorbed these healing vapours.[107] Use of animal and human preparations declined during the eighteenth century but they did not disappear altogether and a number of leading physicians continued to recommend ingredients like cow and horse dung, crabs' eyes and claws, crushed oyster shells, woodlice, millipedes and cobwebs in small doses. This can be seen in a remedy suggested by Buchan, who observed how one of his patients was cured of consumption after drinking breast milk:

> It is better if the patient can suck from the breast than to drink it afterwards. I knew a man who was reduced to such a degree of weakness in a consumption, as not to be able to turn himself in bed. His wife was at that time giving suck, and the child happening to die, he sucked her breasts, not with a view to reap any advantage from the milk, but to make her easy. Finding himself however greatly benefited from it, he continued to suck her till he became perfectly well, and is at present a strong and healthy man.[108]

Breast milk, like that of cows or asses, formed part of a light 'cooling' regimen, which could prevent the patient's blood from becoming 'sizy' or 'viscous', enabling it to flow smoothly, thus aiding recovery. Buchan advised those with consumption to confine themselves to a diet of vegetables and asses' milk, which he calculated 'lessened the acrimony of the humours'.[109] John Radcliffe was also a firm believer in taking asses' milk (with candy sugar) for consumption – asses' milk was preferable to that of cows because, he argued, it was easier to digest.[110] Wesley's 'cooling draughts' and remedies for consumption included water, spring water, water-gruel and skimmed milk. For food he recommended nothing but a 'light diet' of butter-milk 'churned' with 'white bread', milk and apples.[111] *Primitive Physic* recommends following a light or 'easy' diet consisting mainly of 'cooling' liquids:

> For diet, *use milk* and *apples*, or *water-gruel* made with fine flour. Drink *cyder-whey*, *barley-water* sharpened with *lemon-juice* or *apple-water*.[112]

He suggested using apples and citrus fruit, especially lemons, due to the fact that the 'bitter' acids contained in this fruit seemed to be particularly good for treating consumption. Like Buchan, he recommended drinking breast milk from a nursing woman: '191. In the last stage, *suck a healthy woman* daily. This cured my Father'.[113]

A light vegetarian diet was advocated by most eighteenth-century physicians, witnessed by Fothergill's *Remarks on the Cure of Consumptions* (n.d.):

> When a cough begins . . . let the quantity of diet, especially solids be lessened; let the deficiency be made up with warm suppings. Barley-water, milk and water, thin gruel, the lightest broths.[114]

Regimen and medicines that 'constricted' the solids, thereby making 'fibres' 'tense', rendered the humours more fluid, which could evacuate the phlegm.[115] Wesley's endorsement of this can be seen time and again in letters like that which was sent in 1763 to Jane Esther Lee, known also as 'Jenny' to her friends in Larne, Ireland. Her sister, Elizabeth, had died of consumption a year earlier in 1762 and, worried that she might have the disease, Jenny wrote to Wesley. His response was to allay her fears by directing her to the 'cooling regime' that had been set down in *Primitive Physic*:

> My Dear Sister,
> If you are likely to fall into a consumption, I believe that nothing will save your life but the living two or three months upon buttermilk churned daily in a bottle. Change of air may do something, if you add riding every day.[116]

Regimen and the 'non-naturals' were inextricably linked and many Georgian medics believed that medicine was completely futile if used without following simple preventative rules. We know Buchan believed that the cure of consumption resided chiefly in a proper regimen, though he also suggested drinking 'bitter' plant decoctions, to 'constrict' the body and its organs, such as ground-ivy, camomile and comfrey-root.[117] According to Jeremiah Wainewright medicines that relaxed the 'solids' and 'fibres' would thicken the fluid, thereby filling the stomach with a 'glutinous slime'. In turn, this weakened digestion and increased the patient's thirst. It was therefore essential to take 'constricting' medicines whilst observing at all times an exact regimen in one's living.[118]

Primitive Physic lists several 'constricting' medicines designed to alleviate or even cure consumption. These included the juice of watercress, used to treat inflammatory and intestinal disorders, especially the lungs, in the Georgian period, as well as ground-ivy or hyssop infusions, which were recommended by John Hill in his *Family Herbal* for coughs and obstructions of the breast.[119] Hyssop has fever-reducing qualities and, indeed, is still used in 'complementary' medicine today to alleviate bronchitis. In the eighteenth century it was used to treat inflammatory disorders. Due to its poisonous nature, ivy has a very powerful effect on the internal organs, blood circulation and heart. As such, it was used by Georgian physicians to treat many different diseases.[120] In common with current medical thinking Wesley prescribed a number of inhalations and vaporizations for relieving pulmonary consumption. It was thought that inhalations acted as a 'balsam' for the lungs and eased a patient's restricted breathing and rasping cough. He suggested inhaling burning frankincense, steam of 'white rosin' and steamed 'spirit of vitriol', the latter of which was commended by Fothergill. Physicians believed that vitriol 'braced' the body and Wesley argued on a number of occasions that it was the best bracer available. The remedy which required his patient to 'cut up a little turf of fresh earth' and inhale its healing properties might now seem quite a strange prescription, though Wesley's direction here was not as eccentric as it appears. It had been put forward by Blackmore in his *Treatise of Consumptions*: turf was considered valuable for treating this disease because of its sulphurous odour. Blackmore argued that sulphur was particularly useful and explained how the 'chymists' had styled it a 'balsam' for 'the lungs' and blood. Turf was remarkable because it 'eminently contributes to the cure of those that are obnoxious to that distemper'.[121]

The sheer variety of remedies given for pulmonary consumption in *Primitive Physic* corresponds with the many different disease definitions for a range of other consumptive distempers. This plurality reflects what is now common knowledge; that *mycobacterium tuberculosis* was a single micro-organism that could infect any part of the body and manifest itself in multiple ways: 'scrofula' and 'King's Evil' affected the lymphatic glands, causing swelling in the neck, 'lupus vulgaris' attacked the skin, 'Tabes mesenterica' – 'tabes' means 'wasting' in Latin – was tuberculosis of the small intestine, whilst 'Pott's Disease' infected bones, specifically the spine. This latter disease, which obviously predated the Georgian period, was renamed during the eighteenth century after the surgeon Percival Pott, who discovered that 'scrofula' was the cause of spinal curvature. Until then, Thomas Dormandy suggests, there had been no satisfactory explanation for hunchbacks.[122] 'Extra-pulmonary' sites of disease could exist independently, but were not in themselves contagious, though they sometimes co-existed with pulmonary consumption, which, of course, spread very rapidly. Blackmore observed that those weakened by consumptive disorders unaccompanied by ulcerated lungs would not necessarily die. These distempers kept the patient 'lean and emaciated', though they may not actually 'exhaust' someone until they reached an advanced age:

> This was the case of KING WILLIAM of glorious memory. That *Great Prince*, as he informed me himself, was from his birth, a weakly child, and all along, liable to a cough, and a copious expectoration; and when he came last into *England*, for happy deliverance of this Nation from *Popish Tyranny* and *Superstition*, his cough was so increased, while he travelled over *Salisbury Plain*, that he apprehended he should scarcely live till the following spring, yet by that time he recovered a better state, though still persecuted with a great cough, and an inordinate discharge of white and pondrous flegm; while notwithstanding as he eat and slept well, so he was free from a Hectick Fever, and all other symptoms of phthisis or consumption.[123]

According to Blackmore, the monarch did not die from pulmonary consumption – dissection of the body after death revealed no ulcers or 'corruption' in his lungs. Blackmore suggested that 'immoderate evacuations', or diarrhoea, was a key factor in cases like this because it 'defrauded the blood' of much needed 'materials'. This, in turn, produced other consumptive disorders.[124] King William died, he suggested, because his blood had been 'defrauded' of the 'chyle', or nourishment, needed to maintain good health. 'Defrauded' blood was indicative of those symptoms associated with consumptive illnesses, which led to the body growing meagre, feeble and exhausted.[125] Close proximity between the symptoms associated with pulmonary consumption and those attending other consumptive illnesses meant that there was sufficient ambiguity when eighteenth-century physicians or medics attempted to formulate a clear diagnosis. In these circumstances the best physicians could do was offer preventive measures to avoid consumption and other consumptive conditions.

From Consumption to Tuberculosis

It was the English physician, Richard Morton, who first suggested in 1689 that pulmonary consumption was associated with 'tubercles'. Before Koch's discovery in 1882 the medical term 'tuberculosis' referred to any disease typified by the formation of 'tubercles', small round swellings or nodules that could form on the surface of the body, internal organs or bones.[126] The confluence of symptoms meant that even pulmonary consumption was not identified as a single disease until the 1820s.[127] French physicians, Gaspard Bayle and René Laënnec, announced in 1803 that consumptive corpses shared a common characteristic, which was that they all had tubercles in their organs.[128] This observation led to consumption eventually being renamed 'tuberculosis' in 1839 by a German Professor of medicine, Johann Lukas Schönlein.[129] In 1873, Thomas Henry Green, physician to Charing Cross Hospital and leading authority on consumption and diseases of the chest, observed that 'acute tuberculosis' was a 'general infective disease', characterized by 'numerous minute nodular lesions' in various organs and tissues.[130]

Koch restricted the definition of 'tuberculosis' from any disease associated with the formation of tubercles, to one specifically caused by *mycobacterium tuberculosis*, the micro-organism, tubercle bacillus. He believed tuberculosis was caused only by a single micro-organism, though it transpired later that the bovine strain, *mycobacterium bovis*, infected cattle and, before developments in pasteurization, could be passed to humans through cow's milk, a potentially lethal source of infection during the early-modern period. Koch thus confirmed with clinical certainty medical and scientific researches that had taken place much earlier, whilst establishing that pulmonary tuberculosis was highly infectious. Benjamin Marten, an English medic and author of *A New Theory of Consumption* (1720), had already speculated that this disease was caused by '*animalcula* or wonderfully minute living creatures', which, after insinuating themselves into the body, brought about the deadly symptoms of consumption. He also believed that close contact with consumptive patients transmitted the illness from one person to another.[131] In 1865 an army surgeon, Jean-Antoine Villemin, demonstrably proved Marten's hypothesis. He ascertained that the sputum of tuberculosis patients contained virulent particles which, when inoculated into rabbits and other laboratory animals, induced diseases similar to that of tuberculosis.[132]

It was Marten who first tentatively suggested that human contagious diseases were transmitted via micro-organisms. He implied that each contagious disease was uniquely specific to its own causative 'animalcula' (later called micro-organisms) and that each type of disease was caused by different micro-organisms. Significantly, Marten suggested that a severe cough or cold would not necessarily become consumptive, unless the animalcula associated with the disease were already present in the blood or bodily fluids. In these circumstances, even a trifling cough or chill would develop into a 'secondary cause', thereby permitting the consumption to proliferate. He also noted that animalcula differed in strength (strain), which affected the levels of contagion – the animalcula responsible for causing consumption required prolonged contact with a person already infected. Marten pointed out that the life cycle of particular animalcula might determine the sequence of symptoms shown in certain diseases.[133] Marten's scientific speculations, as well as laboratory tests carried out much later by Villemin, were confirmed by Koch in 1882, when he isolated the tubercle bacillus microbe. Recourse to bacteriology meant that Koch could show exactly how air and saliva excretions carried live bacteria from the consumptive lungs of suffering patients.

Romantic perceptions, religious metaphors and evangelical cultural expressions about the significance of consumption thus gradually changed as medical science began to reach its unchallenged ascendancy by the last decades of the nineteenth century, though images of pale, emaciated artists in the grip of consumptive disorders have left an indelible and powerfully enduring legacy; even today, Keats's 'death warrant' continues to fire our imagination in films, operas and television period dramas. Scientific developments in bacteriology and micro-biology, like those undertaken by Koch, meant that particular romantic motifs surrounding consumptive patients were undermined by medical thinking, which hypothesized that this disease was an inherited biological degeneracy – a proposition motivated by ethnic, racial prejudices fuelled by eugenic scientific research.[134] Much of this new hard-edged, 'positivistic' scientific medicine, which was a characteristic feature of the Victorian period, also developed in tandem with a return to an approach that was more 'holistic', empirically grounded and humane.

The sanatorium movement, which was growing in popularity, advocated removing those infected with tuberculosis from the community and treating patients in isolation. The principles that underpinned this 'environmental medicine' were not unique, and these methods had already been practised widely by eighteenth-century physicians, and medics like Wesley, who had drawn on the fifth-century BC 'Hippocratic Corpus', *Airs, Waters, Places*, when implementing regimen as a way of life. As we have noted, Wesley's regimen for consumption, which he adapted from a huge range of medical sources, included following a light diet, getting as much clean, fresh air as possible and undertaking regular exercise. Individuals were encouraged to avoid the damp – weather, houses or clothes – while a light diet of vegetables and milk was the most effective way to alleviate the worst symptoms of consumption. For exercise, it was preferable to go horseback riding and we have seen repeated instances of Wesley insisting upon its efficacy in letters to friends and relatives. This regimen of nutritional food, rest, exercise and fresh air was adopted again in the late nineteenth century by way of encouraging recuperation amongst those suffering from tuberculosis. Eighteenth-century advocates of regimen, like Cheyne, Tissot, Buchan and Wesley, argued that modifications in lifestyle and moderation of the 'non-naturals' were the best and most cost-effective way to prevent consumption. Regimen could also mitigate its worst symptoms. These physicians sought to disseminate their precepts as widely as possible, suggesting to readers, cheap and effective ways of staying healthy.

By the end of the nineteenth century, however, this advice was only available to wealthy patients who could afford to stay in a sanatorium.[135] The movement was initiated by a Silesian student, Hermann Brehmer, who, suffering from tuberculosis, was instructed by his physician to convalesce in an environment conducive to health. Brehmer travelled to the Himalayas, where he studied botany, but also made a full recovery from his illness. On returning home to Germany, he studied medicine, which culminated in his dissertation, *Tuberculosis is a Curable Disease* (1854). The basis of Brehmer's medical research led him to open a sanatorium in Gorbersdorf, where patients could enjoy the countryside, following a healthy regimen of good nutrition, gentle exercise, and copious amounts of fresh air to aid recovery. Indeed, to make it easier for patients to complete their prescribed walks, Brehmer had wooden benches fixed into the ground at regular intervals along forest paths – a bold innovation, Dormandy remarks, which survived his age of sanatoria and, judging from the ubiquity of park benches throughout the civilized world, testify to his obdurate faith in a healthy regimen.[136] Brehmer's approach soon became the desideratum for others across Europe and North America wanting to follow his example; a useful barometer of its success can be seen in its depiction in Thomas Mann's novel, *The Magic Mountain* (1924), where the fictional therapeutic community set in the Swiss Alps is clearly modelled on Brehmer's earlier example.[137]

The sanatorium movement relied on methods that had been routinely used in the eighteenth century, which included following a healthy regimen, improved sanitation and hygiene, as well as strengthening the body against the worst symptoms of consumption. The removal of infectious sufferers from the community had a discernible effect on decreasing the incidence of tuberculosis, though patients being treated in specialized clinics or sanatoria could not expect to receive any specific cure. Recently it has been estimated that fifty per cent of patients treated in therapeutic settings actually died within five years of entering.[138] Active surgical procedures, combined with technological advances in radiation and chemotherapy, as well as developments in anti-tubercular compound medicines and vaccines, treatments which could conquer tuberculosis, continued to elude medical scientists and clinicians until well into the twentieth century.[139]

Conclusion: Turning the Tide on Man's Ancient Enemy

Improvements in socio-economic conditions, combined with increased knowledge wrought by medical science in areas like bacteriology, microbiology and pasteurization, with the implementation of preventive measures, such as the Bacille Calmette-Guérin (BCG) vaccination programme during the 1950s, all contributed to the downward trend in incidences of tuberculosis across Europe.[140] Yet optimism that tuberculosis would finally be eliminated was short-lived, for drug-resistant strains of the disease mutated and evolved and this was worsened by poverty and the AIDS epidemic.[141] The aptly named 'deadly alliance' of tuberculosis and AIDS that has been ravaging developing nations across the sub-Saharan African continent, as well as those marginalized in 'higher-resource' countries, such as the poor, or imprisoned, resulted in the declaration of a global health emergency by the World Health Organization in 1993.[142] Keats's 'death warrant' thus continues to haunt us in the modern era so that pulmonary consumption is not a disease confined to the past: the 'deadly alliance' of tuberculosis and AIDS, in fact, means that, currently, every year, approximately eight million individuals contract tuberculosis, with three million eventually dying from the disease.[143]

This worrying development has led some clinical experts to remark that the history of tuberculosis is one of scientific, medical and political failure

– a failure because, despite successful medical advances and the availability of cost-effective treatment, vast numbers continue to die from this disease every year. Turning the tide and ridding the world of one of the most lethal diseases in human history therefore remains the biggest challenge to be faced by medics and policy-makers alike.[144] The Millennium Development Goals, within which the 'Global Plan to Stop TB' has been conceived, identifies poverty as the primary issue facing governments in developing countries who are attempting to curb tuberculosis.[145] But in Western medicine the under-representation of poverty-related diseases in bio-medical research, particularly those chronic and entrenched diseases affecting African countries, has been much lamented in recent years.[146] Clinicians and medical researchers hoping for a more integrated, contextualized approach to poverty-related diseases like tuberculosis welcome the explicitly pro-poor focus of the 'Stop TB Partnership' campaigns, adding, though, that this will only make a difference to individuals if practical steps are taken to remove obstacles preventing access to cheap and effective treatment.[147]

The plurality of symptoms and interchangeable use of disease definitions, which were applied to different consumptive conditions in the Georgian period before nineteenth- and twentieth-century medical, scientific and technological discoveries had taken place, means that historians need to be cautious when making retrospective assessments about early-modern diseases. Tuberculosis today is only a rough approximation of the numerous consumptive illnesses that dogged eighteenth-century life.[148] Moreover, even pulmonary consumption in Wesley's day had a different topography or aetiology and formed part of a much bigger epistemological shift in clinical diagnosis and medical practice. This makes the modern disease of tuberculosis distinct, though a clinically defined core of tubercular symptoms that have remained consistent do allow for striking parallels. What consumption and tuberculosis do share in common is the fact that they are diseases which are largely determined by a range of political, economic, social and cultural factors. René and Jean Dubos summarized this best in 1952 when they argued that tuberculosis is a socio-economic and cultural disease, which transcends conventional medical approaches:

> On the one hand, its understanding demands that the impact of social and economic factors on the individual be considered as much as the mechanisms by which tubercle bacilli cause damage to the human body. On the other hand, the disease modifies in a peculiar manner the emotional and intellectual climate of the societies that it attacks.[149]

René Dubos, who was a key figure in the development of anti-bacterial drugs in the United States during the 1920s and 1930s – drugs which later led to the introduction of successful anti-tubercular medication – contextualized this disease and recognized the limits of relying purely on a medical model.[150] As Richard Coker suggests, these words are particularly pertinent today when tuberculosis continues to represent a major threat to those most marginalized and vulnerable living in 'lower-resource' or developing countries.[151]

The aetiology and treatment of tubercular diseases might well have changed substantially since Wesley first wrote *Primitive Physic* over 200 years ago, but those core values underpinning his medical manual, namely, to provide cheap, safe and effective medicines to the labouring poor, are responsibilities which continue to dog medical practitioners when attempting to understand the wider context of global health and wellbeing. Clinicians and health campaigners have thus started to utilize 'World TB Day', which falls every year on 24 March, as an ideal opportunity to review progress in tuberculosis treatment and control; to evaluate lessons learnt, whilst assessing what needs to be done to bring the disease under control. When marking 'World TB Day' in 2006, a group of medical scientists, practitioners and academics writing articles for *The Lancet* identified a major challenge facing them as the continued need for a sensitive, specific, rapid, cheap and safe diagnostic test for tuberculosis. Moreover, that research into effective diagnostic practices within developing countries had to take a 'multi-disciplinary' approach, which could ensure proper consideration of the social, environmental and economic dimensions of this disease.[152]

Most serious-minded physicians in the eighteenth century resisted extravagant claims and did not pretend to have a miracle cure for pulmonary consumption. Yet philanthropically inclined medics who sought to give hope felt compassion for their patients, and strove, at least, to find meaning in poor health and suffering. They were adamant that regimen was absolutely central to the efficacy of medicine and could potentially head off consumption. Preventative care was a subject of such great importance, Buchan argued, that it had not escaped the attention of physicians in every age. Yet this empirical, holistic method, the very bedrock of ancient medical practice, was, as Wesley decried in 1747, fast becoming a dying art in his age of 'professional' medicine. Indeed, as Maddox rightly points out, in the acrid atmosphere following William Hawes's scathing criticism of *Primitive Physic* in 1776, Wesley himself was forced to concede to the emerging specialization in medicine that has since permeated modern Western culture.[153] By the late nineteenth century, 'professional' medicine had completely divested itself of this method by following a 'positivist', purely disease-led strategy, which spun on a narrowly conceived idea of medical, scientific, and technological knowledge.

Those wanting to retain a fully contextualized approach, which took account of disease, patient and other socio-economic and environmental factors, were now regarded as dissenting practitioners who provided 'alternative' or 'complementary' treatments to the 'professional' medical canon. Nineteenth-century scientists were, in fact, fairly vociferous in articulating their disdain for what they regarded as the deeply unimpressive efforts of Georgian physicians, who, it was thought, failed to make any real gains or progress in the sphere of medical knowledge. This was mainly due to the fact, they believed, that eighteenth-century medical practice was tethered by a combination of 'kitchen-physic' folklore and religious 'superstition'. Historiographical developments in social and cultural histories of medicine have done a great deal to provide a more nuanced picture, which challenges this narrative, though, periodically, these caricatures still crop up. This can be seen in a fairly recent work by Dormandy, whose otherwise excellent historical survey of tuberculosis is marred by his bowdlerized view of eighteenth-century medicine – a view that has long since been unfashionable amongst historians. Treatment for consumption in 'the days of Keats', he says, added its quota to the suffering of patients. This was because Georgian medicine was 'rooted in ignorance':

> Despite the achievements of earlier centuries, there was, as the eighteenth century turned into the nineteenth, still a yawning gap in the minds of doctors between the clinical symptoms and signs on the one hand and the underlying pathology on the other. To bridge that gap would not necessarily bring relief, but without it any advance in that direction was impossible. Almost a century separates the diagnostic revolution in medicine which began that progression from Koch's historic discovery of the cause; and another fifty years would pass before the cause would yield to treatment.[154]

It is through this lens of nineteenth-century 'Whiggish' cultural and medical values that Wesley's *Primitive Physic* has often been assessed.[155] When writing his manual, though, Wesley was not peddling 'alternative' remedies to an established medical canon. Nor was he simply harking back to a 'primitive' age to procure 'magical' cures. In the same way that he sought to revive for his Methodist followers the 'primitive' purity of apostolic times, Wesley wanted to recover an 'ancient standard' in medicine, which he believed could help restore health and life. He deployed this standard in tandem with the best medical science of his day and *Primitive Physic* prescribed remedies that were well within the bounds of 'orthodox' practice.[156]

Over the next year millions of lives in sub-Saharan countries will be cut short by the 'dreaded disease' that struck fear into so many of Wesley's contemporaries. The difference now, of course, is that modern medical practitioners have recourse to both its prevention and cure. Today, more than ever, Western medical science needs to free itself from a triumphant, positivistic, rhetoric, which has kept it hermeneutically sealed from other disciplines and traditions for nearly two centuries. As governments, non-governmental organizations and aid agencies in 'higher-resource' countries attempt to deal with a global context that is bleakly postcolonial, it is, perhaps, not surprising that Wesley's much cherished 'ancient standard' in physic is, again, being rediscovered and recognized by modern medicine for its therapeutic value. As he himself wryly remarked in *Primitive Physic*:

> Yet there have not been wanting, from time to time, some lovers of mankind, who have endeavoured (even contrary to their own interests) to reduce physic to its ancient standard.[157]

Notes

1 John Donne, 'Insultus Morbi Primus'. I Meditation in *Devotions Upon Emergent Occasions* (1623), in John Carey ed., *The Oxford Authors. John Donne*, Oxford, Oxford University Press, 1990, pp. 333–4, p. 333.

2 William F. Bynam, 'Consumption', *The Lancet* 358 (25 August 2001), p. 676; Alimuddin Zumla and Zoë Mullan, 'Turning the Tide Against Tuberculosis', *The Lancet* 367 (18 March 2006), pp. 877–8 at p. 877.

3 Sir Richard Blackmore, *A Treatise of Consumptions and Other Distempers Belonging to the Breast and Lungs*, London, 1724, pp. 135, 28.

4 Blackmore, *A Treatise of Consumptions*, p. 6.

5 John Wesley, *Primitive Physic: Or, An Easy and Natural Method of Curing Most Disease*, 24th edn, London, 1792, pp. 41–3. Unless otherwise stated, this edition will be referred to throughout; Deborah Madden, '"A Cheap, Safe and Natural Medicine": Religion, Medicine and Culture in John Wesley's *Primitive Physic*', *Clio Medica* 83, Amsterdam and New York, Rodopi, 2007, p. 215.

6 Wesley, *The Journal of the Rev. John Wesley, A.M.* (4 vols, London: J. Kershaw, 1827), 8 May 1777, vol. 4, p. 94.

7 Wesley, Letter to Mary Bosanquet, 16 August 1767, in *Letters* (Telford), vol. 5, p. 61.

8 Guenter B. Risse, 'New Medical Challenges during the Scottish Enlightenment', *Clio Medica* 78, Rodopi, Amsterdam and New York, 2005, p. 245.

9 Risse, 'New Medical Challenges', p. 245.

10 Thomas Dormandy, *The White Death: A History of Tuberculosis*, Hambledon Press, London, 1999, p. 22; Risse, 'New Medical Challenges', p. 245.

11 Dormandy, *The White Death*, p. 22.

12 Madden, '"A Cheap, Safe and Natural Medicine"'.

13 Laura Bartels Felleman, 'A Necessary Relationship: John Wesley on the Body-Soul Connection' (Chapter 4) and Robert Webster, '"Health of Soul and Health of Body": The Supernatural Dimensions of Healing in John Wesley' (Chapter 6).

14 Bartels Felleman, 'John Wesley and Dr George Cheyne on the Spiritual Senses', *Wesleyan Theological Journal* (2004), pp. 163–72 and 'A Necessary Relationship' (Chapter 4).

15 George Cheyne, *An Essay of Health and Long Life*, 1st edn, London, 1724, p. 57.

16 For a survey of the most important scholarly work on this subject see the editors' 'Introduction' in Ole Peter Grell and Roy Porter eds, *Toleration in Enlightenment Europe*, Cambridge, Cambridge University Press, 2000, pp. 1–22.

17 Jon Mee, *Dangerous Enthusiasm: William Blake and the Culture of Radicalism in the 1790s*, Oxford, Clarendon Press, 1992.

18 John Valton, MS autobiography and diaries, 1763–93, 6 vols, Methodist Archives, John Rylands Library, Manchester; Valton in Wesley ed., *The Experience of Several Eminent Methodist Preachers; With an Account of their Call to and Success in the Ministry . . . To the Rev John Wesley*, 3rd edn, New York, 1837, pp. 286–321.

19 Michael MacDonald, 'The Fearefull Estate of Francis Spira: Narrative, Identity, and Emotion in Early-Modern England', *Journal of British Studies* 31 (1992), pp. 32–61, p. 60.

20 MacDonald, 'The Fearefull Estate of Francis Spira', 59.

21 For an excellent analysis of Wesley's careful negotiation here, see Paul Laffey, 'John Wesley on Insanity', *History of Psychiatry* 12 (2001), pp. 467–79.

22 Randy L. Maddox, 'John Wesley on Holistic Health and Healing', *Methodist History* 46:1 (2007), pp. 1–33, p. 16; Madden, '"A Cheap, Safe and Natural Medicine"', p. 189.

23 MacDonald, 'The Fearefull Estate of Francis Spira', p. 57.

24 Valton, in Wesley ed., *The Experience of Several Eminent Methodist Preachers*, pp. 300–21.

25 Valton, in Wesley ed., *The Experience of Several Eminent Methodist Preachers*, p. 214.

26 Wesley, Letter to John Valton, 13 October 1784, *Letters* (Telford), vol. 7, p. 243.

27 Wesley, Letter to John Valton, 18 September 1773, *Letters* (Telford), vol. 6, p. 42.

28 Valton, in Wesley ed., *The Experience of Several Eminent Methodist Preachers*, pp. 300–21.

29 Wesley, 'Letter to John Valton, 5 September 1785', *Letters* (Telford), vol. 7, p. 287.

30 Wesley, 'Letter to John Valton, 22 December 1786', *Letters* (Telford), vol. 7, pp. 360–1.

31 P.W. Ott, 'John Wesley on Health: A Word for Sensible Regimen', *Methodist History* 18 (1979–80), pp. 193–204, p. 199.

32 Webster, 'Health of Soul and Health of Body' (Chapter 6).

33 Madden, '"A Cheap, Safe and Natural Medicine"'.

34 Madden, '"A Cheap, Safe and Natural Medicine"'.

35 Wesley, *Primitive Physic*, p. viii; Cheyne, *The Natural Method of Curing Most Diseases of the Body, and the Disorders of the Mind Depending on the Body*, London, Strahan, 1742.

36 Samuel August Andre Tissot, *L'Avis au Peuple sur sa Sante*, 1762, 2nd edn, trans. J. Kirkpatrick, London, 1765. This was the version Wesley used and abridged. Wesley was also familiar with Tissot's other works, *Onanism* (1760), *Treatise On Epilepsy* (1770), *Nervous Diseases* (1782) and *Diseases of the Men of the World* (1770).

37 A. Wesley Hill, *John Wesley Amongst the Physicians*, London, Epworth, 1958, pp. 55–6.

38 Wesley, Letter to John Valton, 12 November 1771, *Letters* (Telford), vol. 5, p. 289.

39 Medical authorities like William Cullen considered 'scrofula' as another form of 'consumption', caused by poor diet and damp conditions. See Risse, *New Medical Challenges*, p. 244.

40 Wesley, *Primitive Physic*, n. 72.

41 William Buchan, *Domestic Medicine*, 1769, 2nd edn, London, 1772, p. 219.

42 Risse, 'New Medical Challenges', p. 244.

43 Dormandy, *The White Death*, p. 40.

44 Clark Lawlor and Akihito Suzuki, 'The Disease of the Self: Representing Consumption, 1700–1830', *Bulletin of the History of Medicine* 74 (2000), pp. 458–94, p. 462.

45 Blackmore, *A Treatise of Consumptions*, pp. 5–6.

46 Wesley, *Primitive Physic*, p. 41.

47 Risse, 'New Medical Challenges', p. 243.

48 John Arbuthnot quoted by Dormandy, *The White Death*, p. 13.

49 Dormany, *The White Death*, p. 22.

50 Lawlor and Suzuki, 'The Disease of the Self', p. 470.

51 Lawlor and Suzuki, 'The Disease of the Self', p. 460.

52 Lawlor and Suzuki, 'The Disease of the Self', p. 460.

53 Lawlor and Suzuki, 'The Disease of the Self', p. 465.

54 Susan Sontag, *Illness as Metaphor*, New York, Vintage Books, 1979, p. 66; Lawlor and Suzuki, 'The Disease of the Self', p. 458.

55 Risse, 'New Medical Challenges', p. 242.

56 Roy Porter, 'Consumption: Disease of Consumer Society?' in John Brewer and Roy Porter eds, *Consumption and the World of Goods*, London, Routledge, 1993, pp. 58–81, p. 67; Lawlor and Suzuki, 'The Disease of the Self', p. 475.

57 Porter, 'Consumption', p. 70.

58 Risse, 'New Medical Challenges', p. 242.

59 Lawlor and Suzuki, 'The Disease of the Self', pp. 470–1; Porter, 'Consumption', pp. 58–81.

60 Juster, 'Mystical Pregnancy and Holy Bleeding: Visionary Experience in Early Modern Britain and America', *William and Mary Quarterly* 57 (2000), pp. 249–88, pp. 272, 271.

61 Valton, in Wesley ed., *The Experience of Several Eminent Methodist Preachers*, p. 231.

62 Juster, 'Mystical Pregnancy and Holy Bleeding', p. 271.

63 Juster, 'Mystical Pregnancy and Holy Bleeding', p. 271; Porter, 'Consumption', pp. 58–81.

64 Porter, 'Consumption', p. 70.

65 Webster, 'Health of Soul and Health of Body' (Chapter 6).

66 Lawlor and Suzuki, 'The Disease of the Self', p. 463.

67 Fothergill, *Remarks on the Cure of Consumptions* [n.d.], taken from vol. iv of 'Medical Observations and Inquiries' (n.d.) in John Eliot, *A Complete Collection of the Medical and Philosophical Works of John Fothergill*, London, John Walker, 1781, n. 391.

68 Buchan, *Domestic Medicine*, p. 218.

69 Blackmore, *A Treatise of Consumptions*; Jeremiah Wainewright, *A Mechanical Account of the Non-Naturals*, London, 1708.

70 Buchan, *Domestic Medicine*, p. 220.

71 Sunny Y. Auyang, 'Reality and Politics in the War on Infectious Diseases' <http://www.creatingtechnology.org/biomed/germs.htm>, accessed 20 September 2007.

72 Blackmore, *A Treatise of Consumptions*.

73 Buchan, *Domestic Medicine*, pp. 219–20.

74 Buchan, *Domestic Medicine*, p. 219.

75 Wesley, 'Letter to Vincent Perronet, 1748', *Letters* (Telford), vol. 2, p. 307. This was also noted by Wesley in his *Journal* for December 1746. N. Curnock ed., *The Journal of the Revd John Wesley*, 8 vols, London, 1909–16, vol. 3, p. 273.

76 The 1745 pamphlet, *Collection of Receipts for the Use of the Poor*, was enlarged and corrected to a 119-page book, *Primitive Physic*, including a 24-page Preface. The diseases increased from 93 to 243, whilst the remedies increased from 227 to 725 – by the 23rd edition this had increased to 288 diseases and 824 remedies. Wesley's name did not appear on the volume until the 9th edition. See E. B. Bardell, 'Primitive Physick: John Wesley's Receipts', *Pharmacy in History* 21 (1979), pp. 111–21, p. 116; Maddox, 'Reclaiming the Eccentric Parent: Methodist Reception of John Wesley's Interest in Medicine' (Chapter 1); Madden, '"A Cheap, Safe and Natural Medicine"', p. 142.

77 This advertisement was printed on the front of every edition.

78 Valton, in Wesley ed., *The Experience of Several Eminent Methodist Preachers*, pp. 214–15.

79 Wesley, Letter to John Valton, 21 April 1780, *Letters* (Telford), vol. 7, p. 17.

80 Wesley, *Primitive Physic*, pp. xii–xiv. For a fuller discussion, see Madden, '"A Cheap, Safe and Natural Medicine"', p. 155.

81 Wainewright, *A Mechanical Account of the Non-Naturals*, p. 27; Madden, '"A Cheap, Safe and Natural Medicine"', pp. 103, 158, 181.

82 K. Dewhurst, *John Locke (1632–1704), Physician and Philosopher: A Medical Biography*, London, Wellcome Historical Medical Library, 1963.

83 Locke, quoted by Dormandy, *The White Death*, nn. 13, 6.

84 Buchan, *Domestic Medicine*, p. xii.

85 Madden, '"A Cheap, Safe and Natural Medicine"', p. 218.

86 Cheyne, *Essay of Health and Long Life*; Buchan, *Domestic Medicine*, p. 228; Madden, '"A Cheap, Safe and Natural Medicine"', p. 218.

87 R. Heller, 'Priest-Doctors as a Rural Health Service in the Age of Enlightenment', *Medical History* 20 (1976), pp. 361–83; Henry D. Rack, 'Doctors, Demons and Early Methodist Healing', in W. J. Sheils ed., *The Church and Healing*, Studies in Church History: 19, Oxford, Oxford University Press, 1982, pp. 137–52; J. Cule, 'The Rev. John Wesley, M.A. (Oxon.), 1703–1791: "The Naked Empiricist" and Orthodox Medicine', *The Journal of the History of Medicine* 45 (1990), pp. 41–63; Madden, 'Medicine and Moral Reform: The Place of Practical Piety in John Wesley's Art of Physic', *Church History* 73:4 (2004), pp. 741–58 and '"A Cheap, Safe and Natural Medicine"'; Maddox, 'John Wesley on Holistic Health and Healing' and 'Reclaiming the Eccentric Parent' (Chapter 1).

88 Madden, 'Medicine and Moral Reform' and '"A Cheap, Safe and Natural Medicine"'.

89 Blackmore, *Treatise of Consumptions*, pp. i–v. Earlier in his career, however, Blackmore had crossed swords with 'Faculty' physicians from the Royal College because of his staunch resistance to their charitable initiatives, which included providing affordable medicines to the poor from Medical Dispensaries.

90 Blackmore, *A Treatise of Consumptions*, p. x.

91 Blackmore, *A Treatise of Consumptions*, p. xii.

92 Blackmore, *A Treatise of Consumptions*, p. xii.

93 Wesley, *Primitive Physic*, p. vii.

94 Buchan, *Domestic Medicine*, p. v, x.

95 Blackmore, *A Treatise of Consumptions*, pp. vi–viii.

96 Blackmore, *A Treatise of Consumptions*, p. xiii.

97 Madden, 'Contemporary Reaction to John Wesley's *Primitive Physic*: Or, the case of William Hawes Examined', *Social History of Medicine* 17:3 (2004), pp. 365–78 and '"A Cheap, Safe and Natural Medicine"'.

98 Porter, *Health for Sale: Quackery in England 1660–1850*, Manchester, Manchester University Press, 1989; Porter ed., *The Popularization of Medicine 1650–1850*, London, Routledge, 1992.

99 Ott, 'Medicine as Metaphor: John Wesley on Therapy of the Soul', *Methodist History* 33 (1995), pp. 178–91; Madden, '"A Cheap, Safe and Natural Medicine"'.

100 Madden, 'The Limitation of Human Knowledge: Faith and the Empirical Method in John Wesley's Medical Holism', *History of European Ideas* 32 (2006), pp. 162–72.

101 Wesley, Letter to John Valton, 12 November 1771, *Letters* (Telford), vol. 5, p. 289.

102 Madden, '"A Cheap, Safe and Natural Medicine"', pp. 119–20.

103 Wesley, Letter to John Valton, 6 January 1784, *Letters* (Telford), vol. 7, p. 203.

104 Wesley, *Primitive Physic*, p. 41.

105 Wesley, *Primitive Physic*, p. xi.

106 Blackmore, *A Treatise of Consumptions*, p. 155; Madden, '"A Cheap, Safe and Natural Medicine"', p. 219.

107 Madden, '"A Cheap, Safe and Natural Medicine"', p. 219; Lawlor and Suzuki, 'The Disease of the Self'; Porter, *Doctor of Society: Thomas Beddoes and the Sick Trade in Late-Enlightenment England*, London, Routledge, 1992.

108 Buchan, *Domestic Medicine*, p. 225; Madden, '"A Cheap, Safe and Natural Medicine"', p. 221.

109 Buchan, *Domestic Medicine*, p. 222; Madden, '"A Cheap, Safe and Natural Medicine"', p. 218.

110 John Radcliffe, *Pharmacopaeia Radcliffeana: or Dr Radcliffe's Prescriptions, Faithfully Gathered from his Original Recipes*, 1715, 3rd edn, London, 1718, p. 13; Buchan, *Domestic Medicine*, p. 226; Madden, '"A Cheap, Safe and Natural Medicine"', p. 219.

111 Wesley, *Primitive Physic*, pp. 41–3; Madden, '"A Cheap, Safe and Natural Medicine"', p. 219.

112 Wesley, *Primitive Physic*, p. 43.

113 Wesley, *Primitive Physic*, p. 43.

114 Fothergill, *Remarks on the Cure of Consumptions*, n.d., in Elliot ed., *A Complete Collection of the Medical and Philosophical Works of John Fothergill*, pp. 390–405, p. 398; Madden, '"A Cheap, Safe and Natural Medicine"', p. 220.

115 Wainewright, *A Mechanical Account of the Non-Naturals*, p. 27.

116 Wesley, 'Letter to Jenny Lee, 26 May 1763', *Letters* (Telford), vol. 4, p. 213.

117 Buchan, *Domestic Medicine*, p. 230.

118 Wainewright, *A Mechanical Account of the Non-Naturals*, p. 27.

119 John Hill, *The Family Herbal, or An Account of all those English Plants, which are Remarkable for their Virtues*, London, 1755, p. 175; Madden, '"A Cheap, Safe and Natural Medicine"', p. 219.

120 Antonín Příhoda, *The Healing Powers of Nature*, Leicester, Blitz Editions, 1998, pp. 90, 97; Madden, '"A Cheap, Safe and Natural Medicine"', p. 220.

121 Blackmore, *A Treatise of Consumptions*, p. 57; Madden, '"A Cheap, Safe and Natural Medicine"', p. 220.

122 Dormandy, *The White Death*, p. 24.

123 Blackmore, *A Treatise of Consumptions*, p. 8.

124 Blackmore, *A Treatise of Consumptions*, p. 1.

125 Blackmore, *A Treatise of Consumptions*, p. 9.

126 *Oxford English Dictionary*, 2nd edn, s.v. 'Tuberculosis'.

127 Richard R. Trail, 'Richard Morton (1637–1698)', *Medical History* 14:2 (April 1970), pp. 166–74.

128 Sunny Y. Auyang, 'Reality and Politics in the War on Infectious Diseases' <http://www.creatingtechnology.org/biomed/germs.htm>, accessed 20 September 2007.

129 Ole Daniel Enerson, 'Johann Lukas Schönlein', <http://www.whonamedit.com/doctor.cfm/353.html>, accessed 20 September 2007.

130 Thomas Henry Green, *An Introduction to Pathology and Morbid Anatomy*, London, 1873, 203, quoted in *Oxford English Dictionary*, s.v. 'Tuberculosis'.

131 Benjamin Marten, *A New Theory of Consumptions*, London, 1720, p. 51.

132 Auyang, 'Reality and Politics in the War on Infectious Diseases'.

133 Margaret DeLacy, 'Marten, Benjamin (*fl.* 1722)', *Oxford Dictionary of National Biography*, Oxford, Oxford University Press, 2004 <http://www.oxforddnb.com/view/article/57715>, accessed 20 September 2007.

134 Richard Coker, *From Chaos to Coercion: Detention and the Control of Tuberculosis*, New York, St Martin's Press, 2000; Katherine Ott, *Fevered Lives: Tuberculosis in American Culture since 1870*, Cambridge, Massachusetts, Harvard University Press, 1996.

135 Frank Ryan, *Tuberculosis: The Greatest Story Never Told*, Worcestershire, Swift Publishers, 1992; Dormandy, *The White Death*, p. 151.

136 Dormandy, *The White Death*, p. 151.

137 Linda Bryder, *Below the Magic Mountain: A Social History of Tuberculosis in the Twentieth Century*, Oxford, Oxford University Press, 1999; Georgina D. Feldberg, *Disease and Class: Tuberculosis and the Shaping of Modern North American Society*, New Jersey, Rutgers University Press, 1995.

138 O. R. McCarthy, 'The Key to the Sanatoria', *Journal of the Royal Society of Medicine*, 94:8 (2001), pp. 413–17.

139 For a full medical history, see Ryan, *Tuberculosis* and Dormandy, *The White Death*.

140 French researchers, Albert Calmette and Camille Guérin, developed the first vaccine in 1921, though widespread use of the vaccine throughout Europe and the United States only took off after the Second World War. Mortality rates in Europe and the United States were declining dramatically from the mid-twentieth century onwards, with deaths related to tuberculosis falling significantly by the 1950s. In Europe, over the course of a century, tuberculosis fell from 500 out of 100,000 in 1850, to 50 out of 100,000 by 1950. Even before the arrival of antibiotics, improvements in public health saw a reduction in deaths caused by tuberculosis, though its status as a dreaded threat remained. Indeed, when the Medical Research Council was founded in Britain on the eve of the First World War, it immediately concerned itself with research into tuberculosis. See, Wallace Fox, Gordon A. Ellard and Denis A. Mitchison, 'Studies on the Treatment of Tuberculosis Undertaken by the British Medical Research Council Tuberculosis Units, 1946–1986', *The International Journal of Tuberculosis and Lung Disease*, 3:2 (October 1999), pp. 231–79.

141 The reduction of public health services in New York, with the emergence of HIV and AIDS, saw a dramatic increase in tuberculosis during the 1980s and 1990s – reaching a peak of nearly 4,000 cases by 1992. Matters in New York were compounded by a sub-epidemic of drug-resistant tuberculosis. Progression of tuberculosis was halted in 1994 by proactive treatments and therapies, with improved centres for disease control and properly observed prevention guidelines. By 2002 tuberculosis rates in New York were curbed, though clinicians continue to express concern about the presence of large numbers of latently infected individuals within the city – particularly when the tuberculosis pandemic in developing or 'lower-resource' countries poses such a major threat to health in those regions. For a fuller analysis, see W. F. Paolo and J. D. Nosanchuk, 'Tuberculosis in New York City: Recent Lessons and A Look Ahead', *The Lancet Infectious Diseases* 4:5 (May 2004), pp. 287–93, p. 287.

142 World Health Organization (WHO), 'Frequently Asked Questions about

TB and HIV' <http://www.who.int/tb/hiv/faq/en/index.html>, accessed 20 September 2007.

143 Zumla and Mullen, 'Turning the Tide Against Tuberculosis', p. 877.

144 Zumla and Mullen, 'Turning the Tide Against Tuberculosis', p. 877; A. Zumla and M. Gandy, 'Politics, Science and the "New" Tuberculosis' in A. Zumla and M. Gandy eds, *The Return of the White Plague: Global Poverty and the 'New' Tuberculosis*, London, Verso, 2003, pp. 237–42.

145 S. Bertel Squire, Angela Obasi and Bertha Nhlema-Simwaka, 'The Global Plan to Stop TB: A Unique Opportunity to Address Poverty and the Millennium Development Goals', *The Lancet* (18 March 2006), pp. 367, 955–7, p. 955.

146 For a fuller discussion, see Madden, 'Medicine, Science and Intellectual History', in Richard Whatmore and Brian Young eds, *Palgrave Advances. Intellectual History*, Hampshire, Macmillan, 2006, pp. 147–70.

147 Bertel Squire, Obasi and Nhlema-Simwaka, 'The Global Plan to Stop TB', p. 955.

148 Bynam, 'Consumption', p. 676.

149 Quoted by Richard Coker, 'Tuberculosis' in Colin Blakemore and Sheila Jennett eds, *The Oxford Companion to the Body*, Oxford, Oxford University Press, 2001, pp. 697–8 at p. 698.

150 Coker, 'Tuberculosis', p. 698.

151 Coker, 'Tuberculosis', p. 698.

152 Zumla and Mullen, 'Turning the Tide Against Tuberculosis', p. 877.

153 Maddox, 'Reclaiming the Eccentric Parent' (Chapter 1).

154 Dormandy, *The White Death*, p. 25.

155 Maddox, 'Reclaiming the Eccentric Parent' (Chapter 1).

156 Cule, 'The Rev. John Wesley, M.A. (Oxon.), 1703–1791'; Madden, '"A Cheap, Safe and Natural Medicine"'.

157 Wesley, *Primitive Physic*, p. viii.

4

A Necessary Relationship:
John Wesley and the Body–Soul Connection

LAURA BARTELS FELLEMAN

There is no Dark Night of the Soul in the Wesleyan Tradition. St John of the Cross and Mother Teresa of Calcutta described this mystical experience as an absence of God that left them with an intense feeling of abandonment and longing. Conversely, the spirituality described by John Wesley was an experience of love, peace, and joy filling the soul. Most of the time, most people of faith should feel happy – the Eternal Sunshine of the Spotless Mind in comparison to the Dark Night of the Soul.[1]

This normative religious experience, the 'life of God in the soul of man' as John Wesley sometimes referred to it, was available to all who repented of their sins, were saved by faith, born again, and pursued inward and outward holiness. The developmental steps in this order of salvation – conversion, justification, regeneration, and sanctification – are discussed, defended, and defined in countless sermons, hymns, poems, and treatises. If these steps were diligently followed, Wesley claimed they normally led to a feeling of happiness in the spiritually mature.

This was not a permanent happy state, however. It could be lost and when this happened the individual entered the 'Wilderness State' and required the counsel of a knowledgeable cleric who could explain the reasons for this loss of faith and the means by which it could be restored. The fading of spiritual consolations was not a higher, more mature stage of faith development, according to Wesley; instead it was usually indicative of a personal shortcoming. Those in a spiritual wilderness needed to review their past conduct for any sins of commission or omission, temptations, or 'spiritual sloth', any one of which could cause this disease of the soul.[2]

Ignorance could also affect the soul and make a person unhappy. A Christian might be misled by a teacher who preached unorthodox interpretations of scripture and whose theology undermined a sound spiritual life. Religious ideas were rarely innocuous; they either enhanced or detracted from one's maturation in faith. Attacking doctrines that contributed to spiritual ignorance was one motivation for Wesley's prolific publishing programme.

An example of this concern can be found in Wesley's writings against the doctrine of necessity. In one treatise, *Thoughts Upon Necessity* (1774), he cited the case of a man whose ideas have caused him to be ignorant of his sins:

> One of these fairly confessing, that 'he did not think himself a sinner', was asked, 'Do you never feel any wrong tempers? And do you never speak or act in such a manner as your own reason condemns?' He candidly answered, 'Indeed I do. I frequently feel tempers, and speak many words, and do many actions, which I do not approve of. But I cannot avoid it. They result, whether I will or no, from the vibrations of my brain, together with the motion of my blood, and the flow of my animal spirits. But these are not in my own power. I cannot help them. They are independent on my choice. And therefore I cannot apprehend myself to be a sinner on this account.'[3]

Thoughts Upon Necessity is primarily Wesley's position on the debate over the freedom of the will, a long-standing philosophical question that in the eighteenth century became focused on theories of causation in mental processes. The main point of contention in this time period centred on the role of motives in relation to volitions – if things like 'appetites, desires, affection, and passions' occurred first and influenced acts of choice, the will was not free or at complete liberty, but was merely an effect produced by a prior cause.[4]

Given his career-long opposition to Antinomianism, it should come as no surprise that Wesley vigorously argued against necessity. Any suggestion that some external or internal principle controlled a person, predetermined actions, and forced one to act a certain way, whether for good or evil, had to be condemned because such ideas could logically lead to three conclusions with the potential to undermine faith: the idea that humans were not morally culpable for their behaviour, or that there were no future rewards and punishments, or worst of all, the idea that God was the cause of all the sin in the world. Those who argued for the necessity of the will denied these charges and countered with their own critique that liberty of the will was inconsistent with the belief in God's omnipotence and omniscience.

In amongst Wesley's summary of the debate over free agency, springs of action, and First and Final Causes, is the statement of the anonymous gentleman claiming that he is not a sinner because his actions, words, and tempers arise from movements in his blood and animal spirits, and vibrations in his brain – bodily functions that are beyond his conscious control. The significance of this statement for the free-will debate becomes evident once it is compared to different theories of the soul's relationship to the body held by three British physicians – William Harvey, Thomas Willis, and David Hartley.

The unidentified man's ideas concerning the nature of sin are based on such medical theories, but as this chapter will show, Wesley concluded that the physicians' anatomical findings did not directly support the doctrine of necessity. This opinion is consistent with other writings in which he explained his views on the faculties of the human soul and their connection to the body.

The Soulful Blood

Dr William Harvey (1578–1657) studied medicine at the University of Padua, practiced at St Bartholomew's Hospital in London, was a member of the Royal College of Physicians and their Lumleian Lecturer in anatomy, and attended both James I and Charles I. He is best known for his publication *De Motu Cordis* (1628), which describes the circulation of the blood as coursing in a circular motion from the right side of the heart to the lungs and then into the left side of the heart where it is pumped into the arteries and flows throughout the body until it finally returns to the heart through the veins.[5]

The scholarship on Harvey emphasizes the Aristotelian influences evident in his anatomical writings, particularly *De Generatione* (1653). Harvey's education both at Cambridge and at Padua would have included instruction in Aristotle's works and the Aristotelian method of observation and experimentation, inductive reasoning, and syllogism. The conclusion that the blood is the instrument of the soul as articulated in *De Generatione* is based upon this methodology.[6]

The first section of this embryology text details Harvey's observations of foetal development in chicken eggs. He recorded seeing a small point of blood first appear on day four following fertilization and begin to pulse. Exposure to cold air caused the pulse to slow and, when touched with a needle or finger, the *Punctum saliens* withdrew from the irritant. Over the next three days the blood drop developed into a foetus that could move and stretch its body parts, parts that at this stage entailed little more than the limb buds, the neck, and the head with its globs of tissue that eventually would become the brain and eyes.[7]

Based on these observations and experiments, Harvey reasoned that by the fourth day the foetus was animated by a kind of soul that he called the Vegetable Soul because there was evidence of reactive motion, growth and nourishment, which were activities that were also observable in plants. Shortly thereafter, the further development of the foetus suggested to him that a more advanced soul, the Animal Soul, was in operation with all its powers of sensitivity and movement.[8] The mental powers of reasoning, memory, and imagination he attributed to yet a third soul, the Rational Soul.

The division of the soul into three operations or functions, vegetable, animal and rational, is a commonplace in the medical literature of Harvey's time. What is distinctive about his argument is his identification of the blood as the means by which the soul works within the body. Typically, seventeenth-century physicians held that spirits were derived from the blood and then these rarefied byproducts, empowered and guided by the soul, carried out the activities of nutrition, sense, motion, and reasoning.

Harvey rejected this explanation because his embryological research uncovered no evidence of these supposed spirits at work in the developing foetus. Instead all he witnessed was the presence of the blood, appearing first, moving first, coursing into every part of the body, and providing the heat and nourishment that sustains life.

Harvey concluded:

> For such is the soul, that it is not altogether a body, nor yet wholly without a body; it comes partly from without, and is partly born at home: in some sort it is a part of the body, and in some the beginning and cause of all things which are contained in the Animal body; namely, nutrition, sense, and motion . . . And therefore it comes all to the same reckoning, whether we say, that the soul and the blood, or the blood with the soul, or the soul with the blood, doth performe all the effects in an Animal.[9]

Harvey reasoned that the soul must be the cause of all the effects he observed occurring within the chicken egg and put forward several analogies to illustrate the relationship between the foetus, the blood, and the soul. The soul could adhere to the blood, in the way a flame could adhere to lamp oil. The blood's power to influence the growth and health of the foetus exceeded the ability of a material element and must be caused by the 'Omnipotent Agent' in a manner analogous to the power exerted by the Sun and Moon, a power that affects life on Earth, that surpasses the merely elemental, and that must be caused by the Divine.[10]

Harvey's categorization of causality as material, efficient, formal and final is another indication of the influence of the Aristotelian tradition. In *De Generatione* Harvey identified the material cause as the fertilized egg containing matter from both parents; the efficient cause as the thing altering the egg into, in this case, a chicken; the formal cause as the form assumed by all members of this species; and the final cause as the chicken itself, the *telos* towards which the egg moves. Ultimately, God is the final cause who providentially guides all things to their proper end.[11]

The soul is identified as the efficient cause of conception, and Harvey mentioned his plans to publish a treatise on the soul and the brain, a work that in the end was never written. In his chapter 'Of the Conception', Harvey made a few comments about the brain and cognition – that the brain is the organ of the Rational Soul, that phantasms, appetites, and ideas are conceived in the brain after it is stimulated by outer objects, and that our ideas are imitations of these objects, which can sometimes stimulate our appetite for things in the physical world.[12] The remaining physicians to be considered pick up where *De Generatione* left off, and develop their own theories on how the immaterial soul uses the brain to produce mental ideas.

The Still Brain

There is some speculation that our next physician, Thomas Willis (1621–75), may have met Dr Harvey while the two were stationed in Oxford during the Civil War. Harvey was there as the King's physician and Willis as a medical student at Christ Church and a volunteer soldier. After the war's end, Willis established a medical practice based in Oxford and pursued his interests in comparative anatomy and chemistry with other virtuosi of experimental philosophy. He would eventually publish several works based on his research, would be elected to the university's Sedleian Chair of Natural Philosophy, and would become a founding member of the Royal Society, all while maintaining a lucrative medical practice. His best-known work was *Cerebri Anatome* (1664), which was the most detailed description of the parts of the brain and nervous system, complete with illustrations, available at that time.[13]

Willis, like Harvey, observed dissections of animals, fish, and insects and drew physiological conclusions based upon comparative anatomy, but his biochemical explanations of physical processes reflect a new trend in academic medicine.[14] His reliance upon anatomical and chemical investigations is evident in the theory of the soul advanced in his work *De*

Anima Brutorum (1672). In this work Willis repeated the description of the brain and nervous system he first detailed in *Cerebri Anatome* and then compared them to distillation equipment. Chemists of that period distilled various compounds by boiling ingredients, drawing off the steam, and cooling it until a liquid condensed in a separate container called an alembic. This resulting liquor was considered to be the rarefied essence of the original compound, and some physicians experimented with these liquors to see if they could be used to treat diseases and ailments.

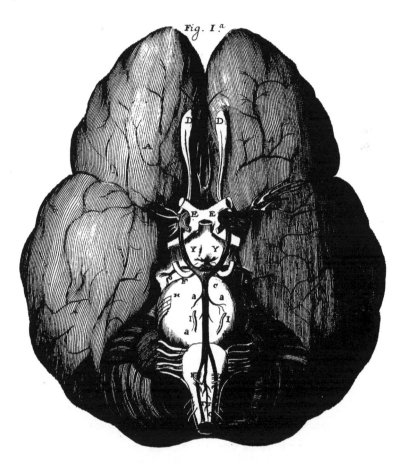

Illustration from Thomas Willis's *The Anatomy of the Brain* (*Cerebri Anatome*, 1664) depicting the arteries entering the cortical folds at the base of the brain. Taken from Thomas Willis, *Dr. Willis's Practice of Physic*, trans. Samuel Pordage, London, Printed for T. Dring, C. Harper, and J. Leigh, 1684, p. 50. Courtesy of the Houghton Library, Harvard College Library, Med. 273.16F* (Wing/W2854). Image published with permission of ProQuest LLC (Early English Books Online). Further reproduction is prohibited without permission.

Willis suggested that the body's production of animal spirits was analogous to the distillation process. Purportedly, animal spirits form when the warmth of the blood causes elements in the blood to separate. The structure of the carotid arteries allows only the most light-weight and spirituous parts of the blood to rise up into the head. The blood vessels in the head distil the blood particles and further refine them into a purified form that next flows into the cortical folds of the brain and cerebellum. These folds serve as alembics that collect the resulting animal spirits. The spirits then ooze throughout the body by way of the nerves carrying commands from the brain to the muscles.

The animal spirits also flow from the sensory organs and communicate sense data back to the brain. This means that the animal spirits are vital to the operation of the corporeal soul that senses the outside world and moves the body, as well as to the function of the rational soul, the immaterial Mind located in the brain that imagines, remembers, and desires.[15] The corporeal soul controls the flow of the animal spirits that convey sensory impressions to the mind. Willis imagined the rational soul seated in the brain awaiting messages from the corporeal soul through the animal spirits:

> ... therefore we may affirm, this purely Spiritual, to sit as in its Throne, in the principal Part or Faculty of it, to wit, in the Imagination, made out of an handful of Animal Spirits, most highly subtil, and seated in the Middle or Marrowie part of the Brain: Because, when as the Species, or every sensible Impression, of which we are any ways Knowing, being inflicted any where on the Humane Body, is carried to the Imagination or Phantasie, and there all the Appetites or Spontaneous Conceptions, or Intentions of things to be done, are excited, the Intellect or Humane Mind, presiding in this Imperial seat, easily performs the Government of the whole Man.[16]

In some ways this is a very conventional argument. As has already been noted, Harvey also attributed cognition to the relationship between the rational soul and the brain, and the notion of animal spirits was widely held by the physicians of his time. The use of the distillation analogy to conceptualize the body's production of animal spirits is also found in many medical texts and should not be seen as an innovation on Willis's part.[17] Nonetheless, the second part of Willis's treatise, in which he drew on his familiarity with chemical experiments, both to explain how the impairment of the corporeal soul can impact the rational soul and to suggest treatments for the resulting pathologies, did make an original contribution to medicine.

The rational soul can easily govern the body and carry out its will as long as the flow of animal spirits remains constant and regular. However, if the corporeal soul and the body it is joined to become diseased, the mental functions will suffer as well. Willis identified frenzy, melancholy, and madness as diseases of the corporeal soul that also affect the rational soul and that occur when the flow of animal spirits is disrupted. The animal spirits are too rarefied and lightweight to be observed, Willis explained, and he offered little physical evidence from his anatomical experiments to account for the presence of animal spirits in the body. He instead used chemical analogies to explain the symptoms he saw in patients.

Frenzy is the permanent loss of ratiocination. Willis theorized that it was caused by the overheating of animal spirits. Sulphur and turpentine are the examples he cited of liquors that can shoot flames into the alembic if the fire under the distillery is too intense. In an analogous way, if the blood is too hot, the animal spirits can rage through the brain like an uncontrollable fire and impair reasoning. Willis followed this description of frenzy with three pages of cures and antidotes including, among others, recipes for making a cherry-lemon-pearl julep, distilled spring water with boiled apples, and tincture of coral dissolved in milk and orange juice.[18]

Melancholy happens when the animal spirits, which are normally light and transparent, darken or clump together as happens when distilled vinegar turns into a useless opaque phlegm. Consequently, the sensory image communicated to the rational soul by the animal spirits does not reflect the object's true appearance but is darker than the original and in shadows. This distorted image then develops into dark and depressed thoughts. Madness is likened to the agitated waters produced when arsenic is distilled. Various pills, powders, and syrups are recommended to clear up sooty animal spirits, and for agitated spirits the use of chemical agents that induce purging is prescribed.[19]

The Musical Mind

Dr Willis's chemical cures focus on the pathologies of the mind, but our next theorist offered an explanation of how the body and soul work together to produce normal mental operations. David Hartley (1705–57) is considered a physician, although he did not receive the doctoral degree in medicine. He read theology and medicine at Cambridge and was licensed to practise as a Fellow of the University. His publications demonstrate his range of interests, which included treaties on smallpox inoculations and remedies for bladder stones. He is still remembered for his contribution to physiological psychology in his work *Observations on Man* (1749). With Hartley we enter the era of Newtonian physics and find one example of how the laws of universal attraction and repulsion influenced physiological theories.[20]

While Wesley and Hartley were contemporaries, there are few clues to the quality of their relationship. In a journal entry dated 4 February 1745 Wesley noted receiving from Hartley an account of the death of Dr George Cheyne (1671–1743), a well known physician and medical writer. A more indirect indication of their acquaintance is the copy of the *Observations* contained in the Methodist Archives with the inscription 'To the Rev. Charles Wesley from the author, June 26, 1753.'[21]

Like Harvey and Willis, Hartley's text is concerned with accounting for the causes of sensation and motion. Unlike the former physicians, however, Hartley identified the instrument of the soul as neither the blood nor the animal spirits, but as the vibration of the ether within the pores of the medullary substance (the myelin sheaths of the nerves and spinal cord and the white matter of the brain). Furthermore, while Willis and Harvey based their theories of the soul and the body on the results of extensive physical experimentations, Hartley's work can be viewed as the product of a mental exercise that analysed and synthesized the implications of Newton's ether hypothesis.

It is Newton's conceptualization of the ether and its properties that informs Hartley's 'Doctrine of Vibrations.' The ether, 'a certain most subtle spirit which pervades and lies hid in all gross bodies', was mentioned in Newton's *Principia* (1687) and *Optics* (1704), and in a letter he wrote to Robert Boyle. Such a medium, with the ability to transfer energy from one point to another, enabled Newton to account for action at a distance (e.g., the gravitational force exerted upon the planets by the sun). Assuming that this medium was universally present, Newton proposed that the ether might permeate the human body and be responsible for the transmission of impulses from the nerves to the brain and from the brain to the muscles.[22]

In the *Observations*, Hartley used Newton's theory to explain how an external, physical object can create an internal, mental impression upon the brain. He hypothesized that every object gives off ether particles with a repulsive force that can cause ether particles in the nerves to oscillate, analogous to the transfer of vibrations from one string of a musical instrument to adjacent strings.[23]

This vibratory action of particles is the mechanism of all the senses – hearing, seeing, feeling, tasting, and smelling, as well as automatic and voluntary bodily motions. Automatic motions include the movement of the heart, lungs, and intestines and are performed when the sensitive soul sends vibrations through the ether in the medullary substance of the spinal cord and nerves to the organs and muscles. Examples of voluntary motions would be walking, speaking, or handling objects. These motions are initiated by the rational soul and originate in the vibration of the ether in the brain's white matter.[24]

In addition to explaining sensation and motion, the *Observations* goes on to explain how the thinking process is built up from vibrations. Hartley called this the Doctrine of Association, and John Locke is identified as the influence behind the Association of Ideas theory. It should be pointed out that Hartley did go beyond the conclusions of the *Essay on Understanding* (1690) when he conceived of associations giving rise to the understanding through a mechanical process of vibration.

The mechanics of cognition begin when repetitive sensory data create an afterimage that lingers in the brain. This lingering image, or simple idea, becomes associated with other simple ideas in the mind if these sensory images commonly reach the brain at the same time. For example, the sight of a piece of fruit generates a simple idea of the fruit's colour, a perception that might trigger vibrations associated with other simple ideas such as how the fruit tastes, and how it smells.[25]

When the vibrations of various simple ideas become associated with one another they form complex ideas – beauty, honour, morality, or a sense of self would all be examples of complex ideas in Hartley's system.[26] Therefore, the various mental faculties of the rational soul (imagination, memory, understanding, will, affections, etc.) are in essence associated vibrations from various simple and complex ideas that have become linked together over the course of a lifetime.

Ultimately, the complex idea of the love of God ('theopathy' in Hartley's terminology) should regulate all the sensations and ideas and become the dominant experience in a person's life so that every experience becomes associated with and interpreted in light of the love of God.[27] Religion can also contribute to this regulator process by explaining God's will and encouraging the development of the willpower to follow the Divine purpose.[28] Like Harvey and Willis before him, Hartley identified God as the ultimate causal force in the world, 'the Cause of Causes', and 'the only Cause and Reality'.[29]

Hartley conceded that the 'doctrine of vibrations and association' was a mechanical explanation of the work of the sensitive soul and the rational soul, but he denied that this implied the materiality of the soul. The immateriality and immortality of the soul was a first principle that

Hartley assumed and did not seek to prove. That this soul is in some way related to the body is another point Hartley saw no need to defend: 'it is sufficient for me, that there is a certain connexion, of one kind or other, between the sensations of the soul, and the motions excited in the medullary substance of the brain; which is what all physicians and philosophers allow'.[30]

All physicians and philosophers would not have been in agreement with Hartley's conclusion that this physiological psychology was evidence in favour of the necessitarian argument. Recognizing how controversial his necessitarian position would be, Hartley tried to craft a compromise by distinguishing between practical free-will and philosophical necessity. Free-will, in the common vernacular, meant the liberty to choose between options and control voluntary motions. Hartley's argument goes behind these voluntary acts to the forces producing them. The will cannot make the ether vibrate or control the process of association; it is independent of these physical processes. Therefore, at the level of everyday, practical experience, the will might feel self-determined, but when considered from a philosophical standpoint, the will is shown to be just one link in a chain of events.[31]

When the Dissenting clergyman, scientist, and social activist Joseph Priestley published an abridgement of the *Observations* he left out Hartley's physiology of vibrations and instead focused on the theory of association and philosophical necessity. Priestley announced his intention to publish the abridgement the same year (1774) in which, according to the historian of science Robert Schofield, 'Priestley began a series of philosophical, metaphysical, and theological publications relating to the doctrine of free will, the operations of the mind, and the relation between body and soul'.[32] Hartley had been deceased for many years when John Wesley came out with his rebuttal of the doctrine of vibrations, but given Priestley's efforts to reintroduce part of the *Observations* the reason for Wesley's timing becomes clearer.

The Wesleyan Diagnosis

Thoughts Upon Necessity came out at the beginning of this Hartleian resurgence. The tract begins in a traditional, scholarly way, with a kind of 'history of ideas' review. The Manichees, the Stoics, the Westminster Council, Jonathan Edwards, Lord Kames, David Hartley, even Adam and Eve are covered in this survey of ancient and modern necessitarians.

After this overview of philosophers, theologians, and one physician,

Wesley quoted the above-cited anonymous man whose attitude exemplified the logical consequences of the doctrine of necessity. This gentleman saw his actions, words, and tempers as the unavoidable result of bodily processes that he could not help, that were not under his power, and that were independent of his choice. Because his behaviour was not volitional, 'They result, whether I will or no', he did not consider himself to be a sinner.

This usage of the physicians' theories is contrary to the conclusions reached by Harvey, Willis, and Hartley. The publications of Harvey and Willis do not defend a necessitarian viewpoint. The topics of human will-power and volition are not covered in Harvey's anatomical texts. Willis identified the will as a function of the rational soul, which was distinct from the corporeal soul and bodily appetites. Hartley realized his theories did imply necessity, but even so he still held individuals responsible for their sinful actions.[33]

Wesley identified the unnamed man's comments as an indirect consequence of the physicians' writings on the body–soul connection:

> The author of two volumes, entitled 'Man', rationally rejects all the preceding schemes, while he deduces all human actions from those passions and judgments which, during the present union of the soul and body, necessarily result from such and such vibrations of the fibres of the brain. Herein he indirectly ascribes the necessity of all human actions to God; who, having fixed the laws of this vital union according to his own good pleasure, having so constituted man that the motions of the soul thus depend on the fibres of the body, has thereby laid him under an invincible necessity of acting thus, and in no other manner. So do those likewise, who suppose all the judgments and passions necessarily to flow from the motion of the blood and spirits. For this is indirectly to impute all our passions and actions to Him who alone determined the manner wherein our blood and spirits should move (par. II.3).

The anonymous man's conclusions might represent the popularizations of medical body–soul theories, or at least, Wesley's fears concerning how the masses would misconstrue the physicians' ideas.

In 'A Thought On Necessity' Wesley chastized Hartley's decision to put his theory before the public:

> but since he saw, this destroyed that very essence of morality, leaving no room for either virtue or vice, why did he publish it to the world? Why? Because his brain vibrated in such a manner, that he could not

help it. Alas for poor human nature! If this is so, where is 'the dignity of man'? (par. 1.4)

Wesley argued that this undignified image of humanity as powerless over bodily motions that determined choice and action was both dangerous and false, and he offered an alternative to this mechanical, clock-work vision of human behaviour.

The argument in Wesley's anti-necessity publications contains no objection to the physicians' characterization of the soul as linked to the body and as particularly dependent upon the brain. As he stated in *Thoughts Upon Necessity*:

For who can deny, that not only the memory, but all the operations of the soul, are now dependent on the bodily organs, the brain in particular? insomuch that a blow on the back part of the head (as frequent experience shows) may take away the understanding, and destroy at once both sensation and reflection; and an irregular flow of spirits may quickly turn the deepest philosopher into a madman. We must allow likewise, that while the very power of thinking depends so much upon the brain, our judgments must needs depend thereon, and in the same proportion. It must be farther allowed, that, as our sensations, our reflections, and our judgments, so our will and passions also, which naturally follow from our judgments, ultimately depend on the fibres of the brain (par. IV.2).

This agreement with medical theory is not a new stance for Wesley. It is consistent with the opinion he expressed in the sermon 'Wandering Thoughts' published in 1762, and one he would reiterate near the end of his life in the 1790 sermon 'Heavenly Treasure in Earthen Vessels'. The soul was connected to the body, especially to the brain; concussions and mental illnesses were evidence of this dependency.

This interrelatedness meant the body could be affected if the soul was in distress. If, over an extended period, the soul experienced temptations or sorrows a person's physical health could be weakened.[34] Nervous disorders were another example of the body–soul relationship. If the body consumed too much alcohol, tea, or meat or if it remained asleep for too long, an individual's mental state could suffer. Failure to rise early (Wesley suggested getting up at four in the morning) was the primary reason there were more people suffering from nervous disorders than ever before. If an early-morning wake-up call did not produce a cure, giving the body an electric shock might restore a person's mental health.[35] (This is *not* a forerunner of the modern alarm-clock.)

Nervous disorders, even madness, could be caused by another form of bodily excess – masturbation. Wesley warned of the dangers of 'self-pollution' in his extract of a work by the Swiss physician Dr Samuel Auguste Andre David Tissot (1728–97). While the doctor implied that some help was possible if the patient consulted a medical professional, Wesley deleted this advice from his edition and instead only recommended the patient cease self-pleasuring, repent, and trust in God. A complete recovery was impossible – Tissot and Wesley both agreed on the prognosis – but at least the process of physical wasting could be halted if the self-abuse stopped. Otherwise, the patient faced an incurable disordering of the nerves.[36]

The prospects for those who suffered from different diseases of the soul were more hopeful. Some ailments of the mind could be treated by physical means. In addition to electrification or early rising, Wesley's collection of medical remedies, *Primitive Physic* (1747), also recommends a breakfast of thyme tea or a tincture of valerian root as treatments for nervous disorders. Lunatics should also try an electric shock or chemical concoctions such as decoction of agrimony or boiled juice of ground-ivy with sweet oil and white wine. Those suffering from raving madness could be fed apples for a month or a diet of bread and milk.[37]

Wesley's familiarity with medical literature can also be found in his *Survey of the Wisdom of God in Creation* (1763). The animal spirits theory of nerve function is recounted, including the two main objections to this theory – that there is no evidence for the existence of animal spirits and that the nerves may not be 'hollow canals' but instead more like solid threads. Hartley's alternative theory of nerve vibration is also mentioned, but Wesley did not commit himself to either theory. Questions are raised in the text as to whether the nerves vibrate or transmit animal spirits and, if animal spirits do exist, whether or not they are composed of blood or ether, but no conclusions are reached. The 1784 sermon 'The Imperfection of Human Knowledge' repeats this list of unanswered questions and adds the hypothesis that the animal spirits might be a kind of 'electric fire'. *The Desideratum* (1759) also speculates that 'electric ether' might move through the nerves. The equation of nerve function with electricity was a theory that received increasing attention from eighteenth-century British physicians and scientists.[38]

The *Survey* does reject the notion that God can endow matter with the power of thought as some Lockeans claimed, but it does not offer an alternative theory, instead only stating that 'the Union of the Soul and Body is another of those things which Human Understanding cannot comprehend'.[39]

The soul is an immaterial spirit – Wesley's writings consistently make that point; it perceives physical sensations, governs bodily motions, thinking, and the will, and it survives the death of the body. His description of the soul is similar to that of the physicians with the difference that Wesley did not attribute the involuntary bodily functions to a lower vegetable or corporeal soul. The only acknowledgement of an Aristotelian cause in the *Thoughts* is in reference to humanity's inability to do anything wise or good unless enabled to do so by the 'First Cause'.[40]

Wesley conceded that 'perceptions in the soul' follow 'motions of the body' and that 'without God we can do nothing' but this did not prove the case for necessity. His argument in *Thoughts* emphasizes two points: first, we are not helpless in the face of bodily functions because God, being omnipotent, has power over our souls and bodies and at any time can alter the way bodily functions develop into sensations, reflections, reasoning, passions, or actions.

Second, Wesley had no doubt that God would help individuals in the exercise of their wills because, in addition to being all-powerful, God is also all-loving. Human beings are not mechanical devices passively reacting to physical sensations or divine compulsions. Such an anthropology is inconsistent with the idea of a God of grace. Our conscience, which helps us judge our behaviour, is the one example of God's grace that Wesley identified in the treatise.

God can assist our wills (our conscience is one form this assistance takes) 'if we choose he should'. The emphasis on our volitional acceptance of Divine cooperation is consistent with other statements made by Wesley on 'responsible grace': 'I am not careful therefore about the flowing of my blood and spirits, or the vibrations of my brain; being well assured, that, however my spirits may flow, or my nerves and fibres vibrate, the Almighty God of love can control them all, and will (unless I obstinately choose vice and misery) afford me such help, as, in spite of all these, will put it into my power to be virtuous and happy forever'.[41]

Wesley's argument in 'A Thought on Necessity' puts forward additional counterpoints to the necessitarian position. Instead of focusing on the omnipotence of God and responsible grace, in this work Wesley discussed the limitations of human reason and willpower and differentiated between 'those who are without God in the world' and 'real Christians' who see God. In order to understand how these subjects relate to the debate over the freedom of the will we must turn to other examples from his writings where he defined these terms and explained his conception of faith as a spiritual sense of God and the things of God.

From the Natural Man to the Real Christian

Wesley argued that the necessitarians' inaccurate description of human experience resulted from their failure to account for God's involvement in the world: 'but in truth this their wisdom is their folly; for no system, either of morality or philosophy, can be complete, unless God be kept in view, from the very beginning to the end'.[42] Not that Wesley presented a complete philosophical system in any of his publications either, but there is enough consistency between his writings that, at a minimum, a Wesleyan order of salvation can be constructed. For the purpose of this chapter only the steps in the salvation process related to the free-will debate are presented in detail. This means that human reason and the will are explained from a Wesleyan perspective, but not the transformations he described salvation promoting in other faculties of the soul, such as the affections, imagination, aesthetic sensibility, and memory.

A logical beginning point for this soteriological system is with the 'Natural Man,' a term Wesley used to refer to humanity in its post-Fall state (or 'natural state') apart from the grace of God. The natural man is completely cut off from God, an atheist with no knowledge of God, or in other words, one of 'those who are without God in the world'.[43]

The reasoning ability of the natural man, his understanding, is as the physicians described it – sensory information is passed to the brain and the mind builds ideas about the physical world out of this data. Wesley concurred with the physicians' conclusion that our judgements, tempers, words and actions depend upon the impressions received by the brain from the five physical senses.

Because the natural man's understanding is limited to his perceptions of the physical world, he cannot form accurate ideas or judgements about things of a spiritual nature. His sensory organs do not have the capacity to perceive the spiritual realm: they can only detect the material world. The natural man can learn about the physical world; 'the eyes of his understanding' are open to material objects but his mind is completely cut off from incorporeal objects.[44]

Wesley compared the natural man to a toad trapped inside a tree. The toad has sensory organs, but they cannot help it form ideas about the world outside the tree. Without the ability to see, hear, taste, smell and feel physical objects the brain is given no impressions to work with, the mind has no information on which to base judgements and opinions, and the toad's voluntary actions are not responses to stimuli from the outer world. The toad is unaware that life exists beyond the tree and has no relationship to that reality.

As with the toad imprisoned in a tree, the natural man is imprisoned in the flesh and a 'veil of blindness' separates him from God and the things of God.[45] The natural man cannot understand what he does not perceive, and he cannot respond to a reality he is unable to detect. His will is devoid of any divine guidance. The soul's faculty of understanding dictates the choices of the will, and in the case of the natural man this means that his will is fixated on worldly things.[46] Acting upon physical sensations, responding to the things that are pleasing to the five senses and avoiding the things that are not, this is all his will is capable of as long as he is deadened to the presence of a spiritual reality.

The moral law cannot guide his will or help him judge his actions because it has been almost totally effaced from his spirit as a result of the Fall.[47] The natural man has no personal sense of moral good or evil. Consequently, he is limited to an existence that is solely determined by his connection to the physical world, the drives, desires, and tempers that reality evokes, and the actions that arise from motivations devoid of morality. The will of the natural man is 'free only to evil' and under the necessity to sin.[48]

In spite of being in this debased condition, the natural man is not completely unaware that some sort of Divine Being exists. He cannot inwardly discern the existence of God, but his impaired reasoning is capable of making some intellectual leaps. Wesley saw examples of this faulty understanding among 'heathens' who had gained some limited knowledge about God. The 'eyes of their understanding' saw the Creation and inferred that there must be a Creator who is 'powerful and wise, just, and merciful', who has the power wisely to judge the actions of people, and consequently, justly punish or mercifully reward them based on their actions or dispositions. Wesley also speculated that oral traditions might have been passed down from Noah and his sons to succeeding generations and this could have preserved some knowledge about God and the things of God. Finally some knowledge about God can be received from the 'witness in the hearts' of all people, which, Wesley wrote, imparted some faint awareness of God.[49]

This witness that 'enlighteneth every man that cometh into the world' Wesley identified as 'preventing grace'. This grace restores some capacity for free-will to the natural man and with this liberty he is free to respond to God's grace or not. Preventing grace is also equated with 'natural conscience', our ability to know the difference between right and wrong.[50] Even though the moral law has been almost entirely erased from the inward spirit, Wesley taught that God's grace was able to assist even the limited understanding of the natural man in matters of morality.[51]

Wesley went so far as to call preventing grace the first stage of the salvation process. The natural man is not self-determined, he is not free from sin, his will and understanding are corrupted, and he is powerless over his desires, affections, and tempers. However, if the natural man were to continue to respond to the promptings of grace a slight feeling of conviction could develop, followed by repentance, then justification and finally sanctification.[52] Human understanding and will are transformed at each of these developmental stages.

Conviction and Repentance: At this point the natural man becomes convicted of sin. By grace, he becomes aware of God and of the moral law, and this insight gives him a new self-understanding. He now realizes that he has no willpower over his desires, no ability to resist physical temptations. At this point in the salvation process he understands that there is another, better way to live. He repents of his old behaviours, but even so he cannot make himself consistently choose a healthier lifestyle.[53]

Justification and Sanctification: In an act of faith, the natural man gives up his attempts to change his attitudes and behaviours through his own efforts and trusts in God's willingness to help him. The will continues to struggle against sin; the justified are conscious of the fact that they are not completely free from the power of sin.[54] Gradually, the believer can reach a stage of salvation where the will responds only to the promptings of the divine. The sanctified eventually understand holiness and are enabled to live in accordance with this divine standard. It is at this stage in the order of salvation that we meet the 'real Christian' who knows God's will and is graciously empowered to resist sinful impulses.

Christian Perfection: At this stage self-will is forgotten and the real Christian is focused on trying to do the will of God. The body may experience physical pain, the mind may be perplexed, anxious, and affected by nervous disorders, but the will can still be steadfastly devoted to following God's commands and living out the example of Christ.[55] The transformation of the understanding is not as thorough as that of the will. The real Christian is still prone to errors in judgement, mistaken ideas, and ignorant opinions, all of which can mislead the will.[56] Perfect love volitionally expressed towards God and neighbour, not perfect understanding, is the promise for which the real Christian strives. Salvation does not depend upon having clear ideas; faith is the only condition for redemption, and Wesley had a very specific definition of saving faith and its degrees.[57]

Faith as a Spiritual Sense

The Sense of the Spiritual World

There can be an intermediary stage between the natural man and the real Christian, an 'infant' degree of saving faith that Wesley modelled on Cornelius in the Book of Acts: 'but what is the faith which is properly saving? Which brings eternal salvation to all those that keep it to the end? It is such a divine conviction of God and of the things of God as even in its infant state enables everyone that possesses it to "fear God and work righteousness"'.[58]

This description of the 'infant state' of saving faith, 'fear God and work righteousness,' is based on Acts 10:35 (where Peter acknowledges that Cornelius is saved). Wesley labelled a person who feared God and worked righteousness 'a servant of God'. While not the highest degree of faith, it was sufficient for salvation. At the real Christian stage of faith, believers can sense the inward witness of the Spirit that assures them of forgiveness, and they feel God's love in their hearts whereas the servants of God fear but do not love God.[59] Only when this fear is transformed into love and assurance can the person be called a child of God.[60]

These various dimensions of the working of the Holy Spirit, perceived by an individual and producing emotions ranging from a feeling of dread to one of assurance, are identified by Wesley as the sense of the spiritual world. At the beginning of his career, Wesley did not have a clear understanding of this witness of the Holy Spirit and the effect it could have on an individual. At one point he entertained the notion that the Christian's dramatic experiences of love, joy, and happiness were simply by-products of the imagination or the animal spirits. Eventually this became a point of controversy between Wesley and the Moravians, and it contributed to his decision to dissociate from them.[61]

The real Christian's love for God was not a product of the imagination nor did it result from overheated animal spirits, Wesley concluded. Nor was it like the theopathy described by David Hartley, which was produced by physical sensations that become associated together and formed a complex idea. Wesley taught that Christian love arose from faith and was a reaction to the experience of God's love and forgiveness.

Real Christians have an inward demonstration, evidence, and conviction of their redemption made possible by faith. Wesley expanded the Hebrews 11:1 definition of faith, 'the substance of things hoped for, the evidence of things not seen', and described it as:

the demonstrative evidence of things unseen, the supernatural evidence of things invisible, not perceivable by the eyes of flesh, or by any of our natural senses or faculties. Faith is that divine evidence whereby the spiritual man discerneth God and the things of God. It is with regard to the spiritual world what sense is with regard to the natural. It is the spiritual sensation of every soul that is born of God.[62]

Faith, according to this definition, is the inward sense of God and the spiritual world, a sense that does not come through natural faculties. The eye', 'ear', and 'palate' of the soul see, hear, taste, and feel God. Faith is a spiritual sense, analogous to the five physical senses, and it functions in a similar way – it communicates impressions of divine things to the mind that can then be developed into ideas, judgements, and reasoning. This faith-inspired understanding can then serve as a more accurate guide to the will.

Wesley used the analogy of a child in a womb to illustrate the difference between a person without faith and a new-born Christian. The developing foetus has sensory organs but the amount and kinds of physical impressions this little one takes in are too indirect for it to get a clear idea of what life outside the womb is like. Once the baby is delivered, the five physical senses are fully operational and it has a direct encounter with the outer world, just as the person who is born again by faith suddenly has an inward experience of God made possible by the regeneration of the spiritual senses.

This theory of a 'new class of senses . . . the avenues to the invisible world' opened up in the real Christian is not without precedent in the eighteenth century. In fact the abovementioned Dr George Cheyne in his work *Philosophical Principles of Religion, Natural and Revealed* (1715) also described the existence of 'divine senses' that could perceive God and the spiritual world. Cheyne wrote that the human spirit is dependent on these senses for knowledge of spiritual objects just as the faculties of the rational soul are dependent on the physical senses for its understanding of the material world. Cheyne found the Lockean theory of human understanding incomplete because it only considered the 'natural and lapsed Man' and not the religious knowledge available to those in a 'regenerated, redintegrated and reestablished Estate' who can sense the spiritual world.[63]

The Sense of the Invisible World

In addition to the spiritual world, the faithful, including the servant of God, can also sense the invisible world. In this world Wesley included such unseen things as the human soul, holy and evil angels, God, Christ, and the Holy Spirit. The spiritual senses perceive that the soul is an immaterial spirit that is prone to follow sinful inclinations, tempted by demons, and aided by the angels and the Trinity. God's attributes of goodness, power and wisdom are also detected by the spiritual senses. Eventually, faith reveals that God is everywhere, the soul of the universe.[64]

This sense of God's presence pervading the creation humbles the pride and transforms behaviours and attitudes towards nature and animals. Wesley wrote of the possibility that real Christians might reach a stage of faith where their spiritual senses allow them to see God in all things (including the natural resources they utilize), and to treat all of God's creatures as their neighbours, cohabitants on this planet that deserve to be treated with love and mercy.[65]

The Sense of the Eternal World

In his description of the eternal world Wesley stated that 'by faith Christians perceive the souls of the righteous, immediately received by the holy angels', 'the souls of unholy men, seized the moment they depart from the quivering lips by those ministers of vengeance, the evil angels', the coming of the Lord, and the execution of the Last Judgement. Even those with the faith of a servant can sense the eternal world.[66]

This perception of things eternal allows Christians to judge their actions and attitudes by a new standard. Instead of depending upon the physical senses to alert them to things that appear or sound good, with their spiritual senses they are able to discern what has lasting, eternal value. Wesley taught that the sanctified regulate their will so that its actions are consistent with their sense of the ways of heaven and this helps to prepare them for their eternal home.[67]

Heavenly Employments

Even death will not bring an end to the real Christian's growth in knowledge of the divine and sense of spiritual things. The holy dead continue on in the order of salvation to the stage of glorification. Wesley was uncertain how the dead would increase their understanding without the brain and the sensory organs, but he did offer some conjectures.

First, the holy dead will be able to learn from many different conversation partners: the wise ones who lived before them, angels and archangels, and Christ. What is more, they will never forget what they learn in these discussions because for Wesley such forgetfulness is just a consequence of the body's limitations. Once free of the flesh, the dead will 'swiftly increase in knowledge' including their knowledge of God, whom they will be able to perceive directly once the hindrance of 'the veil of flesh and blood' is removed.[68]

Besides enlightening conversations, the dead will also be aided by a new set of senses that will give them the ability to peer into the essence of material objects and view things that were invisible to them while they were alive. Wesley listed 'fields of ether . . . thrones, dominions, prince-doms, virtues, powers', and the angels, both good and bad, as possible objects the dead will be able to observe with their new senses.[69] In addition to these new perceptions, the knowledge of the holy dead will also be aided by a new ability to travel throughout the universe and contemplate God's Creation and God's acts of providence.[70]

Such expectations for the afterlife are found in other publications famil-iar to Wesley. For example, a work by the Swiss naturalist Charles Bonnet (1720–93), *Conjectures Concerning the Nature of Future Happiness*, which Wesley published in 1790, contains similar descriptions of new sets of senses being opened up, the perception of new objects, and the ability to move throughout the universe after death. The main difference between Bonnet and Wesley is Wesley's teaching that the spiritual senses are operational in this life for those who have faith while Bonnet described their functions beginning following death.[71]

Spiritual Respiration

The demise of the body does not bring about an end to the life of the soul or the soul's ability to respond to the grace of God. There is no guarantee that faith will develop to this stage, however. As long as the spiritual senses remain open, the individual will be able to sense God and appro-priately react to God's will, but if these avenues of the soul are ever closed, growth in faith will cease. If the reaction of the soul to God, also referred to as spiritual respiration in several Wesley sermons, were to cease then the ability to grow in our understanding of God and the will to turn away from sin would both come to an end.[72]

Many things can adversely affect faith's sense of the spiritual, invisible, and eternal worlds in Wesley's estimation. If the soul stops reacting to God (a negative, inward sin) a process begins that can lead to a positive, inward sin (anger, envy, pride, etc.) that results in the commission of an outward sin. This movement from negative to positive to outward sin brings about a loss of faith and shuts down the spiritual senses.[73]

Friendships with worldly individuals can also darken the spiritual senses and cause the will to revert to its preoccupation with things that please the physical senses.[74] On the other hand, Christianity is a social religion, and interactions with people of different degrees of faith provide opportunities to practise such virtues as meekness and peace-making – exercises that keep the spiritual senses healthy. Therefore, a balance between solitude and sociability, time spent with believers and time spent with doubters, is in order.[75]

The doctrine of necessity can also cut off spiritual respiration. It had to be combatted because it contributed to spiritual ignorance by promoting a view that the soul is bombarded by physical impressions and motives it must passively follow or, alternatively, that the soul is overwhelmed by the will of God. Such a philosophical system could cause individuals to despair of ever growing in faith, and such hopelessness would make them less mindful of trying to lead a holy life and of avoiding sins of commission and omission. With each sinful action, word, or temper the spiritual senses darken until finally one enters the Wilderness State where one's ability to perceive God, and the invisible, spiritual, and eternal worlds, is completely occluded and faith is lost. The doctrine of necessity was just as dangerous as the doctrine of predestination; both could lead to antinomianism and apostasy.[76]

Wesley as Physician of the Soul

The Anglican-Calvinist clergyman Augustus Toplady wrote a response to Wesley's *Thoughts Upon Necessity* in which he parodied the tract as a chemical cure for necessity poisoning. 'The Doctor's three-penny freewill Powder' was now for sale at the Foundry, Toplady noted, and he wrote an advertising jingle Wesley could sing as he hawked his 'spiritual Medicines':

> Come, buy my fine Powders; come buy dem of Me;
> Here be de best Powders dat ever you see.[77]

This caricature of Wesley as a 'quack' doctor or empiric selling his questionable wares to a naive public spoofed his free-will position as well as the *Primitive Physic* and some of the potentially dangerous recipes Toplady thought it contained. Wesley's qualification to offer either philosophical or medical advice is called into question by Toplady's *Scheme*.

Toplady's criticism is accurate in the sense that Wesley's rebuttal of the necessitarians did not address the nature of the causal relationship they saw between motives and volitions. In fact, it is fair to say that Wesley changed the terms of the argument. 'Necessity' becomes the necessity to sin, and Wesley agreed that the natural man is under this compulsion as long as he is separated from God. 'Liberty' becomes the freedom to not sin once the soul is saved and faith gives one the ability to know God and follow God's will.

As the leader of a spiritual renewal movement, Wesley's concentration on the life of the soul and the obstacles to its healthy development are comprehensible. However, the main point in the necessitarian argument was not whether or not the will can be freed from the power of sin, but whether the will or an inward motivation determines actions and choices. Neither *Thoughts Upon Necessity* nor 'A Thought on Necessity' makes a contribution to this conversation, leaving Wesley open to Toplady's charge of philosophical ignorance.

The causal quandary is side-stepped, but Toplady's conclusion that Wesley is a spiritual 'quack' is open to debate. Historians of medicine have pointed out that one of the ways university-trained physicians distinguished their work from that of an empiric was by emphasizing the physician's ability to offer a philosophical explanation of the causal factors involved in health and disease. The medical doctor with formal education was supposed to be able to distinguish between ailments with similar symptoms, to know what had caused an illness, what parts of the body were affected, in what ways they were affected, and what treatment to use. In addition the university physician should be able to describe to the patient the interaction between body, pathology, and remedy and explain how this interaction was part of a universal pattern of causes and their related effects.[78]

Wesley can speak this language when it comes to diseases of the soul. There are numerous examples in his *Journals* and sermons where he made a distinction between someone whose rants express a sorrow over sin, as opposed to a lunatic who may be demon-possessed, or a raving madness caused by a physical illness. A different intervention is called for in each case – the cleric assures the convicted of redemption, prays over those afflicted by evil spirits, and entrusts the mad to the care of a medical doctor and the Good Physician 'who can give life and salvation to all to whom thou hast given no understanding'.[79]

Lunacy and madness are the exceptions to Wesley's rule about happiness and true Christian faith. Even a real Christian can temporarily lose sanity in the midst of demonic torments. The brain and nerves of the mad may be so disordered that the understanding is ruined and beyond cure and consolation. In both cases the soul is overwhelmed and the feeling of happiness suspended, but this does not mean saving faith is lost.[80] Wesley did not equate mental illness with the experience of the Wilderness State.

The Wilderness State is a spiritual ailment with a variety of symptoms (the loss of faith, love, joy, peace, and power over sin) and a variety of causes. Knowledge of the common causes of the disorder and their related cures is what sets the true physician of souls apart from the 'spiritual mountebanks'. Instead of merely prescribing 'the blood of the covenant ... the promises of God' as the antidote in all cases, the spiritual doctor is aware that different causes require different cures. Sins of commission and omission, or inward and outward disobedience, require repentance; temptations require perseverance and reassurance; and ignorance requires orthodox teachings.[81]

Perhaps Toplady was right about *Thoughts Upon Necessity*; in a way it is an inoculation against the doctrine of necessity: a diluted version of ideas that could infect faith. Rather than wait for the epidemic of necessity to break out, Wesley was proactive and distributed a shot of evangelical orthodoxy to strengthen Methodist immunity. His confidence in this treatment is based not on the mastery of philosophical tenets but on professional experience.

His published works record the story of a religious leader who learned how to lead people to a faith experience marked by happiness and who, over the course of the Revival, discovered how to maintain them in this state of spiritual well-being. As long as the Methodists followed a regimen that kept the avenues of their souls open and clear, Wesley expressed optimism that they would enjoy spiritual health for ever.

Notes

1 Wesley quoted these lines from the Alexander Pope poem 'Eloisa to Abelard' in 'An Earnest Appeal to Men of Reason and Religion', *Works*, vol. 11, p. 46, n. 3.
Eternal sunshine of the spotless mind;
Each prayer accepted, and each wish resign'd; . . .
Desires composed, affections ever even,
Tears that delight, and sighs that waft to heaven.
2 Wesley, *Thoughts Upon Necessity* (1774), *Works* (Jackson), vol. 2, pp. 205–12.
3 Wesley, *Works* (Jackson), vol. 10, pp. 458, 459. I would like to thank Dr Randy Maddox for referring me to Sermon 128 'The Deceitfulness of the Human Heart', *Works* vol. 4, p. 151, par. 3, note 5, where the anonymous man is identified as Francis, Earl of Huntingdon, son of Selina, Countess of Huntingdon. See also *Works* vol. 4, p. 122, note 8.

4 James A. Harris, *Of Liberty and Necessity: The Free Will Debate in Eighteenth-Century British Philosophy*, Oxford, Clarendon Press, 2005, pp. 1–18.

5 Geoffrey Keynes, *The Life of William Harvey*, Oxford, Clarendon Press, 1966, and Gweneth Whitteridge, *William Harvey and the Circulation of the Blood*, London, Macdonald, 1971.

6 George Kimball Plochmann, 'William Harvey and his Methods', *Studies in the Renaissance* 10 (1963), pp. 192–210; Walter Pagel, *William Harvey's Biological Ideas: Selected Aspects and Historical Background*, New York, Hafner, 1967; Walter Pagel, *New Light on William Harvey*, London, Karger, 1976; Roger French, *William Harvey's Natural Philosophy*, Cambridge, Cambridge University Press, 1994 and Thomas Fuchs, *The Mechanization of the Heart: Harvey and Descartes*, trans. Marjorie Grene, Rochester, NY, University of Rochester Press, 2001.

7 William Harvey, *Anatomical Exercitations Concerning the Generation of Living Creatures*, London: printed by James Young for Octavian Pulleyn, 1653, pp. 90–112.

8 Harvey, p. 101.

9 Harvey, pp. 459, 460.

10 Harvey, pp. 459, 460.

11 Harvey, pp. 264–71, 551–4.

12 Harvey, pp. 539–56.

13 Hansruedi Isler, *Thomas Willis 1621–1675, Doctor and Scientist*, New York, Hafner, 1968; Kenneth Dewhurst, *Willis's Oxford Lectures*, Oxford, Sandford Publications, 1980; and Robert G. Frank, Jr., *Harvey and the Oxford Physiologists*, Berkeley, University of California Press, 1980.

14 Audrey B. Davis, *Circulation Physiology and Medical Chemistry*, Lawrence, KS, Coronado Press, 1973; Harold J. Cook, *The Decline of the Old Medical Regime in Stuart London*, Ithaca, Cornell University Press, 1986; Allen G. Debus, *Chemistry and Medical Debate*, Canton, MA, Science History, 2001.

15 'Anatomy of the Brain', *Dr. Willis's Practice of Physick*, London: Printed for T. Dring, C. Harper and J. Leigh, 1684, pp. 65, 72–5.

16 Thomas Willis, *The Soul of Brutes*, London, Printed for T. Dring, C. Harper and J. Leigh, 1683, p. 41.

17 R. J. Forbes, *A Short History of the Art of Distillation from the Beginnings up to the Death of Collier Blumenthal*, Leiden, Brill, 1970, p. 39.

18 Willis, *Soul of Brutes*, pp. 181–7.

19 Willis, *Soul of Brutes*, pp. 189, 195, 206.

20 A. H. T. Robb-Smith, 'Cambridge Medicine' in *Medicine in Seventeenth Century England*, ed. Allen G. Debus, Berkeley, University of California Press, 1974, pp. 327–69; Martha Ellen Webb, 'The Early Medical Studies and Practice of Dr. David Hartley', *Bulletin of the History of Medicine* 63 (1989), pp. 618–36; Richard C. Allen, *David Hartley on Human Nature*, Albany, State University of New York Press, 1999; Roy Porter, *Flesh in the Age of Reason*, London, W.W. Norton, 2003, p. 347–61.

21 Randy L. Maddox, 'Charles Wesley Family Book Collection', on-line guide, The Methodist Archives, John Rylands Library, MAW CW66–67 <www.library.manchester.ac.uk/specialcollections/methodist/using/charleswesley/> accessed 20 March 2008.

22 *The Works of the Honourable Robert Boyle*, London, printed for A. Millar, 1744, vol. 1, pp. 70–3; C. U. M. Smith, 'Hartley's Newtonian Neuropsychology', *Journal of the History of the Behavioral Sciences* 23:2 (1987), pp. 123–36; William T. Clower, 'The Transition from Animal Spirits to Animal Electricity: A Neuroscience Paradigm Shift', *Journal of the History of the Neurosciences* 7:3 (1998), pp. 208–9; Wes Wallace, 'The Vibrating Nerve Impulse in Newton, Willis and Gassendi: First Steps in a Mechanical Theory of Communication', *Brain and Cognition* 51 (2003), pp. 66–94. Newton's description of the ether is taken from the *General Scholium* to the third edition of the *Principia* quoted in Smith, p. 124.

23 David Hartley, *Observations on Man, his Frame, his Duty, and his Expectations*, Bath and London, Samuel Richardson, 1749, vol. 1, pp. 15, 21–3. Allen, pp. 83–104.

24 Hartley, vol. 1, pp. 81–112, 243–63.

25 Hartley, vol. 1, pp. 65, 66.

26 Hartley, vol. 1, pp. 65, 75. Allen, p. 333.

27 Hartley, vol. 2, pp. 309–15.

28 Hartley, vol. 2, p. 53.

29 Hartley, vol. 1, pp. 114, 508; vol. 2, p. 313. Willis referred to God as the 'First Mover', *Soul of Brutes*, pp. i, ii.

30 Hartley, vol. 1, pp. 33, 34, 511, 512.

31 Hartley, vol. 1, pp. 504–7; vol. 2, pp. 53–70.

32 Robert E. Schofield, *Mechanism and Materialism*, Princeton, Princeton University Press, 1969, p. 263. His intellectual biography, *The Enlightened Joseph Priestley: A Study of his Life and Work from 1773 to 1804*, University Park, PA, Pennsylvania State University Press, 2004 offers a scholarly overview of this series.

33 Willis, *Soul of Brutes*, pp. ii, 42, 43; Hartley, pp. vii, viii, 509.

34 *Works* (Jackson), vol. 2, p. 225, par. II.3.

35 *Works* (Jackson), vol. 7, pp. 29, 70; vol. 8, pp. 313, 317; vol. 14, p. 244; John Wesley, *The Desideratum, or Electricity Made Plain and Useful*, London, Bailliere, Tindall and Cox, 1871, 43.

36 James G. Donat, 'The Rev. John Wesley's Extractions from Dr. Tissot: A Methodist *Imprimatur*', *History of Science* 39 (2001), pp. 285–90.

37 John Wesley, *Primitive Physic*, 22nd edn, Philadelphia, Printed by Parry Hall, 1791, pp. 106, 107, 108, 113, 114.

38 Clower, pp. 209–13.

39 *Survey* 1763, vol. 1, pp. 21, 92; vol. 2, p. 255. See John Yolton, *Thinking Matter*, Minneapolis, University of Minnesota Press, 1983 for more on British theories on the materiality of the soul.

40 *Works* (Jackson), vol. 7, pp. 226, 227; vol. 10, p. 477.

41 *Thoughts*, *Works* (Jackson), vol. 10, p. 474. Randy L. Maddox, *Responsible Grace: John Wesley's Practical Theology*, Nashville, Abingdon Press, 1994.

42 *Works* (Jackson), vol. 10, p. 473, par. 4.

43 *Works* (Jackson), vol. 1, p. 411; vol. 5, pp. 110, 202; vol. 6, pp. 25, 58.

44 'Eyes of the understanding' is a Wesleyan synonym for Human Understanding taken from Ephesians 1:18. See *Works* (Jackson), vol. 5, p. 469; vol. 11, p. 15 where this phrase is used in reference to reasoning.

45 *Works* (Jackson) vol. 5, p. 102; vol. 6, pp. 70, 274; vol. 8, p. 5. Wesley did not offer any details on the nature of this veil. The imagery is found in 2 Corinthians 3:13–16.

46 *Works* vol. 4, pp. 294, 298.

47 *Works* (Jackson) vol. 5, pp. 99, 436.

48 *Works* (Jackson) vol. 10, p. 392.

49 *Works* (Jackson), vol. 4, pp. 51, 52, pars. 8, 9.

50 *Works* (Jackson), vol. 6, p. 44; vol. 10, pp. 232, 392. This definition of preventing grace can also be found in *Works* (Jackson), Sermon 85, vol. 6, p. 512; and Sermon 105, vol. 7, p.189. In *Thoughts On Necessity* Wesley refers to the conscience as an 'umpire' or 'inward judge' (par. IV.5).

51 *Works* (Jackson), vol. 6, p. 512; vol. 12, p. 453.

52 *Works* (Jackson), vol. 3, pp. 203, 204, par. II.1.

53 *Works* (Jackson), vol. 5, pp. 102, 443, 449; vol. 8, p. 428; vol. 9, p. 496; vol. 11, pp. 486–8.

54 *Works* (Jackson), vol. 1, p. 341, par. 10.

55 *Works* (Jackson), vol. 6, p. 433; vol. 11, pp. 368, 371, 372, 377, 384, 399, 422; vol. 12, pp. 207, 346.

56 *Works* (Jackson), vol. 3, p. 73, par. I.3.

57 *Works* (Jackson), vol. 4, p. 175, par. 15.

58 *Works* (Jackson), vol. 3, p. 497, par. I.10. This conception of justification is significantly different from an earlier one found in the sermon 'The Spirit of Bondage and the Spirit of Adoption' where knowledge of the moral law caused the servant to fear God and this fear was a sign that he was not yet justified.

59 *Works* (Jackson), vol. 3, p. 497, par. I.10, p. 489, par. I.12, and p. 500, par. II.4.

60 *Works* (Jackson), vol. 4, pp. 34–6.

61 *Works* (Jackson), vol. 1, pp. 204, 256, 257, 330; vol. 2, pp. 213, 215.

62 *Works* (Jackson), vol. 11, p. 46, pars. 6 and 7.

63 George Cheyne, *Philosophical Principles of Religion, Natural and Revealed*, London, Printed for G. Strahan, 1733, vol. 2, pp. 110–13.

64 *Works* (Jackson), vol. 4, pp. 30–32, pars. §5–7.

65 *Works* (Jackson), vol. 5, pp. 281, 283; vol. 7, pp. 98, 233, 257; vol. 14, pp. 300, 302.

66 *Works* (Jackson), vol. 4, pp. 32–5, pars. 8–13.

67 *Works* (Jackson), vol. 6, p. 196; vol. 7, pp. 260, 261.

68 *Works* (Jackson), vol. 4, p. 192, par. 6.

69 *Works* (Jackson), vol. 4, pp. 192, 193, par. 7.

70 *Works* (Jackson), vol. 4, p. 193, par. 7 and 196, par. 11.

71 Charles Bonnet, *Conjectures Concerning the Nature of Future Happiness*, London, New Chapel, City Road, 1790, pp. 5–9, 14, 16–20.

72 *Works* (Jackson), vol. 5, pp. 226, 227, 232; vol. 6, p. 70.

73 *Works* vol. 1, pp. 434–6, pars. I.8 and II.1.

74 *Works* (Jackson), vol. 3, p. 147, par. 10.

75 *Works* (Jackson), vol. 1, pp. 533–8, pars. I.1–9.

76 For the development of Wesley's critique of predestination see W. Stephen Gunter, *The Limits of 'Love Divine'*, Nashville, Abingdon Press, 1989, pp. 227–66.

77 Augustus Toplady, *The Scheme of Christian and Philosophical Necessity Asserted*, London, printed for Vallance and Simmons, 1775, pp. iii–vi.

78 King, 4, pp. 182–232; Cook, 20; and Andrew Wear, *Knowledge and Practice in English Medicine*, Cambridge, Cambridge University Press, 2000, pp. 116–46.

79 *Works* (Jackson), vol. 1, p. 231; vol. 6, p. 378; vol. 7, p. 330; vol. 11, p. 225.

80 *Works* (Jackson), vol. 1, p. 231; vol. 4, pp. 221, 267, 321; vol. 6, pp. 378, 433; vol. 7, p. 330.

81 *Works* (Jackson), vol. 2, pp. 205–17.

5

'This Curious and Important Subject':
John Wesley and *The Desideratum*

LINDA S. SCHWAB

John Wesley's 1760 work, *The Desideratum: Or, Electricity made plain and useful. By a Lover of Mankind, and of Common Sense*, has elicited a wide range of evaluations from scholars of the last half-century.[1] This little (72-page) book on the medical applications of electricity has been praised (with a somewhat backhanded compliment) as 'an example of his most "scientific" writing', and pilloried (with a mild qualification) as appearing 'on the surface, terribly amateurish'.[2] On the strength of it, Wesley has been credited with being (along with contemporaries Richard Lovett and Jean Paul Marat) one of 'the real pioneers of electrotherapy', and playing 'a major role in [its] development' – and has also been almost completely ignored.[3] *The Desideratum* might be among Wesley's attempts 'to improve medical practice without upsetting medical order' – or part of a strategy aimed at inculcating 'the principles of obedience and subordination to religious and political authority'.[4] Discussion of its place (if any) in the history of medicine has been complicated and often compromised by a persistent and critical misunderstanding: that the only contemporary application of electricity in medicine is electroconvulsive therapy ('electroshock') for psychiatric illness.

However, the recent rapid growth of electrotherapy for chronic pain and other disorders associated with the peripheral nervous system and its acceptance as standard treatment for a wide range of medical conditions place Wesley's work in a new context. In addition, as several of the essays in this volume illustrate, there is a new appreciation for and interest in understanding eighteenth-century science on its own terms, and not as an imperfect version of 'real science', the science of today.

In light of both of these developments, it is time to re-examine what Wesley set out to do when he wrote *The Desideratum*. Some of the most obvious questions one might ask of the work have been among the least addressed: how Wesley used the sources available to him, the extent of his personal contribution to the clinical accounts included in *The*

Desideratum, and how he understood the relevant medicine of his day, especially 'nervous diseases'. Almost all of the available studies of *The Desideratum* focus on its relation to the medical practice of its day, but it is equally important to understand its setting in the context of electrical research and technology.

'Living in an electrical century'

The London season of 1747 was more than metaphorically brilliant. 'Was you ever electrified?' asked that tireless correspondent, Mrs Elizabeth Carter of Miss Catherine Talbot, and went on to offer her the intriguing details:

> We have an itinerant philosopher here who knocks people down for the moderate consideration of sixpence, and men, women and children are electrified out of their senses. This is at present the universal topic of discourse. The fine ladies forget their cards and scandal to talk of the effects of electricity.[5]

In the same year, William Watson, recently awarded the Royal Society's Copley Medal and known as England's leading 'electrician', demonstrated the velocity of electricity in experiments that sent a charge across Westminster bridge and back through the Thames and through a four-mile circuit at Shooter's Hill just outside London. Nor was electricity merely a local sensation. In Philadelphia, Benjamin Franklin passed the spring and summer pursuing a well designed series of significant electrical experiments on the newly discovered 'Leyden Jar' (he as yet had no thoughts of kites and keys), forwarding his results to Peter Collinson, a member of the Royal Society, in a series of letters.[6] Late in the year, in Geneva, Switzerland, professor Jean Jallabert carried out a remarkable cure of a locksmith's paralyzed arm by repeatedly and gently stimulating the atrophied muscles with small electric shocks.[7] And in the autumn of 1747, John Wesley, who had published the first edition of *Primitive Physic* that summer, also 'went with two or three friends, to see what are called the electrical experiments' and recorded his responses in his *Journal*:

> How must these [experiments] also confound those poor half-thinkers, who will believe nothing but what they can comprehend? Who can comprehend, how fire lives in water, and passes through it more freely than through air? How flame issues out of my finger, real flame, such as sets fire to spirits of wine? How these, and many more as strange

phenomena, arise from the turning round a glass globe? It is all mystery: If haply by any means God may hide pride from man![8]

From the ridiculous to the sublime, the signs of a new science were everywhere. Furthermore, it was a rapidly changing science. In Britain, in America and on the Continent, investigators from professors to skilled amateurs, worked solo and in teams – and, of course, competed – to discover and demonstrate the properties of electricity, its roles in nature, and its effects on the human body: in short, to show how it might be understood, its destructive potential tamed and its powers applied. As one of these investigators would ask, 'Does it not appear . . . that we are living in an electrical century?'[9]

It is difficult to find a contemporary analogy both for the rapid flowering of electrical science in the eighteenth century and for its cultural pervasiveness. Perhaps the closest comparison is the development of modern physics in the first four decades of the twentieth century (indeed, the classic survey of electricity in the eighteenth century makes the connection explicit in its subtitle, 'A Study in Early Modern Physics'[10]) – but, although relativity and quantum mechanics captured popular interest, particularly in the engaging figure of Albert Einstein, neither was a game that anyone could play. The many applications of computers suggest a parallel cultural pervasiveness, but key names in the development of that new science are not well known nor their works widely read.

But although these recent advances offer no direct parallel to the growth of electrical science in the eighteenth century, they do afford indirectly relevant models of rapid scientific change. Non-scientists are apt to regard scientific progress as a smooth process working at a steady rate. Such is rarely, if ever, the case. Rapid advances – the kind of situation in which a whole field of study is born or reshaped within a decade or two – take place when a number of insightful and creative investigators are engaged in exploring phenomena that suggest a dramatically new or different interpretation of how the world works (as in twentieth-century physics) or a broad and diverse range of hitherto inaccessible but highly useful applications (as in computer science). Electricity in the eighteenth century met both criteria at the same time.[11] It is especially important to emphasize that the cultural pervasiveness of electricity made it an important feature of everyday life and thought for educated people in Wesley's milieu, and not merely a specialty for natural philosophers.

By the middle of the eighteenth century, it was clear that the discoveries in electricity had indeed significantly changed the understanding of nature. In 1755, a professor at the University of Uppsala saw the studies in electricity up to that time as culminating in and being given meaning by Benjamin Franklin's demonstration of the electrical nature of lightning three years previously: 'forty years ago, when one knew nothing about electricity but its simplest effects, . . . who would have believed that it could have any connection with one of the greatest and most considerable phenomena in Nature, thunder and lightning?'[12] Exercising a not unreasonable national pride, an Englishman might have dated the beginning of the new electrical science to the first, rather than the second, decade of the century. From 1704 to 1709, Francis Hauksbee, chief experimentalist to the Royal Society under Isaac Newton, published a series of experiments on light and electricity in the Society's *Philosophical Transactions*, and both in the experiments themselves and in his methods and apparatus Hauksbee set the pattern for studies to come.[13] Following on the work of Robert Boyle, Hauksbee devised a way to test what substances would give off light in a vacuum by constructing a simple friction assembly inside a glass chamber evacuated by an air pump. The interesting results obtained, especially from amber and glass, prompted Hauksbee to build an electrical machine, the basic design of which was followed in almost all those made and used in the eighteenth century. The operation of the machine was simple and direct: a glass globe or cylinder was turned by a crank and pulley system as it was being rubbed (by hand). The electrostatic energy collected on the glass produced various visible effects such as light and sparks. Hauksbee also found that a fine glass tube, rubbed vigorously with paper, attracted bits of thin brass leaf and produced a breeze-like sensation when brought near the face.

While Hauksbee was busy generating (so to speak) new demonstrations of the properties of electricity for the meetings of the Royal Society, a Canterbury dyer and versatile self-taught scientific amateur called Stephen Gray was also engaged in electrical experiments. His studies on the sorts of things that could and could not be electrified, and the distance over which an electrical charge could travel, became a full-time occupation when he was admitted as a pensioner of the Charterhouse in 1719. Over the next ten years he found that many different objects, when suspended by silk cord (which today we recognize as a non-conductor), could transmit the electrical properties along their length. In 1729, Gray's imaginative persistence in seeking new conductors culminated in his suspending a small 'charity boy' – a pupil at the Charterhouse school – by silk cords, applying a charged glass rod to the boy's bare feet, and drawing sparks from the boy's nose. Both the electrical properties of human beings and new vistas in the entertainment potential of electrical experiments were simultaneously demonstrated.

Had Gray carried out this famous experiment a decade earlier, that 'charity boy' might have been John Wesley, who was a student at the Charterhouse from 1714 to 1720. (Wesley retained a life-long fondness for Charterhouse, and would later note the Charterhouse connection of this famous experiment.)[14] Despite missing a childhood opportunity for direct involvement in electrical research, however, Wesley reached Oxford in an era when the teaching of physics was more and more by demonstration and experiment. Indeed, Oxford could lay claim to the first use of this innovative method, thanks to John Keill, and his successor the Revd Jean Théophile Desaguliers (who was soon to succeed Hauksbee as chief experimenter of the Royal Society). Both were dedicated followers of Isaac Newton whose personal as well as intellectual influence continued to dominate the field of natural philosophy (Newton lived until 1727). Teaching physical science by demonstrations exemplified Newton's commitment to experiment – as Newton famously said, 'I frame no hypotheses' – over against Descartes's more speculative natural philosophy; followers of Newton were therefore keen to pursue 'matters of fact' and to steer clear of 'hypotheses'. Nor did one have to be actively engaged with natural philosophy to share the commitment to observation and experience: 'matters of fact, based on first-hand experience and reliable reports . . . , were held to be basic to both historical and scientific knowledge.'[15]

By the time of Wesley's matriculation the teaching of physics – that is, Newtonian mechanics – through a course of logically progressing demonstrations was well established not only at Oxford but also at Cambridge.[16] Although contemporary scholar Samuel Rogal claims that Wesley had 'no formal training in the natural or physical sciences,' there is evidence that he not only had access to first class education in these areas, but also took advantage of it.[17] John Whitehead, the physician and local preacher who was Wesley's friend and early biographer, noted specifically that at college Wesley 'studied with a good deal of care' not only Euclid's geometry and Newton's *Opticks* but also the work of the above-mentioned Keill, whose textbook of natural philosophy (originally published in Latin) became available in English in 1720.[18] In addition, John Cule mentions that Wesley's physics notebook still exists.[19]

Over the next two decades, much of the most significant work in electricity took place on the Continent, with the elaboration of theoretical frameworks taking place largely in France and work on instrument design in Germany.[20] The discovery that revolutionized the field, however, came from the Netherlands. In 1746, Pieter van Musschenbroek, a staunch Newtonian who taught a demonstration-based course in mechanics at the University of Leiden and also participated in the family business of building scientific instruments, reported that when a glass jar of any size or shape was used to collect the electricity produced by friction, a very powerful charge could be obtained by completing a circuit from the inside to the outside of the jar, a charge so strong one would not willingly suffer it a second time.[21] The operation of this simple condenser, known ever after as a 'Leyden Jar', could not be explained by any theory of the day, and like Gray's 'flying boy' it proved irresistible to experimentalists and entertainers alike. Readers of *Philosophical Transactions* and *The Gentleman's Magazine* (John Wesley read both) could follow the rapidly accumulating number of experiments on electricity.[22] Almost anyone of even modest means, whether man or woman, adult or youth, who was eager to see or take part in electrical demonstrations could find a way to do so.[23] The age of electricity had unmistakably arrived.

'Having procured an apparatus on purpose . . .'

Although the tone of Wesley's 1747 comments on 'the electrical experiments' is one of wonder and amazement at the paradoxical nature of this newly discovered form of fire, he did not stop there and simply marvel at the mystery. That he had been reading the leading figures in British electrical science is implied in the sources listed in *The Desideratum*; he quickly recognized most significant work of the time, the 'experiments and observations' of the American investigator Benjamin Franklin, as is evident from his *Journal*:

> *Sat.* 17 [Feb 1753]. – From Dr. Franklin's Letters I learned,
> 1. That electrical fire (or ether) is a species of fire, infinitely finer than any other yet known.
> 2. That it is diffused, and in nearly equal proportions, through almost all substances.
> 3. That as long as it is thus diffused, it has no discernible effect.
> 4. That if any quantity of it be collected together, whether by art or nature, it then becomes visible in the form of fire, and inexpressibly powerful.
> 5. That it is essentially different from the light of the sun; for it pervades a thousand bodies which light cannot penetrate, and yet cannot penetrate glass, which light pervades so freely.
> 6. That lightning is no other than electrical fire, collected by one or more clouds.

7. That all the effects of lightning may be performed by the artificial electric fire.

8. That any thing pointed, as a spire or tree, attracts the lightning, just as a needle does the electrical fire.

9. That the electrical fire, discharged on a rat or a fowl, will kill it instantly: But discharged on one dipped in water, will slide off, and do it no hurt at all. In like manner the lightning which will kill a man in a moment, will not hurt him, if he be thoroughly wet. What an amazing scene is here opened for after-ages to improve upon![24]

Since 'Dr. Franklin's Letters' played a significant role for Wesley in writing *The Desideratum*, it is worth exploring this brief entry. Although Benjamin Franklin had been sending reports of his experiments to Peter Collinson to be read before the Royal Society since 1747, they had not appeared in the *Philosophical Transactions*.[25] Seeking a wider audience, Collinson took them to Edward Cave ('Sylvanus Urban'), publisher of *The Gentleman's Magazine*, who not only published them together as a pamphlet, but also featured some of the discoveries in his magazine in advance.[26] The first printing of the first edition of Franklin's *Experiments and Observations* was in 1751, and a second printing, *Supplemental Experiments and Observations on Electricity*, which differed from the first only in an expanded section of errata, took place in 1753.[27] In 1753, Franklin received honorary doctorates from both Harvard and Yale, and late in the year would also receive the Copley medal, all in recognition of the importance of the material in his 'Letters.'

Even a cursory examination of Wesley's summary and Franklin's original text shows that Wesley did not merely abstract and summarize this work, but rather studied it carefully in order to present Franklin's findings as a whole. Franklin's landmark work is, after all, a series of letters: unlike a modern scientific paper, he did not begin with a theoretical part that reviews recent work on the subject and lays out a series of experiments designed to evaluate a particular hypothesis. Instead, Franklin's letters began with a series of observations on the power of 'points' (the experiment used a household bodkin) to '*throw off* as well as *draw off* the electrical fire' (observations that proved central to the invention of the lightning rod), and did not turn to 'opinions and conjectures' until the sixth piece in the pamphlet.[28] Wesley selected ideas and phrases from the sixth piece, which begins with the general observation that 'electrical matter consists of particles extremely subtile'.[29] For the most part, Wesley followed the order of the topics treated in 'Opinions and Conjectures' simply moving the biological observations to the conclusion of his list so as to progress from the essential nature of 'the electrical fire (or ether)' through its manifestations in the world and conclude with its effects on living creatures. We will find him using precisely this order for the 'philosophical' part of *The Desideratum*, which also draws heavily on Franklin's work.

But how did Wesley come to the idea of using electricity as a cheap, safe and versatile medicine? It seems to have occurred almost simultaneously to many of those who were exploring electricity that its strong physiological effects on living things – observed with plants as well as animals – would indicate that it could be useful in treating disease. Indeed, the second-century medical author Galen, whose work defined European medicine throughout the medieval era and was still considered authoritative by many in Wesley's day, noted that the sting of the electric ray, or 'torpedo fish', treated headache by 'numb[ing] the senses'.[30] Electrotherapy seems to have been in use at the University of Halle in 1744–5, at the Edinburgh Royal Infirmary in 1751 and at Shrewsbury Hospital in 1754.[31] By this last time, however, John Wesley had already heard directly about successful electrical treatments and recommended the use of 'electrification' as a 'new remedy':

> *Sat.* 20 [Jan 1753]. – I advised one who had been troubled many years with stubborn paralytic disorder, to try a new remedy. Accordingly, she was electrified, and found immediate help. By the same means I have known two persons cured of an inveterate pain in the stomach; and another of a pain in his side, which he had had ever since he was a child. Nevertheless, who can wonder that many gentlemen of the Faculty, as well as their good friends, the apothecaries, decry a medicine so shockingly cheap and easy, as much as they do quicksilver and tar-water?[32]

This was precisely the area in which electricity intersected with one of Wesley's main concerns, health care for the poor. It may not be coincidental that the very next entry in Wesley's *Journal* after his review of Franklin's work was '*Wed.* 21. – I visited more of the poor sick.' Indeed, by this time he had already been running what amounted to a free clinic at the Foundry for some time, and having written of it in 1748:

> But I was still in pain for many of the poor that were sick; there was so great expense, and so little profit . . . I saw the poor people pining away, and several families ruined, and that without remedy. At length I thought of a kind of desperate expedient. 'I will prepare, and give them physic myself.' For six or seven and twenty years, I had made anatomy

and physic the diversion of my leisure hours; though I never properly studied them, unless for a few months when I was going to America, where I imagined I might be of some service to those who had no regular physician among them. I applied to it again. I took into my assistance an apothecary, and an experienced surgeon; resolving, at the same time, not to go out of my depth, but to leave all difficult and complicated cases to such physicians as the patients should choose. I gave notice of this to the society; telling them, that all who were ill of chronical distempers (for I did not care to venture upon acute) might, if they pleased, come to me at such a time, and I would give them the best advice I could, and the best medicines I had.[33]

What seems to have been the decisive step in convincing John Wesley that electrical treatment was not only among the best available medicines – perhaps, indeed, the best, given its versatility – but also ideally suited for use in a free clinic was a book on the medical applications of electricity, which appeared in 1756. Bearing the resounding partial title *The Subtil Medium Prov'd; or, that Wonderful Power of Nature, so long ago conjectur'd by the Most Ancient and Remarkable Philosophers, which they call'd Sometimes Aether, but oftener, Elementary Fire, verify'd*, this book by Richard Lovett, a lay clerk at Worcester Cathedral then in his sixties, is commonly regarded as the first work in English on electrotherapy.[34] Lovett's book comprises four 'Dialogues', the first two 'showing that all the distinguishing and essential qualities ascribed to ether by [the ancient] and the most modern philosophers, are to be found in electrical fire, and that, too, in the utmost degree of perfection', to quote the rest of the title, and the third and fourth on the uses of electricity in medicine, including reports of his own experiments and the cases he treated. That Wesley found this work highly influential is clear both from the weight placed upon it in *The Desideratum* and the speedy introduction of an electrical apparatus into his practice.

So it was that, a little over nine years from his first journal entry on electricity, John Wesley entered the brand-new field of electrotherapy himself. His involvement grew rapidly, as did his conviction of the value of this new treatment:

Having procured an apparatus on purpose, I ordered several persons to be electrified, who were ill of various disorders; some of whom found an immediate, some a gradual, cure. From this time I appointed, first some hours in every week, and afterward an hour in everyday, wherein any that desired it, might try the virtue of this surprising medicine. Two or three years after, our patients were so numerous that we were obliged to divide them: So part were electrified in Southwark, part at the Foundry, others near St. Paul's, and the rest near the Seven-Dials: The same method we have taken ever since; and to this day, while hundreds, perhaps thousands, have received unspeakable good, I have not known one man, woman, or child, who has received any hurt thereby: So that when I hear any talk of the danger of being electrified, (especially if they are medical men who talk so,) I cannot but impute it to great want either of sense or honesty.[35]

By the end of 1759, he was completing his own work on 'this curious and important subject', *The Desideratum: Or, Electricity made plain and useful. By a Lover of Mankind, and of Common Sense*, which was published (anonymously) early in 1760.

'This unparalleled remedy'

The Desideratum did not remain anonymous for long. In the same year, a correspondent of many aliases asked Wesley, in the public forum of the *London Magazine*, '"Why did you meddle with electricity?" For the same reason as I published the "Primitive Physic", – to do as much good as I can', Wesley responded.[36] His 'Preface' to *The Desideratum* says as much. This brief (five-page) introduction has received far more attention from scholars than the work it introduces, an imbalance that has tended to skew how it is read at a few significant points.

In outline, the ten paragraphs that constitute the 'Preface' are a clear, concise statement of what Wesley intended to cover, why the subject is significant, and what he hoped to accomplish through the work. What he intended to cover was the best recent work on electricity:

In the following tract, I have endeavoured to comprise the sum of what has been hitherto published, on this curious and important subject, by Mr. Franklin, Dr. Hoadly, Mr. Wilson, Watson, Lovett, Freke, Martin, Watkins, and in the monthly magazines. But I am chiefly indebted to Mr. Franklin for the speculative part, and to Mr. Lovett, for the practical: tho' I cannot in every thing subscribe to the sentiments either of one or the other.[37]

Although few readers today would recognize any name other than Franklin, all of the other authors were well known at the time. What is more, their contributions outlined an extremely productive decade of work in electricity. William Watson published at least one paper a year on this subject in *Philosophical Transactions* from 1744 to 1753. Benjamin Martin, John Freke (Martin's opponent), Benjamin Wilson and Francis Watkins all published substantial essays on electricity in the banner year of 1746; Wilson published a full treatise in 1750, Freke in 1752, Franklin's outstanding work appeared in 1753, and Wilson teamed with Dr Benjamin Hoadly in a series of experiments on electrical resistance published in 1756. That was also the year of Lovett's first work on the medical applications of electricity, which he followed with a second part in 1759 and an appendix in 1760. Wilson continued to publish until 1780 and Lovett summed up his own work and interests in *The Electrical Philosopher* in 1774.[38] By 1760, the central importance of Franklin's work was widely recognized: Wesley's emphasis on Franklin would have received agreement from all investigators in the field.

Nor is his statement of the emphasis he has chosen to put on the medical side as unscientific, or antiscientific, as it is sometimes taken to be. Following the idea that he did not agree completely with either Franklin or Lovett, Wesley wrote:

> Indeed I am not greatly concerned for the philosophical part, whether it stand or fall. Of the facts we are absolutely assured . . . But who can be assured of this or that hypothesis, by which he endeavours to account for those facts? Perhaps the utmost we have reason to expect here is an high degree of probability. I am much more concerned for the physical part, knowing of how great importance this is: how much sickness and pain may be prevented or removed, and how many lives saved by this unparalleled remedy.[39]

Far from 'dismiss[ing] the philosophical (or scientific) considerations of electricity', or being opposed to theory as a result of lack of interest in mathematics, Wesley was here clearly commenting on the state of electrical research, still dogged by many inexplicable observations.[40] Although Franklin's theory of electricity as one 'fluid' (the presence or absence of which could be described as positive or negative) had largely won out over the idea of two different kinds of electricity, the phenomenon of induced charge remained both a theoretical puzzle and a practical complication.[41] But the 'physical' – we would say physiological – effects of electricity could be applied in useful ways without necessarily understanding them in full, and that was what Wesley proposed to show. That Wesley did not dismiss theory in favour of practice is immediately obvious upon turning to the body of *The Desideratum*, in which the first part – the 'philosophical' part – is actually slightly longer than the second, or 'physical', part.

But what gave urgency to the 'physical' part for Wesley was the dire situation in medical care, especially for the poor. The preference of physicians for 'exotics' over 'simple remedies' inevitably led, Wesley believed, to the rejection of any new agent that is efficacious in a broad range of diseases.[42] Sharp remarks about physicians and apothecaries occur throughout Wesley's works.[43] Nowhere is this more pointed than in his sermon, 'On the Use of Money', written in 1744, preached again in 1758 and 1759, and published in 1760:

> And are not they partakers of the same guilt [of harming the neighbour in his body], though in a lower degree, whether surgeons, apothecaries, or physicians, who play with the lives or health of men, to enlarge their own gain? Who purposely lengthen the pain or disease which they are able to remove speedily? Who protract the cure of their patient's body in order to plunder his substance? Can any man be clear before God who does not shorten every disorder 'as much as he can' and remove all sickness and pain 'as soon as he can?' He cannot: For nothing can be more clear than that he does not 'love his neighbour as himself'; than that he does not 'do unto others as he would they should do unto himself'.[44]

It is surely not coincidental that, as Wesley preached this sermon and prepared it for publication in the same time period as he was preparing *The Desideratum*, its thoughts should inform the purpose of the latter work, and, indeed, the same sense of a medical crisis compounded by greed and lack of neighbourly love recurs throughout the Preface.[45] In the years when the intellectually curious were following the newest developments in electricity, disease, especially among the poorest of the poor, was ravaging London to an extent that some writers compared with the plague years.[46] In the first half of the century, eight London hospitals were built or renovated to serve the poor, and in the twelve months preceding May 1748, these hospitals treated more than 30,500 patients.[47] After 1750, the situation improved somewhat, especially for young children, but there was still a serious shortfall of medical practitioners, even including laymen.[48] Although John Wesley enjoyed cordial personal relations with some physicians, and had a surgeon and an apothecary at the Foundry, his personal experience among the poor apparently made this an emotional as well as a practical issue for him.[49] It was also always a spiritual issue as well, as it was for many of the time who were concerned with the life of piety and compassion.[50] As we will see, Wesley's personal experience among the sick poor included not only visitation but also direct involvement in their treatment.

Having reviewed the 'simple remedies' previously scorned by physicians and apothecaries, Wesley then turned to describing electricity's remarkable record of success in treating a broad range of ills but also the sometimes 'unaccountable' responses to its use. For example, in 'paralytic' cases, initially encouraging results were often followed by relapse, whereas frequently in 'rheumatic' cases, after some initial deterioration, there was eventually a lasting improvement.[51] But there was one particular application in which one could accurately call electricity 'the Desideratum, the general and rarely failing remedy, in nervous cases of every kind (palsies excepted)'.[52] This statement has led many a twentieth-century reader to conclude that Wesley was proposing the use of electricity primarily for the treatment of mental disease or psychological conditions.[53] Although Wesley elsewhere called physicians' use of the word 'nervous' 'a good cover for learned ignorance',[54] here he immediately turned to the possible connections between electricity and hypotheses about the structure and function of peripheral nerves:

> Perhaps if the nerves are really perforated (as is now generally supposed) the electric ether is the only fluid in the universe which is fine enough to move through them. And what if the nervous juice itself be a fluid of this kind? If so, it is no wonder that it has always eluded the search of the most accurate naturalists.[55]

As we will see, these ideas fit within a descriptive model of human physiology that is still recognizable, although differing in emphasis from that most familiar in the West today.

In the last three paragraphs of the 'Preface', Wesley brought together each of its main themes under the idea with which he began, that the current state of electrical knowledge had come about by the sharing of results among many individuals. In view of the expected rejection of electrical treatment by the 'Gentlemen of the [medical] Faculty' and the apothecaries,

> let men of sense do the best they can for themselves, as well as for their poor, sick, helpless neighbours ... And if a few of these lovers of mankind, who have some little knowledge of the animal economy, would only be diligent in making experiments, and setting down the more remarkable of them, in order to communicate them to one another, that

each might profit by the other's labour: I doubt not, but more nervous disorders would be cured in one year, by this single remedy, than the whole *English Materia Medica* will cure by the end of the century.[56]

Finally, Wesley pointed out that his work was intentionally 'little more than an extract from others' prepared 'for the use of those who have little time or money to spare', and urged 'some who has more leisure and ability than me' to write a detailed practical work on electricity 'which might be a blessing to many generations.'[57]

'From a thousand experiments'

One of the reasons that so much less has been written on the body of *The Desideratum* than on its 'Preface' may be that, on the first reading (or the first three) one's eyes glaze over. For the first part in particular, it is almost a disadvantage to know anything about electricity. The reader is soon immersed in an unfamiliar scientific vocabulary, positive and negative are defined in a sense precisely opposite to the way those terms are used today, and, early on, the properties of electricity are confused with those of oxygen (which was not discovered and described as an element until the middle of the next decade). Furthermore, since Wesley did not cite sources in the modern way, readers have sometimes assumed either that none of it is Wesley's work, or that all of it is, including the experiment of sealing a cat in an oven with a lighted candle, which is instead a slightly modified summary of one of Robert Boyle's best-known experiments.[58]

However, if one takes Wesley at his word – that he was 'chiefly indebted to Mr. Franklin for the speculative part, and to Mr. Lovett, for the practical' – the confusions begin to clear.[59] A careful reading of Franklin's *Experiments and Observations on Electricity* not only shows how Wesley used Franklin's work to anchor this part of his book but also suggests where Wesley's conceptual framework for understanding electricity differed from Franklin's and gives the reader a clearer picture of the audience that Wesley had in mind in writing the book.[60]

As noted above, not until the sixth piece in his *Experiments* did Franklin review his own work to date in an orderly and 'philosophical' way; this piece, dating from 1749, is titled 'Opinions and Conjectures'.[61] For the person who wants primarily to know what electricity is, rather than how to carry out experiments with it, this would be the place to begin – and as Wesley's 1753 *Journal* entry shows, he took 'Opinions and Conjectures' as the theme and outline of all of Franklin's *Experiments*.[62]

However, although the general plan of this section in *The Desideratum* follows the order of his 1753 summary, Wesley expanded upon the summary in significant ways. In order to understand his own contributions to this part it is helpful to examine exactly how Wesley used Franklin's *Experiments*. This may at first appear to be easy to do, because John Wesley often quoted directly or paraphrased very closely from his source. But if one actually correlates the material step by step, as Wesley would have had to do, it becomes evident that a great deal of work was required to craft an overview in which the ideas 'follow upon one another in a simple and clear manner designed to please'.[63] After an introduction of 12 paragraphs, which will be treated in more detail below, Wesley addressed three issues using Franklin's work: the properties of electricity, the Leyden Jar and the effects of electrical shocks, and electrical phenomena in nature, principally lightning.

Wesley's description of the general qualities of what Franklin called 'electrical matter', paragraphs I.13–28 in *The Desideratum*, at first follows closely the order as well as the content of Franklin's 'Opinions and Conjectures'. Wesley then drew from two other letters of Franklin's to say more about the particular ability of 'points' to draw charge, the natural quantity of electricity in different kinds of matter, resistance and the limit to electrification. He returned to 'Opinions and Conjectures' to talk about the strength of the electrical atmosphere that surrounds an object, filling in, again, from Franklin's other letters.[64] Some of these letters postdated the 1751 edition of Franklin's *Experiments*, so Wesley would have had to refer to newer editions than the one he first read. Next, in I.29–31, Wesley gathered together information about the properties of the Leyden Jar, the effects of electrical shocks on birds, small animals and humans, the power of an electric shock to reverse the polarity of a compass needle and penetrate a thick stack of paper, and experiments showing that the reservoir of electricity is the earth and that dry and moist air conduct electricity differently. These subjects are found to range among several of Franklin's letters.[65] This transition to atmospheric effects allowed Wesley to consider at length (in I.32–42) the phenomenon of lightning and, more briefly, other observations about possible roles of electricity in nature. This portion drew heavily on Franklin's letter on 'Thunder-gusts', using 30 of its 56 paragraphs on lightning and another six on the *aurora borealis*, and of course included the famous 'kite' experiment (a separate letter), as well as a discussion of lightning rods (from 'Opinions and Conjectures').[66]

In using Franklin's work as a basis for explaining electricity, Wesley dealt with few of Franklin's actual experiments. He was, however, careful to mention things of practical significance, for example the construction of the Leyden Jar and the use of lightning rods. To the latter he appended a short discussion of a question much debated in the day, that is, whether such protective devices contravened the will of God. He concluded that it was 'no more an impeachment of his Providence, when we foresee a storm of lightning and rain, to shelter our house (as far as we are able) from the one, than to shelter ourselves in that house from the other'.[67] In light of the criticisms of Wesley as lacking interest in theory, it is particularly notable that he was careful to include two of Franklin's 'thought experiments': one visualizing the ability of points to draw off charge as being like pulling the hairs from a horse's tail one at a time, and the other a simple quantitative example illustrating the conservation of charge in a Leyden Jar.[68]

In reading this part of *The Desideratum*, one is reminded of Whitehead's observation that, among academic subjects, Wesley showed the least aptitude for writing about history because it required dealing with masses of detail.[69] But in this case, did Wesley skim over much of Franklin's experimental work because he found it uninteresting, because he saw it as unnecessary detail for a 'plain and useful' description, because he believed its conclusions were more probable than certain, or because his understanding of electricity was shaped by a somewhat different conceptual framework from Franklin's? That Wesley lacked the temperament for appreciating experiment is not borne out in *The Desideratum*, since he gave over the remainder of the 'speculative' part to brief accounts of the experiments of (in order) Watson, Wilson, Martin and Watkins, emphasizing their work on the relationship between electricity and fire and, in the case of Martin, electricity's effects on human circulation.[70] Wesley stressed throughout *The Desideratum* that his aim was a clear, plain and logical (and, one might infer, uncluttered) exposition of electricity for those most interested in its therapeutic usefulness. His contention that 'the utmost we have reason to expect here is an high degree of probability'[71] agreed with Franklin, who not only continually revised his ideas about electricity based on his own work and that of others but also pointed out that one doesn't need a complete understanding of electricity to use it in practical ways, any more than one needs a complete understanding of the physics of gravity to build a shelf capable of keeping one's china from falling to the floor.[72]

This leaves open, however, the issue of Wesley's conceptual framework for understanding electricity. When one reads *The Desideratum* and Franklin's 'Opinions and Conjectures' side by side, one is immediately struck by just such a difference. Franklin began his summary, as noted above, by describing the 'electrical matter', and introduced the idea of electricity as a fluid within a few paragraphs. Thereafter, he described the properties of electricity in both particulate and fluid terms, for example, noting that electricity fills common matter as water fills a sponge, but within the pores of matter, the particles of electricity are so oriented as to minimize their mutual repulsion, that is, on the corners of an equilateral triangle, the dimensions of which are determined by the quantity of electricity in matter.[73] Wesley's 12-paragraph introduction to Part I of *The Desideratum* sets out a very different conceptual framework for the start:

> From a thousand experiments it appears that there is a fluid far more subtle than air, which is everywhere diffused thro' all space, which surrounds the Earth and pervades every part of it. And such is the extreme fineness, velocity, and expansiveness of this active Principle, that all other matter seems to be only the body, and this the soul of the Universe . . . This great machine of the World requires some such constant, active, and powerful Principle, constituted by its Creator, to keep the heavenly bodies in their several courses, and at the same time give support, life, and increase to the various inhabitants of the earth. Now as the heart of every animal is the engine which circulates the blood thro' the whole body, so the sun, as the heart of the world, circulates this fire thro' the whole universe. And this element is not capable of any essential alteration, increase, or diminution. It is a species by itself; and is of a nature totally distinct from that of all other bodies.[74]

This emphasis on electricity as an elemental energy, for which Wesley used George Berkeley's expression 'the soul of the universe', was also consistent with the Newtonian language of 'ethers'.[75] But, rather than beginning his 'plain and useful' work with a digression into abstruse philosophy, Wesley's introduction immediately placed the subject of electricity into a coherent and self-consistent framework capable of connecting both experimental results and natural phenomena (recall his emphasis on Franklin's work on lightning) to animal physiology, thereby giving a rationale for electrotherapy in medicine. That framework drew in a significant way on the great discoveries of the preceding century that had made British medical science the world standard.

William Harvey's 1628 work on the circulation of the blood inspired a generation of colleagues and protégés to explore the role of vessels in human anatomy and physiology. In the 1650s and 1660s, associates of Harvey published major texts on the circulation of bile and of lymph, on the function of spleen, glands and nerves, and on cerebral anatomy.[76] By the 1680s, British books on anatomy and physiology dominated Western medicine.[77] All of these discoveries – which rapidly opened new avenues

for investigation in other sciences – rested on meticulous work in anatomy, carried out by dissection. By John Wesley's university days, it was
accepted as a matter of course that anyone who was interested in medicine
must read anatomy. Eunice Bonow Bardell's careful study of Wesley's
diary notes from Curnock, in addition to an unpublished letter in the
Herrnhut archives, suggest that Wesley's anatomy studies must have been
more than just 'the diversion of [his] leisure hours'.[78] While in Georgia,
Wesley not only read and discussed a new book on anatomy with Swiss
Huguenot physician Jean Regnier, but also attended the autopsy of a
member of the Moravian community, whose leader commented that 'Mr
Wesley . . . understands anatomy very well.'[79] And what all the anatomical studies of the time emphasized, following on the brilliant work of
Harveian research physicians, was that the vessels and their fluids were
key to understanding the human organism. Such a conceptual framework
emphasized the harmonious working of the body as a whole through the
several networks that provide communication among its parts. In this, the
as yet unknown fluid proper to the nerves must play a key role. Electricity
– which could remain invisibly bound to air or water, which could flow to
or from the earth through a human being, and which, among its effects,
noticeably accelerated the pulse and the motion of blood through the
vessels – appeared to be a very convincing candidate for the role of the
hitherto elusive 'nervous juice'.[80] This is the framework that pulls together
Wesley's thoughts on 'ethereal fire', his selections from Franklin and other
'electricians', and his preference for physicians like Thomas Sydenham
and George Cheyne who focused on the body as a 'well-working' whole.[81]

'The grand instrument of life'

These key attributes – the power of electricity, its apparent ability to com-
bine with and be 'tempered' by air and water, and its marked effect on
circulation – render it, according to Wesley's brief introduction to the
'practical' part of The Desideratum, 'the grand instrument of life', with
the kind of pervasive influence proposed by Berkeley. However, believing
that 'plain matters of fact weigh more than nice speculative reasoning',
Wesley went immediately to brief remarks about 'the disorders in which
[electrification] has been of unquestionable use', and thence to case
studies of actual treatments.[82] In this section Wesley was, as he noted in
the 'Preface', just as indebted to Lovett as he had been to Franklin in the
preceding part.

Indeed, a careful comparison with The Subtil Medium Prov'd suggests that Wesley relied on Lovett for more than the technical aspects of electro-therapy. Nor was he unwise to do so. Although Richard Lovett apologized in his preface for his own lack of classical education, which he feared might be evident in poor grammar, to today's reader his style is straightforward and engaging, his presentation clear and his overall approach more 'scientific' (in the modern sense) even than Franklin's, with appropriate use of original experiments and careful recording of clinical data.[83] In an age when science was not yet subdivided into specialties or fenced off from the curious by years of formal training, significant contributions were often made by 'amateurs': Franklin earned his living as a printer, Wilson as a painter and Martin as a maker of scientific instruments, to name a few. Against this background, Richard Lovett's experience marked him as a capable and serious student of electricity. He had attended the lectures of the Royal Society's chief experimenter Desaguliers,[84] met with William Watson to discuss the apparent acceleration of fluid flow by electricity (and devised his own experiment to test Watson's proposal),[85] gathered and analysed literature reports of electrical treatment and compiled seven years of his own case studies.[86] Furthermore, he had thought carefully about the rationale for electrical treatment, how it might act physiologically, and why it sometimes succeeded and sometimes failed in treating the same condition.

John Wesley's *Desideratum* shows a debt to Lovett in many of these areas. Wesley followed an ordering of topics similar to Lovett's in his introductory paragraphs.[87] Like Lovett, he considered electricity and 'ethereal fire' to be synonyms.[88] He attributed the vital functions of air to this 'fire' and gave an important role to Berkeley in making this connection.[89] Furthermore, in reading Lovett one sees clearly and fully laid out the circulation-based physiology that is implied by Wesley. Lovett had his imaginary interlocutor ask in Dialogue IV, 'Wherein do you imagine the specific quality of the electrical virtue chiefly to consist?' and answered by proposing that it promotes unobstructed, 'free circulation'.[90] Increased circulation of the blood could reduce inflammation and disperse 'clogs' (sometimes used of situations where we might today say 'toxins').[91] Increased circulation of nervous fluid, 'whether it be the nervous fluid of anatomists, or this fluid ether', could reverse numbness, and even raise spirits in a way similar to exercise.[92] In short, it was the cause of all the organs performing their proper functions harmoniously, leading to a healthy body.[93]

This fuller picture of optimum bodily function helps a great deal in understanding Wesley's briefer account of nervous diseases. Upon listing 44 'disorders in which [electrification] has been of unquestionable use', running alphabetically from 'agues' and 'blindness' to 'tooth-ach' and 'wen', Wesley commented,

> It will easily be observed that a great part of these are of the nervous kind; and perhaps there is no nervous distemper whatsoever, which would not yield to a steady use of this remedy. It seems therefore to be the grand *Desideratum* in physic, from which we may expect relief . . . even in many of the most painful and stubborn disorders to which the human frame is subject.[94]

To the modern reader, for whom the occasional antiquated names (such as 'King's Evil' for tubercular abscess or 'bronchocele' for goitre) are enough of an obstacle, there is nothing 'easy' in observing the number of 'nervous' diseases in the list. It is this that has led some readers to suppose that Wesley meant diseases of hysterical or psychosomatic origin.[95] On the other hand, if one simply counts those diseases that clearly involve the peripheral or central nervous systems, in other words, that involve pain, loss of nerve or muscle function, or seizures, almost half of the conditions listed qualify. Using Lovett's understanding of a close relationship between the circulatory and nervous systems, several more might be added.

One might well wonder, then, since Wesley drew so heavily from Lovett in this part of the *Desideratum*, what he himself contributed. The answer is simple, definite and surprising: nearly half of the case studies in the *Desideratum* come from Wesley's own clinics, and, given the level of detail, most of them seem to be from Wesley himself.

It is not difficult to verify this. As Wesley moved down the alphabetical list of illnesses, giving one or more examples of treatment for each one, he put in quotes each one that was abstracted from Lovett's book, followed by the citation 'Mr. L.' Of the 97 case studies, 27 are directly attributed to Lovett. Nine other studies come from Sweden; we learn from *The Subtil Medium* that Dr Zetzell communicated several of these from Uppsala through the *Gentleman's Magazine* of July 1755.[96] Another case came from 'Mr. Floyer, a surgeon in Dorchester' via Lovett, as well as the case of a man with a palsied tongue from the hospital in Edinburgh. Three accounts, all of them dealing with eye diseases, came from 'a gentleman in Newcastle upon Tyne', and a detailed description of the course of treatment for a West Indian woman, deaf as the result of a cold, from Benjamin Wilson's book.[97] Eight of the remaining short cases or general treatment notes in *The Desideratum* appear also to be from Lovett.[98]

It is the other 45 cases that are of particular interest. They follow the same general form: the person's name (occasionally initials), address, sometimes age, and sometimes occupation are given first; then the disease, a brief description of the symptoms, and the duration of the condition, concluding with the treatment given and the result. Richard Lovett, in *The Subtil Medium Prov'd*, scrupulously applied a similar pattern, always giving the patient's name, address, illness, duration of illness, the result of treatment and the exact manner of treatment. When Wesley quoted Lovett's cases, he omitted many of the details, particularly the names, noting that 'whoever desires to see a more circumstantial account of many of the preceding cases, with the names of most of the patients and their places of abode, may consult Mr. Lovett's treatise.'[99] The named cases that Wesley does list, however, have London (not Worcester) addresses, most of which are readily correlated with one of the four clinic locations that Wesley noted in his *Journal*.[100] Indeed, the areas of the Foundry and Seven Dials account for most of them.

Furthermore two of the cases have a direct connection to John Wesley. William Matthews, 32 years old, who was treated for epilepsy, was one of the masters at the Foundry school.[101] Silas Told, who had also been one of the schoolmasters at the Foundry, and became best known as the preacher of Newgate Prison, also resorted to the clinic for heart palpitations of many years' duration.

> In February 1757 while I was electrifying for a pain in my stomach (which was wholly removed by one shock) he came in and said, 'My heart is very bad, and I think I will try it too'. He did so, receiving a shock through the breast, and has been ever since perfectly well.[102]

The conclusion is almost unavoidable that, given Told's close association with Wesley over much of his colourful career, the 'I' of this passage is, as elsewhere throughout the book, Wesley himself.[103]

Whether or not Wesley treated all of the cases himself, and the occasional variations in the record-keeping protocol suggest that others took a hand as well, these 45 case studies provide a fascinating glimpse of clinic visitors. Twenty-five of them are female, 20 male; the youngest was seven (Samuel Rennee, a weaver's son, treated for persistent headache); the oldest 86 (Michael Hayes, Westminster, treated for ankle pain). One suffered a work-related injury: William Jones, a plasterer from Seven Dials, fell from a scaffold on a Thursday and was severely bruised. Carried to the clinic by friends on Saturday, he walked home after one brief treatment and returned to work on Monday. The largest group of patients were associated with the fibre and fabric trades: five women (warper, throwster, mantuamaker, quilter, and silk winder) and three men (two weavers and a tailor). There were three cabinet-makers and one chair-maker, rope-maker, leather-pipe maker, gardener and excise officer with his wife. Among women, there were three servants, a charwoman (who had also sought help at two charity hospitals previously), a nurse and a tallow-chandler's wife. One child's father was a gun-maker at the Tower.[104]

Were the clinic visitors the truly poor? The silk weavers (and, presumably, allied crafts, such as the throwsters who prepared the silk thread) have been called 'one of the most chronically depressed of the skilled occupations', while cabinet-makers and chair-makers made only slightly more per week.[105] Between 1756 and 1773, crops were poor, and the rise in bread prices, although not so high in London as elsewhere, pushed those who were always on the edge of subsistence, such as women domestics and the elderly, closer to disaster.[106] The 1760s were 'the most remarkable decade of industrial disputes of the whole century', especially among the silk-weavers and throwsters of Spitalfields and Bethnal Green, just east of the Foundry.[107] These indications suggest that the people who sought help at Wesley's clinics could have included some of London's most desperate labourers and marginalized poor.

As to the treatments and outcomes in *The Desideratum*, according to the custom of the time only the successes are described. Therefore, many authors today dismiss these accounts, especially the more dramatic ones, such as the cure for blindness.[108] Rogal goes even further to claim that 'Wesley trod upon dangerous ground, probably without ever realizing so'. Noting that Franklin had accidentally given himself very serious shocks on two recorded occasions, he speculated that if Franklin could not 'control his devices', probably Wesley could not do so either.[109] How should a modern reader evaluate the treatments described in *The Desideratum*? Were they safe? Could they have been effective?

In order to address these questions, one must first understand the sort of apparatus used at the time for electrotherapy. One of Wesley's electrical machines is on display in his house by the Chapel on City Road, London.[110] About the size of today's portable sewing machine, the apparatus is supported on non-conducting glass legs. A leather pad presses lightly (its pressure can be adjusted using a thumbscrew) against a piece of black silk covering a glass cylinder. When the operator turned the glass cylinder by a crank, frictional (static) electricity was collected on the comb-like points of a metal arm. At the other end of the arm is a thin vertical rod about nine inches long that terminates in a metal ball. Although Max W. Woodward suggests that the patient took hold of the metal ball,

Lovett indicated that this method was rarely used.[111] Drawings of the time show that 'directors' (glass-encased wire or chain electrodes) were hooked to the vertical rod, allowing precise placement and a degree of fine control in 'drawing sparks' from the patient. Alternatively, the static charge could be accumulated using a Leyden Jar and the directors connected to the jar to administer a shock. Both Lovett's and Wesley's instructions on treatment discuss the use and placement of these 'chains'. The often-reproduced illustration from a 1799 text shows such a treatment in progress on a child, using an apparatus that is basically similar to Wesley's but larger, with some additional features.[112] The size of the jar sets an upper limit on how much charge can be accumulated by turning the cylinder. A period Leyden Jar of about a pint capacity is displayed with Wesley's machine, and the size of the machine would appear to make a larger jar impractical. As a result, the shocks from a friction machine like Wesley's could be, as he claimed, painless, no greater than those we sometimes experience from the static charge accumulated in walking across a wool rug in wool socks. Lovett held that the only reason for painful treatment was 'unskilful management . . . if not downright foul play' from the operator. Since the accumulated charges could be reduced by using a smaller jar, he apparently employed an eight-ounce jar, and recommended a four-ounce one in conditions where pain was already a symptom.[113] The strength of the shock, as Lovett noted, could also be controlled by the operator's touch: the quicker the touch of the rod or chain, the milder the shock.[114]

In contrast to this method, where control and repeated application of very small shocks was the rule, Benjamin Franklin used Leyden Jars of six to nine gallons capacity for his experiments, frequently connecting them in series.[115] It is not surprising that completing the circuit by inadvertent contact would produce a painful and even stupefying shock. Contrary to Rogal's claim that 'there exists no easy means for determining the differences in the strength of the electrical shock' between Franklin's accident and Wesley's (or Lovett's) protocol, the size of the Leyden Jars employed makes comparison easy.[116] Franklin himself noted that the two six-gallon jars he used contained 40 times the electricity of a 'common phial'.[117] Stanley Finger and Franklin Zaromb contend that his accident was the first report of the kind of shock-induced amnesia that would later be recognized as a concomitant of electroconvulsive therapy.[118]

Such straightforward evidence that Wesley's methods had nothing in common with 'electroshock' treatment for psychiatric illness would come as no surprise to authors in the field of electrotherapy who have long recognized Wesley as a leading figure in their own gentler art. In

considering John Wesley's work, Ruth Richardson observes that 'physio-
therapists especially find [electrotherapy] valuable for a wide range of
physical ailments, including pain, chest conditions (such as asthma),
Raynaud's disease, bowel and bone disorders, and wound healing. The
list bears similarities to Wesley's.'[119] Dennis Stillings credits Wesley's
empirical studies of pain relief with setting the stage for the brief and
tantalizing use of electro-acupuncture in early nineteenth-century
Europe.[120] Moreover, David Charles Schechter sees his use of electrical
treatment for palpitations, angina and slow pulse as contributing to the
introduction of electro-resuscitation methods in the next decade
(1774).[121] Non-invasive, mild electrical stimulation methods have proven
highly useful for back pain, and promising in the treatment of muscle
atrophy, spinal cord injury, and rheumatoid hand conditions.[122] Recent
work on chronic heart failure has found that peripheral electrical stimulation both increases muscle strength and improves blood flow, as early
work on electricity postulated.[123]

These few examples from a very large body of literature on electrotherapy over the past three decades suggest that the case studies in *The
Desideratum*, far from being a farrago of over-hopeful anecdotes, often
have surprisingly contemporary relevance. This is true even of what might
be initially the least believable case: that of the blind boy treated by
Andrew Floyer, the surgeon of Dorchester. 'He was as blind', wrote
Floyer of the boy's sudden and mysterious loss of vision, 'as if his eyes had
been cut out. Taking the case to be a perfect *gutta serena* in both eyes, I
told his parents, it was my opinion he would never see again.' 'Gutta
serena' denoted any ophthalmological disease that did not render the eye
opaque; it could result from paralysis of the optic nerve or, as seems like-
lier in this case, of the muscles that open and close the iris. Despite the
grim prognosis, Floyer 'determined to try the electric shock'. The lad's
sight gradually returned following each of four daily treatments, and by
the fifth day 'his sight was perfectly restored'. A physician, a surgeon, an
apothecary, two gentlemen and the boy's father attested to the truth of the
account.[124] Because eye diseases were so poorly understood, this treatment was undertaken on no stronger hypothesis than that the optic nerve
might somehow be involved. In the past few years, among the various
approaches to designing a visual prosthesis for the blind, electrical stimulation of the optic nerve has also been explored, and its eighteenth-century
antecedents noted.[125]

'The noblest medicine yet known'

Why, then, has it taken so long for Wesley's work on electricity to be appreciated by scholars, as it is by practitioners in the field of medical electricity, as an early and legitimate contribution to medicine? Several reasons might be adduced: the ambiguous history of electrotherapy, its association with non-standard practitioners, and perceptions of John Wesley as uninterested in a scientific approach and driven by prior theological or other commitments.

It is true that the history of electrotherapy, though exceedingly colourful, has had its dubious moments, or even decades. From the opening of the electrical era in the eighteenth century up to the turn of the twentieth century, advances in the medical applications of electricity were matched and eventually outpaced by new and creative forms of so-called 'quackery'.[126] Following the first edition of *The Desideratum*, newly introduced portable medical machines of several different designs, along with the inclusion of electrotherapy in editions of Wesley's *Primitive Physic*, doubtless provided encouragement, if any was needed, to electrical novices.[127] Wesley had added a mild endorsement, 'it can do no hurt in any case', from Dr Anton De Haen, the distinguished director of clinical instruction in Vienna.[128] The proliferation of devices and operators is suggested in John Wesley's letter recommending 'electrification' to his brother Charles, in which he felt he had to urge Charles not to dismiss it as 'a quack machine'.[129] As Wesley continued to recommend electrification to his correspondents and to use it himself,[130] the accomplishments of electrical medicine in the 1770s alone ran the gamut from its first use to restore heartbeat (the patient was a child, Sophia Greenhill, who had fallen from a window), to the weird and wonderful 'Temple of Health', established by the famous Dr James Graham – or perhaps, one should say, the notorious 'Dr' Graham, sometimes dubbed 'The Emperor of Quacks'. As Turrell observed, when comparing John Wesley, Jean Paul Marat and James Graham, 'of such kind, then, were the godparents of electrotherapy. Can we wonder that this science, introduced to the notice of a critical and captious profession by such sponsors as these, passed through a troubled and neglected childhood?'[131]

And so it went throughout the nineteenth century as well, with researchers elucidating the physiological roles of electricity and electrical charlatans both hard at work. By 1900, quackery seemed to have won out over legitimate medical uses of electricity, and electrical treatment for most purposes other than resuscitation was largely abandoned until the 'crude and violent' method of electroconvulsive therapy began to be applied in the 1930s.[132] In the 1970s, Western interest in electro-acupuncture, dormant for generations, revived as a result of discoveries about the body's own mechanisms for perceiving and controlling pain, and exploration of electrotherapeutic methods for a wide range of conditions began to follow. Even so, the tendency to marginalize electrotherapy, assigning it to non-physician professionals, has held back both research and application in some areas, especially pain management.[133] Today, when school sports departments own electric defibrillators and electrical stimulation for back pain is standard treatment, the long association of electrotherapy with quackery still casts a shadow over the early history of electrical medicine.

As a result, writers both then and now have been keen to establish a hard-and-fast line between 'professional' and 'alternative' medicine and their practitioners. This distinction is not always an easy one to make for the eighteenth century. The anatomical studies of Harvey's school represented the work of an elite, and these advances – especially after 50 years – were little reflected in the quality of medical practice. Among graduate physicians, for whom there were no national standards, several systems of thought and practice prevailed.[134] Both physicians and patients were apt to prefer the old remedies, however dangerous and distasteful they might be.[135] To add to the diversity, surgeons and apothecaries provided care similar to that of physicians, and the most convenient treatment of all might well come from a lay medical practitioner in one's village or neighbourhood; often this lay practitioner was a clergyman.[136] Turf wars were inevitable.

Reading *The Desideratum*, it may at first appear that one such war was between Wesley and the recognized medical practitioners. Despite his pointed remarks about the aloofness of the medical elite and the overly intimate relationship between physicians and apothecaries, Wesley's book itself reveals that not all of the 'regular' doctors rejected electrotherapy: besides the case study from surgeon Floyer and reports from Dr Zetzell in Sweden, an unnamed apothecary provided electrical treatment on a house call.[137] The practice of electrotherapy was not a dividing line between 'professionals' and 'irregulars'; instead, it cut across categories from the start, and continued to do so. By the end of the century, when 'electrical dispensaries' were becoming common in hospitals, surgeons and apothecaries usually ran these clinics, and the majority of physicians stayed with familiar methods.[138]

Furthermore, it is significant that *The Desideratum* never came in for the kind of scathing attack of the kind that Dr William Hawes directed at *Primitive Physic*. One might note that Hawes, as founder of the Royal

Humane Society, would later call for electrical shock to be administered in all resuscitation attempts, a further indication of the acceptability of electrical medicine to at least some 'regular' practitioners.[139] Hill took as negative Joseph Priestley's review of Wesley's electrical medicine in his 1767 work, *The History and Present State of Electricity with Original Experiments*:

> This account of the medical use of electricity by Mr Lovett and Mr Wesley is certainly liable to an objection which will always lie against the accounts of those persons, who, not being of the faculty, cannot be supposed capable of distinguishing with accuracy either the nature of the disorder or the consequence of a seeming cure. But, on the other hand, the very circumstance of their ignorance . . . supplies the strongest argument in favour of its innocence at least. If in such unskilful hands it produced so much good and so little harm, how much more good and how much less harm would it possibly have produced in more skilful hands?[140]

However, these comments come at the end of a long and overall positive treatment of, first, Lovett's work and then Wesley's, and Priestley immediately negated this objection by listing the cases in which Dr De Haen had confirmed Wesley's and Lovett's claims. Here one learns that Wesley's quotation from De Haen in *Primitive Physic* came from the doctor's magisterial work *Ratio Medendi*, the one that had earned him the post at Vienna.[141] Priestley concluded by echoing Wesley's appeal that 'some physician of understanding and spirit' might establish a 'room' for such treatments, adding that 'it would certainly be more for the honour of the faculty, that the practice should be introduced in such manner, than that it be left to some rich Valetudinarian, who may take it into his head that such an operation may be of service to him.'[142]

'Plain matters of fact weigh more than nice speculative reasoning'

As J. W. Haas Jr. has pointed out, the long history of portraying John Wesley as biased against science, resistant to essential features of its practice and driven by doctrinal commitments has been justified and supported by 'isolated statements abstracted from his work and have not taken into account the philosophical perspective which undergirded his theology and science or the role that science played in his work.'[143]

Although *The Desideratum* is among the least studied of his works related to science or medicine, it has elicited responses that illustrate precisely the problems of reading Wesley out of context of which Haas speaks. For example, failure to realize that Wesley's involvement in medical electricity was clearly connected to and developed out of his long-standing interests in natural philosophy and anatomy has led Paola Bertucci to propose that it was a 'change in composition of electrical audiences' from salon culture to the lower classes that first attracted Wesley's attention and suggested to him both a new proselytizing strategy and a way to inculcate the value of obedience in lower-class Methodists.[144] Reading the text of *The Desideratum* through this hermeneutic of suspicion – Bertucci refers to Wesley's 'concoction of electrical theories' – misses the sense that Wesley was writing about observable phenomena at all: 'mixed with air, the dreadful powers of electricity were mitigated and turned into healing ones, just as human passions when tempered according to the dictates of Methodism would result in political obedience and social harmony'.[145] The most succinct refutation of such a reading is the detailed, careful and thoughtful work that Wesley carried out in presenting an orderly review of Franklin's *Experiments and Observations*; after all, sometimes a spark is only a spark.

Rogal interprets the influence of Wesley's prior commitments in a different way. In his analysis, Wesley

> simply lacked the time and the patience (perhaps even the interest) to wrestle with others' philosophical and/or scientific observations. Simply, if he could not filter any fact or consideration, old or new, through his biblically founded system of right versus wrong, of good versus evil, then he had no use for it . . . Once Wesley realized the supposed value of electricity as a healing agent, he could readily accept the product and abandon the concept to the scientists, the experimenters and the philosophers.[146]

It is certainly true that John Wesley applied his time and energy to preaching the gospel, and in making this activity, in its many forms, his primary commitment, he cut himself off from direct involvement with the community of experimenters. (One might compare Priestley, whose primary time commitments were clearly to experiment, teaching, interaction with the scientific community and writing, and for whom ministry came in at a distant second place.) Again, however, direct engagement with Wesley's sources for *The Desideratum* shows that he did indeed 'wrestle with others' . . . scientific observations', to a degree that can only indicate personal interest in the subject matter. As to his intellectual or imaginative inability to participate 'in the type of drawn-out and often abstract theories and experiments required of the serious and legitimate scientific methods of his day', in both Franklin and Lovett he studied experimenters whose accounts of their work were crisp, direct and placed in a clear but minimal theoretical framework.[147] That much of the work on electricity in this era is repetitive is less a consequence of the 'style' of science in the day than an indication of how difficult it was to sort out the influence of subtle effects such as induction.

Wesley's rejection of theory has often been assumed because of his lack of interest in mathematics. As Schofield expressed it, 'he was ignorant of science – in the way that most people who are not scientists, who do not experiment, who ignore or dislike mathematics, will be ignorant – but he did not dislike or ignore science.'[148] Those who take this tack rest their case on Wesley's two published comments on the subject. The first is from the sermon 'The Use of Money':

So I am convinced, from many experiments, I could not study, to any degree of perfection, either mathematics, arithmetic, or algebra, without being a deist, if not an atheist: and yet others may study them all their lives without sustaining any inconvenience. None, therefore, can here determine for another; but every man must judge for himself, and abstain from whatever he in particular finds to be hurtful to his soul.[149]

The other comes from the *Survey of the Wisdom of God in the Creation*, in the preface to which Wesley stated his intent to write 'in the most clear, easy, and intelligible manner, that the nature of things would allow: particularly free from all the jargon of mathematics, which is mere Heathen Greek to common readers'.[150] As Haas observes, taken in the fuller context given here, the former comment is pastoral counsel, not a normative statement about the value of mathematics, and the second reflects a dividing line still observed: science books for general readers go light on mathematics.[151]

In addition, as Haas also observes, 'eighteenth-century science had a decidedly non-mathematical character'.[152] This was particularly true in English-speaking countries. When the German scientist Franz Aepinus sent his 1759 essay on magnetism and electricity to Benjamin Wilson, the Englishman was nonplussed by Aepinus's heavily mathematical treatment of Franklin's one-fluid model: 'the introducing of algebra in experimental philosophy is very much laid aside with us, as few people understand it; and those who do, rather chose to avoid that close kind of attention'.[153]

For years to come, British scientists would prefer geometrical, rather than algebraic, descriptions of physical phenomena.[154]

Similar selective quotation also shapes the discussion of Wesley's receptiveness to theory more generally. Three comments related to his work on electricity are often selected: his 1747 response to the 'electrical experiments' as 'all mystery', certain to 'confound those poor half-thinkers, who will believe nothing but what they can comprehend'; his claim, in *The Desideratum*, to be 'not greatly concerned for the philosophical part, whether it stand or fall . . . Perhaps the utmost we have reason to expect here is an high degree of probability'; and finally, his *Journal* response to Joseph Priestley's

> ingenious book on Electricity. He seems to have accurately collected and well digested all that is known on that curious subject. But how little is that all! Indeed the use of it we know; at least, in some good degree. We know it is a thousand medicines in one: In particular, that it is the most efficacious medicine, in nervous disorders of every kind, which has ever yet been discovered. But if we aim at theory, we know nothing. We are soon *Lost and bewilder'd in the fruitless search.*[155]

Time indeed showed that Priestley's bold attempt to join earthquakes and volcanic eruptions to lightning as electrical phenomena was 'fruitless', and the 'all' then known about electricity was puzzlingly incomplete. As Priestley acknowledged in the preface to the first edition, 'natural science' as a whole was scarcely past the foothills of an immense range of possible knowledge.[156]

Taken as separate items, each of these statements seems, to the modern reader, to slight 'theory'; taken together with others from Wesley's works pertaining to natural history, joined to the many references to the limits of human knowledge in the *Sermons*, and placed in the context of the works to which they responded, they outline a coherent picture of human reason, as both Haas and Deborah Madden have shown.[157] Adhering to 'an enlightened empirical method that privileged fact over theoretical speculation' in medical practice certainly put Wesley in the respected company of Locke, Boyle, and Sydenham.[158] This English empirical tradition aimed at offering the clearest and most direct way to safe and efficacious treatments, which were in very short supply in that era.[159] An empirical approach has also characterized modern work in electrotherapy, in which several significant advances in improving pain relief or muscle strength came from the trial-and-error approach.[160] In a larger view, Wesley's caution toward theoretical speculation served as a useful corrective to a too-exalted view of human reason. This becomes very clear in comparing Wesley's approach to reason and human understanding with Priestley's in the preface to the latter's work on electricity. Priestley's account of the 'human understanding . . . grasping at the noblest objects, and increasing its own powers', daily (!) improving 'the security and happiness of mankind', not to mention the activities of 'human abilities' and 'human imagination', soon begin to sound firmly divorced from actual human beings.[161] In such a context, Wesley's emphasis on the limits of human understanding provides a realistic re-grounding of human abilities in the complexities of real people, as well as a theological counterpoint that exalts an active and involved God over an absentee landlord or deified reason.

'Let every candid man take a little pains, to understand the question before he determines it'

Critiques of Wesley's grasp of and interest in theory share some interesting common features. First, such critiques define 'theory' in the modern scientific sense of a framework of observations and related principles, established by repeated experiment, that provides a consistent and unifying explanation for physical or biological phenomena. Context makes clear that, in the eighteenth century, 'theory' was more closely related to a speculative description based on (frequently) unrelated principles. Second, they implicitly assume that 'theories' will always have, or be capable of, mathematical expression, making robust use of algebra and calculus. On the contrary, many significant modern theories are expressed in spatial, dynamic, or temporal terms, and although expression in terms of an equation is usually possible, it may not be the first resort in either using or explaining the theory.

Finally, there is often a tendency to confuse scientific models with more general metaphors. There are no uninterpreted observations in science; every investigator or, for that matter, reader, fits observations of nature into some conceptual framework capable of including, in a coherent and self-consistent way, as wide a range of known observations as possible. A metaphor, on the other hand, usually denotes a simple correspondence, relating two unrelated things for the purposes of comparison.

Making these distinctions helps us to appreciate Wesley's theoretical framework for understanding the effects of electricity on disease, beginning with a branch of knowledge in which he had cultivated a reasonable expertise, human anatomy. The immense influence of William Harvey and his school shaped an understanding of anatomy in which communication of fluids by vessels played a driving role. The model of the human body most familiar to us in the West is of organ systems that may be studied and often treated as quasi-independent units. Control by the nervous system is often pictured as flowing from the central nervous system (brain and spinal cord) through the peripheral nerves to a target organ.

Which is 'right'? Both and neither. Each model has explanatory strengths and weaknesses. Although the organ-based understanding remains dominant in the West, there is today a greatly enhanced appreciation of the wide range of communication methods within the human body. David Stewart attributes Wesley's practical grasp of homeostasis – which did not receive formal expression until more than a third of the twentieth century had passed – to medical intuition.[162] Such a grasp of physiological self-regulation would be a natural consequence of a circulation-centred anatomy, as the holistic ideal of a 'well-working' body indicates. Once the reader becomes aware that in the eighteenth century the importance of communication by vessels overrode the individual significance of organs, Wesley's medical works, and also Lovett's, Cheyne's and many others, become more understandable and their complementary perspective intriguing.

Wesley frequently carried these ideas over into his sermons.[163] One of the most striking examples of the vessel-based understanding of anatomy and physiology occurs in Wesley's late sermon 'What is Man?':

Nay, what am I? With God's assistance, I would consider myself. Here is a curious machine, 'fearfully and wonderfully made'. It is a little portion of *earth*, the particles of which cohering, I know not how, lengthen into innumerable fibres, a thousand times finer than hairs. These, crossing each other in all directions, are strangely wrought into membranes; and these membranes are as strangely wrought into arteries, veins, nerves, and glands; all of which contain various fluids, constantly circulating through the whole machine. In order to the continuance of this circulation, a considerable quantity of air is necessary. And this is continually taken into the habit, by an engine fitted for that very purpose. But as a particle of ethereal *fire* is connected with every particle of air, (and a particle of water too,) so both air, water, and fire are received into the lungs together; where the fire is separated from the air and water, both of which are continually thrown out; while the fire, extracted from them, is received into, and mingled with, the blood . . . Without this spring of life, this vital fire, there could be no circulation of the blood; consequently, no motion of any of the fluids, of the nervous fluid in particular (if it be not rather, as is highly probable, this very fire we are speaking of).[164]

Here the all-important vessels, 'arteries, veins, nerves and glands', built up from fibrous membranes, carry 'various fluids, constantly circulating through the whole machine', and this dynamic vital process depends on 'the ethereal fire' – Wesley's synonym for electricity – which is presented as the probable fluid of the nerves. It is a coherent model, and its picture of the energetics of respiration (expressed in today's language as electrical potentials) and the role of nerves in heart and circulatory function is clearly part of the lineage of modern physiology. It is not a 'parable of electric fire',[165] but a theoretical model powerful – that is, broad-based – enough to suggest a rationale for electrical therapy and to indicate the cases in which it might be particularly useful: those using its ability 'to pervade the finest arteries and nerves, to dilate their obstructed or contracted orifices; as well as to restore the tone of any muscle or fibre'.[166] It was, after all, 'real flame, such as sets fire to spirits of wine', not a metaphor, that intrigued John Wesley on his first visit to 'the electrical experiments'.[167]

Therein lies a neglected but suggestive connection to questions of deep concern to today's scientist-theologians. As an outstanding representative of that group, John Polkinghorne, writes:

Classical Christian theology from Augustine onwards, and most powerfully expressed in the writings of Aquinas, sought to preserve the uniqueness of divine action by speaking of God's primary causality, exercised in and under the secondary causality of creatures. No explanation was given of how this happens; it was simply said to be the case. Any attempt to exhibit the 'causal joint' by which the double agency of divine and creaturely causalities related to each other was held to be impossible, or even impious.[168]

Although the originator of the phrase 'causal joint', Anglican theologian Austin Farrar, held to the classic view that the mystery of divine action is beyond human reason to grasp, Polkinghorne proposes that 'creation is not so distanced from its Creator that the character of its history and process affords no clue to the nature of God's interaction with it.'[169] Although it is beyond our ability fully to understand such a connection, we may reasonably examine specific physical processes that are inherently unpredictable – not ones about which we simply do not yet know enough, but ones with 'built-in' unpredictability – to see if they suggest any insight as to what such a connection might be like. In so doing, intellectual daring and intellectual humility must be in balance. In particular, 'if we are not content to live with an acknowledgement that there are phenomena that are beyond our contemporary powers of explanation, we shall have a truncated and inadequate grasp of reality.'[170] Although research after John Wesley's time revealed much about electricity that had earlier seemed intrinsically inexplicable, his willingness to propose it as the 'constant, active, and powerful Principle, constituted by its Creator, to keep the heavenly bodies in their several courses, and at the same time give support, life, and increase to the various inhabitants of the earth', balanced by his continual caution about the limits of human understanding, appear to be an instance of such humble exploratory thinking at the brink of the modern world.[171]

'A blessing to many generations'

But finally, in light of these varied features, what does *The Desideratum* add to our understanding of John Wesley's place in science and medicine? It shows him to be a perceptive reader of current scientific literature, and a skilful and painstaking reviewer, though not a participant in the scientific community. It allows one a practical yet comprehensive glimpse of how Wesley viewed the human person, and a picture of him at work in his clinics that is far more detailed and vivid than the sparse observations in his *Journal*. It opens to the reader an aspect of his life and times – the 'electrical century' – that is of new and intense interest to scholars, and newly appreciated by today's practitioners of electrical medicine.

It is, however, his call for the cooperative efforts of 'men of sense' and 'lovers of mankind' to explore the medical uses of the new medium, to 'take a little pains, to understand the question before he determines it' by giving it a try and keeping track of the results obtained that sets this work in our contemporary context.[172] In making these appeals, Wesley became part of the process of technology transfer that Michael Brian Schiffer identifies as central to the wide dispersal of electricity-related activities throughout eighteenth-century life.[173] Like Lovett and Priestley, who both called for the forming of groups of common interest (in medical and scientific electricity respectively), to share results freely, Wesley too offered his skill and experience as a guide to help novices with what seems to have been perceived as a steep learning curve, even for the well-educated.[174]

But it was not Wesley's intent to propagate this difficult new technology for interest's sake alone: rather, to answer critical needs for health care among the poor. We might detect encouraging signs of a lasting influence for Wesley's work today in such movements as parish nursing programmes. In this light, we must surely be dismayed that a recent study 'suggests that although physicians who practice among the underserved may explain their work in religious terms, religious physicians do not appear to disproportionately care for the underserved'.[175] And we might encourage our Christian brothers and sisters who have special expertise in a new or difficult technology to look for ways to share its benefits with the needy. In short, considering Wesley's work as a whole, although *The Desideratum* offers unique insights into Wesley's scientific and medical interests and a suggestive connection to his theology of nature and the human person, we might hope that its most lasting contribution will prove to be to the philosophy of health care, where its driving concern – the widest possible access to safe, inexpensive and effective ways of getting and keeping well – is increasingly, if still imperfectly, appreciated.

Notes

The author thanks Mr John Liardo, of the Buffalo Public Library, for assistance with the resources of the 'Milestones in Science' Collection in the Rare Book Room.

1 John Wesley, *The Desideratum: Or, Electricity made plain and useful. By a Lover of Mankind, and of Common Sense*, London, printed and sold by W. Flexney under Gray's Inn Gate, etc., 1760. (All references are to this, the first edition.) The 1871 edition is available on-line at <http://books.google.com>. This 1871 edition lists the original edition as 1759; however, 1759 was the date of Wesley's 'Preface', and the date of publication was 1760.

2 Robert E. Schofield, 'John Wesley and Science in 18th Century England', *Isis* 44 (1953), pp. 331–40, p. 336; Samuel J. Rogal, 'Electricity: John Wesley's "Curious and Important Subject"', *Eighteenth-Century Life* 13 (1989), pp. 79–90, p. 71.

3 A. Wesley Hill, *John Wesley Among the Physicians: A Study of Eighteenth-Century Medicine*, London, Epworth, 1958, p. 83; Francis Schiller, 'Reverend Wesley, Doctor Marat and their Electric Fire', *Clio Medica* 15 (1981), pp. 159–76; The classic work in the field, J. L. Heilbron's *Electricity in the 17th and 18th Centuries: A Study in Modern Physics*, Berkeley, University of California Press, 1979, and Mineola, NY, Dover, 1999, gives two brief citations to Wesley's *Journal* but does not mention *The Desideratum*.

4 John Cule, 'The Rev. John Wesley, M.A. (Oxon.), 1703–1791: "The Naked Empiricist" and Orthodox Medicine', *Journal of the History of Medicine and Allied Sciences*, 45 (1990), pp. 41–63, p. 63; Paola Bertucci, 'Revealing Sparks: John Wesley and the religious utility of electrical healing', *British Journal of the History of Science* 39:3 (2006), pp. 341–62, p. 362.

5 *A Series of Letters between Mrs. Elizabeth Carter and Miss Catherine Talbot, from the Year 1741 to 1770*, 2 vols, London, 1809, vol. 1, p. 193.

6 Benjamin Franklin, *Benjamin Franklin's Experiments: A New Edition of Franklin's Experiments and Observations on Electricity*, 'Letter to Peter Collinson' 28 March, 'Letter to Peter Collinson' 25 May and 'Letter to Peter Collinson' 28 July 1747, I. Bernard Cohen, ed., Cambridge, MA, Harvard University Press, 1941, pp. 169–86.

7 Michael Brian Schiffer, *Draw the Lightning Down: Benjamin Franklin and Electrical Technology in the Age of Enlightenment*, Berkeley, University of California Press, 2003, p. 136.

8 John Wesley, *The Journal of the Rev. John Wesley, A.M.*, 16 October 1747, Standard Edition, 8 vols, Nehemiah Curnock ed., London, Epworth, 1909–16, vol. 3, pp. 320–1.

9 Johann Gottlieb Schäffer, *Die electrische Medizin*, Regensberg, 1766, translated and cited by Schiffer, *Draw the Lightning Down*, pp. 5 and 272, n. 8.

10 Heilbron, *Electricity in the 17th and 18th Centuries*.

11 Of course, any discovery or series of discoveries that reshape the view of the universe are bound to have practical consequences, and new technologies can illuminate previously unknown areas of investigation: modern physics made possible both nuclear weaponry and nuclear medicine, and computer science has provided model systems useful in the attempt to understand cognition. However, in these cases, either the pure or the applied science took priority.

12 Samuel Klingenstierna, *Tal* (1755), p. 26, in Heilbron, *Electricity in the 17th and 18th Centuries*, p. 6.

13 These experiments were collected and published by Hauksbee as a book in 1709. After his death, his nephew, also named Francis Hauksbee, published a second edition of the book in 1719 (Schiffer, *Draw the Lightning Down*, p. 26).

14 L. Tyerman, *The Life and Times of the Rev. John Wesley M.A., Founder of the Methodists*, 3 vols, New York, Harper, 1872, vol. 1, p. 19.

15 Barbara Shapiro, 'History and Natural History in Sixteenth- and Seventeenth-Century England: An Essay on the Relationship Between Humanism and Science,' in Barbara Shapiro and Robert G. Frank, Jr, *English Scientific Virtuosi in the 16th and 17th Centuries*, Los Angeles, University of California, 1979, p. 27.

16 Heilbron, *Electricity in the 17th and 18th Centuries*, pp. 13–14, 142, 290.

17 Rogal, 'Electricity,' p. 79.

18 John Whitehead, *Life of John Wesley with Life of Charles Wesley*, 2 vols, Philadelphia, William S. Stockton, 1845, vol. 2, p. 286.

19 Cule, 'Naked Empiricist', p. 47. No source cited. This may be Wesley's notes on Bartholin's *Physica*, discussed in J. W. Haas, Jr, 'John Wesley's Views on Science and Christianity: An Examination of the Charge of Antiscience', *Church History* 63:3 (1994), pp. 378–92, pp. 380–1.

20 For a scientific review of the history, see Heilbron, *Electricity in the 17th and 18th Centuries*; recent works for non-specialists include Schiffer, *Draw the Lightning Down*, and, for a popular audience, Patrice Fara, *An Entertainment for Angels: Electricity in the Enlightenment*, New York, Columbia University Press, 2002.

21 Ewald von Kleist, Dean of the Cathedral at Kammen, actually discovered

the 'Leyden Jar' in 1745, but his account was so poorly written as to be irreproducible.

22 Rogal, 'Electricity,' p. 88, note 1, lists many of the articles that appeared in *The Gentleman's Magazine*.

23 Schiffer's book, *Draw the Lightning Down*, dealing with the role of electrical technology in many different socio-cultural activities and networks, discusses access to demonstrations and apparatus in pp. 67–90 and 91–106, as do Fara, *An Entertainment for Angels*, pp. 9–50, and Bertucci 'Revealing Sparks'. All of these authors note the participation of women as well.

24 Wesley, *Journal*, 17 February 1753, Vol. 4, pp. 53–4.

25 It is a matter of dispute whether the letters were read and briefly discussed but not printed or whether some or most of the letters were not read, owing perhaps to the jealousy of William Watson, the leading figure in electrical science and then President of the Royal Society. For the former (and strongly majority) view, see I. Bernard Cohen, 'Introduction', in Franklin, *Experiments*, chapter III.2, pp. 77–100; for the latter, see Tom Tucker, *Bolt of Fate: Benjamin Franklin and His Electric Kite Hoax*, New York, Public Affairs, 2003, pp. 60–9.

26 For this complex history, see Cohen, 'Introduction', pp. 87–9.

27 Benjamin Franklin, *Experiments and Observations on Electricity, made at Philadelphia in America, by Mr. Benjamin Franklin, and Communicated in several Letters to Mr. P. Collinson, of London, F.R.S.*, London, printed and sold by E. Cave, St John's Gate, 1751, and *Supplemental Experiments and Observations on Electricity, Part II, made at Philadelphia in America, by Benjamin Franklin, Esq, and Communicated in several Letters to P. Collinson, Esq. of London, F.R.S.*, London, Printed and sold by E. Cave, St John's Gate, 1753. A full list of editions is found in I. Bernard Cohen, 'Introduction', chapter 4.1, pp. 141–8.

28 Franklin, 'Letter II', *Experiments*, 11 July 1747, p. 171. Bernard Cohen notes that the first edition reversed Franklin's first two letters, and that the date of this letter was actually 25 May 1747 (it was probably received in London 11 July).

29 Franklin, 'Opinions and Conjectures . . . 1749', *Experiments*, p. 214.

30 Quoted in Dennis Stillings, 'A Survey of the History of Electrical Stimulation for Pain to 1900', *Medical Instrumentation* 9:6 (1975), pp. 255–9, p. 255.

31 Edward Stainbrook, 'The Use of Electricity in Psychiatric Treatment in the Nineteenth Century', *Bulletin of the History of Medicine* 22:2 (1948), pp. 156–77, p. 157; Cule, 'Contributions of John Wesley to Medical Literature', *Histoire des sciences médicales* 17:4 (1982), pp. 328–31, p. 330.

32 Wesley, *Journal*, 20 January 1753, vol. 4, p. 51.

33 John Wesley, 'A Plain Account of the People Called Methodists: in a Letter to the Rev. Mr. Perronet . . . Written in the year 1748', XII.1, 2, 3, *The Works of John Wesley*, 14 vols, London, Wesleyan Methodist Book Room, 1872, reprint, Grand Rapids, Baker Books, 2002, vol. 8, pp. 263–4.

34 Richard Lovett, *The Subtil Medium Prov'd; or, that Wonderful Power of Nature, so long ago conjectur'd by the Most Ancient and Remarkable Philosophers, which they call'd Sometimes Aether, but oftener, Elementary Fire, verify'd . . .* , London, J. Hinton, Newgate Street, 1756; Rogal suggests that the priority belongs to John Neale, *Directions for Gentlemen, who have Electrical Machines, How to proceed in making Their Experiments*, London, 1747, but this

work appears to touch on electrotherapy only in a postscript appealing for clinical accounts (Rogal, 'Electricity', p. 81).

35 Wesley, *Journal*, 9 November 1756, vol. 4, pp. 190–1.

36 Wesley, 'A Letter to Mr T. H., *alias* Philodemas, *alias* Somebody, *alias* Stephen Church, *alias* R. W. Inserted in the "London Magazine" for 1760 page 651' *WJW*, vol. 13, pp. 387–92.

37 Wesley, 'Preface', *The Desideratum*, §1, p. iii.

38 For detailed bibliographic information on these sources, see Rogal, 'Electricity', p. 88, note 1, and Heilbron, *Electricity in the 17th and 18th Centuries*, pp. 501–69. Rogal also observes that Wesley cited no continental sources.

39 Wesley, 'Preface', *The Desideratum*, §2–3 pp. iii–iv.

40 Rogal, 'Electricity', p. 84; Schofield, 'John Wesley and Science in 18th Century England', p. 338.

41 Schiffer, *Draw the Lightning Down*, p. 27.

42 Wesley, *The Desideratum*, pp. iv–v.

43 Turrell dates this 'prejudice against the medical profession' from the 'unfavourable reception . . . [Dr Cheyne] his favourite medical author received at their hands' in 1724. W. J. Turrell, 'Three Electrotherapists of the Eighteenth Century: John Wesley, Jean Paul Marat and James Graham', *Annals of Medical History* 3 (1921), pp. 361–7, p. 361.

44 Wesley, 'The Use of Money', Sermon 50, §I.5, *WJW*, Vol. 6, p. 129; dates according to [Timothy L. Smith, 'Chronological List of John Wesley's Sermons and Doctrinal Essays', *Wesleyan Theological Journal* 17:2 (1982), pp. 88–110, <http://wesley.nnu.edu/wesleyan_theology/theojrnl/16–20/17–15.htm>.

45 Wesley, 'Preface', *The Desideratum*, §3–4 and §8–10, pp. iii–iv and vi–vii.

46 George Rudé, *Hanoverian London 1714–1808*, Berkeley, University of California Press, 1971, p. 84.

47 Rudé, *Hanoverian London*, pp. 84–5.

48 For a brief account of current views on relationships between doctors and lay practitioners in this era, see Deborah Madden, 'Contemporary Reaction to John Wesley's *Primitive Physic*: Or, the Case of Dr William Hawes Examined', *Social History of Medicine* 17:3 (2004) pp. 365–78, pp. 366–8.

49 Wesley, 'A Plain Account . . . 1748'. §XII.2, *WJW*, vol. 8, p. 264.

50 Deborah Madden, 'Medicine and Moral Reform: The Place of Practical Piety in John Wesley's Art of Physic', *Church History* 73:4 (2004), pp. 741–58.

51 Wesley, 'Preface', *The Desideratum*, §5–6, pp. iv–v.

52 Wesley, 'Preface', *The Desideratum*, §7, p. vi.

53 Among those who have examined the question whether Wesley's work on electrotherapy should be considered a precursor to electroshock or other electrical treatment of psychological ills are Stainbrook, 'The Use of Electricity in Psychiatric Treatment in the Nineteenth Century'; Richard A. Hunter, 'A Brief Review of the Use of Electricity in Psychiatry', *The British Journal of Physical Medicine* 20:5 (1957), pp. 98–100; Hill, *John Wesley Among the Physicians*, p. 93; and H. Newton Malony, 'John Wesley and the Eighteenth Century Therapeutic Uses of Electricity', *Perspectives on Science and Christian Faith* 47 (1995), pp. 244–54, pp. 245, 251–2.

54 Wesley, 'Thoughts on Nervous Disorders', 1784, §I.1, *WJW*, vol. 11, p. 515.

55 Wesley, 'Preface', *The Desideratum*, §7, p. vi.

56 Wesley, 'Preface', *The Desideratum*, §9, pp. vi–vii.

57 Wesley, 'Preface', *The Desideratum*, §10, p. vii.

58 Rogal, 'Electricity', p. 79, represents the view that all of Wesley's scientific work (presumably including *The Desideratum*) was a simplified summary of other writers; Dennis Stillings, 'John Wesley: Electrotherapist', *Medical Instrumentation* 8:1 (1974), p. 66, mistakenly reads Boyle's experiment as Wesley's. That cats were safe around Mr Wesley is evident from Flowers's chapter on 'Environmental Stewardship' in the present volume.

59 Wesley, 'Preface', *The Desideratum*, §1, p. iii.

60 Franklin, *Experiments*, pp. 169–279, 300–1.

61 Franklin, 'Opinions and Conjectures . . . 1749', *Experiments*, pp. 212–36.

62 See note 24, above.

63 Schofield, 'John Wesley and Science in 18th Century England', p. 336.

64 So as to keep the focus on the overall organization of this section of *The Desideratum*, the specific paragraph correlations will be listed in these notes rather than the text. References to the individual letters of Franklin are given both in Cohen's numbering (see note 6) and by the date of the original letter to facilitate the use of different sources. Wesley's §I.13–17 include Franklin's 'Opinions and Conjectures' (hereafter 'O & C') §1–6, 9–10, 15–17. Wesley's §I.18–24 draw from Franklin's Letters II (25 May 1747) and XII (September 1753). Wesley's §I.25–28 draw from Franklin's 'O & C' §33, 35 and Letters VIII (from E. Kinnersley, 3 February 1752) and VII (to Cadwallader Colden, 1751).

65 Wesley's §I.29, on the Leyden Jar, draws on Franklin's Letter III (28 July 1747). For Wesley's §I.30, on physiological and other effects of a shock, see Franklin's 'O & C' §22; Letter IV (29 April 1749), §28, §20 and §26; and Letter VI (27 July 1750). The source of Wesley's §31 remains to be located.

66 In addition to Letter V, Wesley also touched on Franklin's later thoughts on lightning (Letter XII, September 1753). The 'kite' experiment is Letter XI (19 October 1752) and the proposal of lightning rods to protect buildings comes from Franklin's 'O & C', §20. Franklin made no mention of the 'sensitive plant', *Mimosa*, so this came from Wesley's other reading.

67 Wesley, *The Desideratum*, §I.40, p. 29.

68 Wesley, *The Desideratum*, §I.17, pp. 15–16 and §I.29, p. 21.

69 Whitehead, *Life of John Wesley* vol. 2, p. 302.

70 Wesley, *The Desideratum*, pp. 31–41.

71 Wesley, 'Preface', *The Desideratum*, p. iii.

72 Franklin, 'Opinions and Conjectures', *Experiments*, §19, p. 219.

73 For example, see Franklin, 'Opinions and Conjectures', *Experiments*, §1–11, pp. 213–15.

74 Wesley, *The Desideratum*, §I.1, 4, pp. 9 and 10.

75 Wesley's citation of Berkeley, *The Desideratum*, §I.3, p. 10; reviewing this subject: G. N. Cantor, 'The Theological Significance of Ethers', in *Conceptions of Ether*, New York, Cambridge University Press, 1981, pp. 135–55.

76 Robert G. Frank, Jr, 'The Physician as Virtuoso in Seventeenth-Century England', in Shapiro and Frank, *English Scientific Virtuosi*, pp. 84–92.

77 Robert G. Frank, Jr, 'The Physician as Virtuoso', pp. 97–8.

78 See note 33.

79 Eunice Bonow Bardell, 'Primitive Physick: John Wesley's Receipts', *Pharmacy in History* 21:3 (1979), pp. 111–21, pp. 113–14. Wesley called Jean Regnier 'John Reinier' in his diary.

80 See note 55.

81 Philip W. Ott, 'John Wesley on Health as Wholeness', *Journal of Religion and Health* 30:1 (1991), pp. 43–57, pp. 45–7. Also see Lester S. King, 'George Cheyne, 'Mirror of Eighteenth Century Medicine', *Bulletin of the History of Medicine* 48 (1974), pp. 517–39, pp. 526 and 537, for the importance of vessels in Cheyne's system.

82 Wesley, *The Desideratum*, pp. 41–2.

83 Lovett, 'To the Reader', *The Subtil Medium Prov'd*, p. iii.

84 Bertucci, 'Revealing Sparks', p. 345. Bertucci does not mention that Desaguliers was the chief experimenter for the Royal Society, and therefore the closest Britain could offer to a professional research scientist. Nor does she note that the 'popular magazines' from which Lovett also learned (such as *The Gentleman's Magazine*) were the only venue for sharing experiments outside of *Philosophical Transactions*, and carried much of the important work in electricity in that era.

85 Lovett, *The Subtil Medium Prov'd*, pp. 140–1.

86 For an example of analysis of the literature, Dr Hart's letter to Mr William Watson regarding cases of palsy treated by electricity at Shrewsbury Hospital, see Lovett, *The Subtil Medium Prov'd*, pp. 101–8; seven years' experience, 'To the Reader', *The Subtil Medium Prov'd*, p. i.

87 Lovett, *The Subtil Medium Prov'd*, pp. 1–3; Wesley, *The Desideratum*, pp. 9–12.

88 Lovett, 'To the Reader', *The Subtil Medium Prov'd*, p. iv. Lovett added that electrical fire, fire, electrical ether and ethereal spirit are also synonyms; Wesley simply moved back and forth between the terms.

89 Lovett, *The Subtil Medium Prov'd*, pp. 64–9; Wesley, *The Desideratum*, pp. 10–11, 42.

90 Lovett, *The Subtil Medium Prov'd*, p. 100.

91 Lovett, *The Subtil Medium Prov'd*, pp. 101–2, 116, 122, 137–9.

92 Lovett, *The Subtil Medium Prov'd*, pp. 101, 115.

93 Lovett, *The Subtil Medium Prov'd*, p. 126.

94 Wesley, *The Desideratum*, pp. 42–3.

95 For example, see H. Newton Malony, 'John Wesley and Psychology', *Journal of Psychology and Christianity* 18:1 (1999), pp. 5–18, pp. 8–9, and Hunter, 'A Brief Review of the Use of Electricity in Psychiatry', p. 99.

96 Lovett, *The Subtil Medium Prov'd*, pp. 110–14.

97 Andrew Floyer's treatment of a blind boy: Lovett, *The Subtil Medium*, pp. 116–20; Wesley, *The Desideratum*, p. 44; Robert Moubray, the Scot with the palsied tongue, in Lovett, p. 109, and Wesley, p. 62; the Newcastle and Wilson reports, Wesley, pp. 44–6 and 49–50.

98 Two have not been assigned and may belong to either Wesley or Lovett.

99 Wesley, *The Desideratum*, p. 70.

100 See note 35. Richard Horwood's 1792–99 map, available at <www.oldlondonmaps.com/horwoodpages>, proved helpful in locating some of the streets mentioned. Presumably the Seven Dials clinic was at the chapel on West Street.

101 Wesley, *The Desideratum*, p. 52.

102 Wesley, *The Desideratum*, p. 62.

103 Wesley's *Journal* does not mention an illness around this date, but other entries (see below) show that Wesley often treated himself by this method.

104 Wesley, *The Desideratum*, pp. 43–69.

105 Rudé, *Hanoverian London*, p. 88.

106 Rudé, *Hanoverian London*, pp. 90, 203.

107 Rudé, *Hanoverian London*, pp. 191ff, 197–201.

108 For example, the medical application of electricity as a 'dubious practice', 'laughable or even fraudulent' see Fara, *An Entertainment for Angels*, pp. 66, 90.

109 Rogal, 'Electricity', pp. 80–1. Franklin's report of the mishap he suffered when preparing to kill the Christmas turkey by electrification: Benjamin Franklin, Letter to [John Franklin?], 25 December 1750, <http://www.franklinpapers.org/franklin/yale>.

110 The apparatus is pictured in many of the articles about Wesley's interest in electricity. For an article devoted to the subject, see Max W. Woodward, 'Wesley's Electrical Machine', *Nursing Mirror* 114 (1962), pp. x, xvi. A particularly fine photograph appears in Stillings, 'A survey', p. 257. Collier (Frank W. Collier, *John Wesley Among the Scientists*, New York, Abingdon Press, 1928, illustration facing p. 34) shows the apparatus before restoration, minus the collecting arm.

111 Woodward, 'Wesley's Electrical Machine', p. x; Lovett, *The Subtil Medium Prov'd*, p. 138.

112 For a picture and discussion of the 1799 print, as well as a photograph of one of the extant examples, see http://www.thebakken.org/artifacts/Adams.htm. For more about the use of a frictional apparatus in different therapeutic situations, see Schiffer, *Draw the Lightning Down*, pp. 140–2. Note that the Adams apparatus accumulates a stronger charge by means of a Leyden Jar, and also incorporates an electrometer to measure the strength of the charge. Note also that the child and her mother both look calm, a not-so-subtle suggestion that the method is safe and painless for anyone.

113 Lovett, *The Subtil Medium Prov'd*, pp. 102, 107.

114 Lovett, *The Subtil Medium Prov'd*, p. 131.

115 For this contrast, see Wesley, *The Desideratum*, p. 71; Lovett, *The Subtil Medium Prov'd*, pp. 120–39.

116 Rogal, 'Electricity', p. 81.

117 Quoted in Stanley Finger and Franklin Zaromb, 'Benjamin Franklin and Shock-Induced Amnesia', *American Psychologist*, 4 (2006), pp. 240–8, p. 243.

118 Finger and Zaromb, 'Benjamin Franklin and Shock-Induced Amnesia', pp. 246–7. These authors also contrast Wesley's protocol with Franklin's accident, p. 246.

119 Ruth Richardson, 'John Wesley's Ethereal Fire', *The Lancet*, 358 (2001), p. 932.

120 Stillings, 'A survey of the history of electrical stimulation for pain to 1900', pp. 256–7.

121 David Charles Schechter, 'Historical Notes on Electroresuscitation', *Medical Instrumentation*, 9:6 (1975), pp. 251–4, p. 251.

122 V. Neumann, 'Electrotherapy' (Editorial), *British Journal of Rheumatology*, 32 (1993), pp. 1–2. Modern methods of electrotherapy mentioned in this

and the next article no longer use static electricity; however, their low-current, low-frequency devices retain the aim of painless treatment. For an account of a static instrument of the modern era, and a photograph of a nearly complete glass-cylinder electrostatic treatment kit ca. 1760, see A. D. Moore, 'Electrostatic discharges for treating skin lesions: Does it deserve some new research?' *Medical Instrumentation* 9:6 (1975), pp. 274–5.

123 Petr Dobsák, and others, 'Low-Frequency Electrical Stimulation Increases Muscle Strength and Improves Blood Supply in Patients with Chronic Heart Failure', *Circulation Journal* 70 (2006), pp. 75–82.

124 Wesley, *The Desideratum*, p. 44. Lovett's account is much more detailed, and includes the testimony of the witnesses: Lovett, *The Subtil Medium Prov'd*, pp. 116–20.

125 C. E. Uhlig, S. Taneri, F. P. Benner and H. Gerding, '[Electrical stimulation of the visual system. From empirical approach to visual prostheses]' (English translation of German title provided by abstracting service), *Ophthalmologe* 98:11 (2001), pp. 1089–96, via abstract PMID: 11729743 [PubMed - indexed for MEDLINE].

126 For the eighteenth century, see Schiffer, *Draw the Lightning Down*, pp. 133–60; for the nineteenth, see Stillings, 'A survey of the history of electrical stimulation for pain to 1900' and Stainbrook, 'The Use of Electricity in Psychiatric Treatment in the Nineteenth Century'.

127 Schiffer, *Draw the Lightning Down*, pp. 143–5.

128 Electrical therapy began to be included in Wesley's *Primitive Physic* as early as 1759, with a separate section accorded to it in 1761. See Madden, 'Contemporary Reaction to John Wesley's *Primitive Physic*', p. 366.

129 John Wesley, To Charles Wesley, 26 December 1761, *Letters* (Telford), vol. 4, p. 166.

130 Letters recommending electrification include John Wesley, To Mary Bosanquet, 15 January 1770, *Letters* (Telford), vol. 5, p. 176 (electrification for general use); To Penelope Newman, 23 October 1772, vol. 5, p. 342 (for eye pain); To Thomas Taylor, 30 October 1775, vol. 6, pp. 185–6; To Ann Bolton, 13 July 1774, vol. 6, p. 97 (to get an electric machine); To John Bredin, 17 May 1781, vol. 7, p. 60 (for scorbutic sores); to John Bredin, 19 October 1781, vol. 7, p. 86 (for general use). Notes from Wesley, *Journal*, 11 July 1764, vol. 5, p. 83 (recommended for epilepsy); 26 December 1765, vol. 5, p. 152 (self-treatment for fall from horse); 19 April 1774, vol. 6, pp. 16–17 (recommended electrification to Mr Greenwood for angina); 19 September 1773, vol. 6, p. 3 (self-treatment for shoulder pain); 23 March 1783, vol. 6, p. 400 (self-treatment for cramps and fever).

131 Turrell, 'Three Electrotherapists', p. 367.

132 Hunter, 'A Brief Review of the Use of Electricity in Psychiatry', p. 100. See also Finger and Zaromb, 'Benjamin Franklin and Shock-Induced Amnesia', pp. 246–7.

133 Neumann, 'Electrotherapy', p. 1.

134 Cule, 'Naked Empiricist', p. 41.

135 Cule, 'Contributions of John Wesley to Medical Literature', p. 328.

136 For the diverse scene of eighteenth-century medicine, see Madden, 'Contemporary Reaction to John Wesley's *Primitive Physic*', pp. 366–8, and ref-

erences therein. For the role of clergy, see Madden, 'Medicine and Moral Reform', pp. 743–5; for clergy and laity, see Cule, 'Naked Empiricist', pp. 43–6.

137 Wesley, *The Desideratum*, p. 51. Apparently the apothecary initially 'made light of' the master's suggestion to 'electrify' a servant fallen in a seizure, but he seems to have had the requisite equipment with him.

138 Schiffer, *Draw the Lightning Down*, p. 148.

139 Schiffer, *Draw the Lightning Down*, pp. 157 and 307, note 101.

140 Quoted in A. Wesley Hill, *John Wesley Among the Physicians*, p. 92. Haas takes the overall context as favourable to Wesley, and also notes that elsewhere in a different edition of the same book Priestley 'praised [Wesley's] work'. These other instances are not readily traced in the edition below. John W. Haas, Jr, 'Eighteenth Century Evangelical Responses to Science: John Wesley's Enduring Legacy', *Science and Christian Belief*, p. 6 (1994), pp. 83–102, p. 89.

141 Joseph Priestley, *The History and Present State of Electricity with Original Experiments*, London, C. Bathurst, T. Lowndes, etc., 1775 (4th edition), pp. 384–6.

142 Priestley, *The History and Present State of Electricity*, p. 387.

143 Haas, 'John Wesley's Views on Science and Christianity', p. 380.

144 Bertucci, 'Revealing Sparks', pp. 347–58. Considering that the decade following *The Desideratum* was marked by labour riots among precisely the population that Wesley's clinic served, had the inculcation of obedience been his motive, it clearly failed miserably.

145 Bertucci, 'Revealing Sparks', p. 358.

146 Rogal, 'Electricity,' p. 86.

147 Rogal, 'Electricity,' p. 87.

148 Schofield, 'John Wesley and Science in 18th Century England', p. 340. Bertucci also makes this connection ('Revealing Sparks', pp. 358–9).

149 Wesley, 'The Use of Money', Sermon 50, §I.2, *WJW*, vol. 6, p. 127.

150 John Wesley, *A Survey of the Wisdom of God in the Creation, or A Compendium of Natural Philosophy Containing an Abridgment of that Beautiful Work, 'The Contemplation of Nature.' By Mr. Robert Bonnet, of Geneva. Also an Extract from Mr. Deuten's 'Inquiry into the Origin of the 'Discoveries Attributed to the Ancients'*, 2 vols, Philadelphia, Jonathan Pounder, 1816, vol. 1, p. iv.

151 Haas, 'John Wesley's Views on Science and Christianity', p. 388.

152 Haas, 'John Wesley's Views on Science and Christianity', p. 388.

153 Cited in Fara, *An Entertainment for Angels*, p. 129, from an undated manuscript.

154 Fara, *An Entertainment for Angels*, pp. 130–1. This situation pertained through Faraday's era (whose electrical researches spanned the 1830s).

155 Wesley, *Journal*, 4 January 1768, vol. 5, p. 247.

156 Joseph Priestley, *The Theological and Miscellaneous Works of Joseph Priestley*, 'Preface to "The History and Present State of Electricity, with Original Experiments"', John Towill Rutt ed., 25 vols, Hackney, Smallfield, 1817–31, vol. 25, p. 344.

157 Haas, 'John Wesley's Views on Science and Christianity', pp. 384–6; Deborah Madden, 'The Limitation of Human Knowledge: Faith and the Empirical Method in John Wesley's Medical Holism', *History of European Ideas* 32 (2006), pp. 162–72.

158 Madden, 'The Limitation of Human Knowledge', pp. 165–6.

159 Cule, 'Naked Empiricist', pp. 46, 51–63; James G. Donat, 'Empirical Medicine in the 18th Century: The Rev. John Wesley's Search for Remedies that Work', *Methodist History* 44:4 (2006), pp. 216–26.

160 Neumann, 'Electrotherapy'.

161 Priestley, 'Preface to "The History and Present State of Electricity . . . "', p. 343.

162 David Stewart, 'John Wesley the Physician', *Wesleyan Theological Journal* 4:1 (1969), pp. 27–38 <http://wesley.nnu.edu/wesleyan_theology/theojrnl/01–05/04–3.htm>.

163 Representative analyses are found in Philip W. Ott, 'John Wesley on Health as Wholeness'; Philip W. Ott, 'John Wesley on Mind and Body: Toward an Understanding of Health as Wholeness', *Methodist History* 27:1 (1989), pp. 61–72; Philip W. Ott, 'Medicine as Metaphor: John Wesley on Therapy of the Soul', *Methodist History* 33:3 (1995), pp. 178–91; Haas, "John Wesley's Views on Science and Christianity'; and Madden, 'The Limitation of Human Knowledge'.

164 Wesley, 'What is Man?' Sermon 109, §1, 2, 4, *WJW*, vol. 7, pp. 225–6 ; Smith's date, 2 May 1788 [see note 44].

165 Bertucci, 'Revealing Sparks', p. 360.

166 Wesley, *The Desideratum*, §II.52, p. 70.

167 See note 8.

168 John Polkinghorne, *Faith, Science and Understanding*, New Haven, Yale University Press, 2000, p. 115.

169 Polkinghorne, *Faith, Science and Understanding*, p. 117.

170 Polkinghorne, *Faith, Science and Understanding*, p. 119.

171 Wesley, *The Desideratum*, §I.4, p. 10.

172 Wesley, 'Preface', *The Desideratum*, §9, pp. vi–vii, p. 72 and §II.53, pp. 70–1.

173 Schiffer, *Draw the Lightning Down*, pp. 3–5.

174 On the need for cooperative exploration: Lovett, *The Subtil Medium Prov'd*, pp. 131–2, and Priestley, 'Preface to "The History and Present State of Electricity . . . "', pp. 349–51; on the perceived difficulty of understanding electricity, Lovett, 'To the Reader', *The Subtil Medium Prov'd*, p. ii and Joseph Priestley, *The Theological and Miscellaneous Works of Joseph Priestley*, 'Preface to "A Familiar Introduction to the Study of Electricity"', John Towill Rutt ed., 25 vols, Hackney, Smallfield, 1817–31, vol. 25, pp. 355–6.

175 Farr A. Carlin, Lydia S. Dugdale, John D. Lantos and Marshall H. Chin, 'Do Religious Physicians Disproportionately Care for the Underserved?' *Annals of Family Medicine* 5:4 (2007), pp. 353–60.

6

'Health of Soul and Health of Body':
The Supernatural Dimensions of
Healing in John Wesley

ROBERT WEBSTER

> Therefore expect from Him, not what you deserve, but what you want
> – health of soul and health of body: ask, and you shall receive; seek, and
> you shall find; not for your worthiness, but because 'worthy is the
> Lamb'.[1]

On Monday, 11 August 1740, John Wesley recorded in the published
extract of his journal an episode of an experience that he witnessed in a
society room. According to Wesley's account, about 40 or 50 individuals
who were seeking salvation had gathered for prayer and thanksgiving. As
was his custom, Wesley retired early in the evening but was awakened by
loud shouts and noises at 2.00 a.m. Particularly noticeable was an individual that was identified in Wesley's journal as J—— W——, most likely
Jane Wildbore.[2] Wesley focused on her in his account as an example of
edification for his readers when he described her as one '. . . who had been
always till then very sure that "none cried out but hypocrites" . . . But she
too now cried to God with a loud and bitter cry. It was not long before God
heard from his holy place'.[3] Forty-five years later in 1785, he included
another experience of Jane Wildbore, which described both natural and
supernatural healing, in his famous *Arminian Magazine*. After having lost
the use of her legs due to an accident, coupled with unsuccessful medical
treatments over a four-year span, Wildbore was resolved to seek healing
through the activity of prayer. Her experience was recounted in the version
that appeared in the magazine in 1785:

> How can I attend the means of grace, and get a livelihood in the world,
> without the use of my limbs? She then endeavoured to believe that God
> was *able* and *willing* to restore her to her former soundness, if she
> sought him with all her heart. She also believed that he *would* do it: and
> on that account promised to serve him all the days of her life. Soon

after, being left alone in the house one Sunday evening, it was impressed on her mind to pray for deliverance from her infirmity; but how to get on her knees, and rise up again she knew not. At last she strove to believe that God would help her: and so it was; for by endeavouring to use her hands, she kneeled down, and continued in prayer for a considerable time, and then rose up again. Thus she continued praying and acting faith on God till Tuesday evening, when an excruciating pain went through her feet and legs, which caused her to cry out aloud; but when the pain was over, she found she could move, first her toes, and then her feet and legs. She then got up and walked over the room, blessing and praising God for what he had done: and from that time she has enjoyed the perfect use of her limbs.[4]

Wildbore's experience demonstrates several themes that John Wesley addressed throughout his life. First, the idea of healing illustrated in Wesley's edited account was not opposed to the physical cures that were available through the emerging science of medicine available in the eighteenth century.[5] It was as a last resort that she consulted the possibility of what Wesley called 'that old unfashionable medicine, prayer'.[6] Throughout Wesley's lifetime both natural medicine and spiritual prayers were used together for the health of individuals in different circumstances and a variety of ways. Certainly it is true that there were instances when John Wesley and other Methodists in the eighteenth century seemed impatient and sidelined medical practice in favour of spiritual prayers. Such was the case when John wrote to his younger brother Charles on 28 September 1760, 'I care not a rush for ordinary means', he wrote, 'only that it is our duty to try them. All our lives and all God's dealings with us have been extraordinary from the beginning.'[7] More often, however, Wesley advocated the use of medical techniques alongside prayer as a source for obtaining health for both body and soul.[8] The administration of medicine after society meetings, electrifying himself and others while on preaching tours, and the cure of the infirm with prayer, all fit into a symbiotic understanding of human nature and divine grace, which Wesley advocated during the eighteenth century. Second, the idea of supernatural healing for Methodists living during the Enlightenment took place within a grid that embraced a polyvalent hermeneutic for understanding the means of grace. Prayer, fasting, and constant communion were an integral part of Methodists living in the Age of Reason, and Wesley unabashedly contended that those who faithfully attended to the prudential and instituted means of grace availed themselves to a transcendental reality, which intersected with and influenced human existence. Throughout Methodist narratives collected by both John and Charles Wesley, it was easy to find accounts of experiences that demonstrated the viability of a belief in supernatural healing. Despite particular controversies, like the London disturbances of the 1760s, Wesley continued to assert that the healing grace of God was present for those who prayed, fasted, and communicated. Third, the social dimension of healing was played out in a theatre-like atmosphere with deathbed accounts of Methodists. John McManners, in his study of death during the Enlightenment, rightly points out that disease and death were realities that touched each and every individual: 'a new understanding of the eighteenth century comes to us when we review its history in terms of disease and mortality'.[9] Certainly the Methodists of the eighteenth century faced death like the rest of society. However, few made use of their experiences like the Methodists, who saw themselves fitting into an *ars moriendi* tradition that attempted to value the experience of a good death. In various narratives that depicted the final hours of suffering a glimpse was offered into the state of the departing soul. Occasionally, supernatural healing was demonstrated but at other times a vision into the invisible world was portrayed. In the former, healing was granted to individuals that had been critical of the Methodist vision of justification and sanctification, and thereby served as an example of the mercy of God and an opportunity to renounce their sin, thus experiencing the love of a gracious Saviour. In the latter, as we will note, the desire for healing was eschewed by the faithful in favour of transportation into another realm of existence where peace and harmony were actualized. The deathbed narratives of Wesley's followers are intriguing portrayals that reveal how the Methodists understood both death and life. Additionally, the narratives indicate that the Methodists were not ultimately overcome by the terror of death, but were triumphant with their confidence in the assurance that God's presence was a living reality in their hearts. In this respect, these accounts became commentaries which asserted that death was not a moment of despair but a place which could not eclipse the reality of divine existence.

In the following pages I will deal with these aspects of John Wesley's thought and show how he endeavoured to weave from the text of human experience the reality of God's presence in health and wholeness. More specifically, the nature of supernatural healing will be looked at to show that Wesley was not out of sync with the culture in which he lived, but vitally contributed to important dimensions of both religion and medicine. As a result, it will be demonstrated that Wesley was a man who had interest in both primitive and modern understandings of health and wholeness.

I

A renewed interest has surfaced in John Wesley's knowledge and use of medical theory.[10] His knowledge of seventeenth and eighteenth-century medicine is apparent, not only by his reading of various medical treatises of the period, but also by noting the incorporation and rhetorical use of medical imagery and terminology in his writings. Words like 'physician', 'illness' and 'healing' served a dual function.[11] On the one hand, they signified a continuum that existed throughout human investigation and verification. The identification of a body of knowledge that could be agreed upon by members of society was instrumental for both the accumulation of data in general and the development of science in particular. At this level, truth was considered social as it was recognized, validated and handed down from one generation to another. A similar point has been made by Steven Shapin when he writes: 'the history of truth can be a social history because what we know about the world is arrived at, sustained, and recognized through collective action'.[12] On the other hand, the language that Wesley utilized to signify both illness and healing also asserted ideas that were important for a Methodist self-identification in the eighteenth century. In a journal entry for 24 November 1760, for example, Wesley noted the dual benefits of visiting the sick for the Methodists: 'I visited as many as I could of the sick . . . And that both for our own sake and theirs. For *theirs*, as it is so much more comfortable to them, and as we may then assist them in spirituals as well as temporals. And for *our own*, as it is far more apt to soften our heart and to make us *naturally care* for each other'.[13] Additionally, at the conclusion of his sermon, in which he took his text from Matthew 25:36, the mature Wesley incorporated the New Testament character Phoebe and exhorted his readers to engage themselves in the activity of visiting the sick, particularly noting the eternal dimensions of this discipline for the Methodists:

> Begin, my dear brethren, begin now: else the impression which you now feel will wear off; and possibly it may never return! What then will be the consequence? Instead of hearing that word 'Come, ye blessed . . . . For I was sick and ye visited me', you must hear that awful sentence, 'Depart, ye cursed! . . . For I was sick, and ye visited me not!'[14]

Wesley was not only interested in visiting the sick as a means of pastoral care, but also developed a plan for therapeutically treating various types of illnesses that people struggled with in life. Fundamental to this aspect of his programme was the successful publication of his *Primitive Physic: Or An Easy and Natural Method of Curing Most Diseases* (1747).[15] This little book, which became popular in Methodist piety and practice, was an interesting selection of remedies that could be administered by almost anyone. The *Primitive Physic* was filled with medical advice from various medical authors and Wesley's own experience.[16] For example, for anyone suffering from a chronic head-ache, Wesley advised:

> 396. Keep your feet in warm water, a quarter of an hour before you go to bed, for two or three weeks: Tried.
> 397. Or, wear tender hemlock leaves under the feet, changing them daily:
> 398. Or, order a tea-kettle of cold water to be poured on your head, every morning, in a slender stream:
> 399. Or, take a large tea-cupful of carduus tea, without sugar, fasting, for six or seven mornings: Tried.[17]

Primarily targeted at assessing and dealing with minor ailments, Wesley found support for this type of practice from primitive culture. In the Preface he wrote, "Tis probable, physic, as well as religion, was in the first ages chiefly traditional: every father delivering down to his sons, what he had himself in like manner received, concerning the manner of healing both outward hurts and the diseases incident to each climate, and the medicines which were of the greatest efficacy for the cure of each disorder'.[18] This resonated with great numbers of people, and Wesley's little book went through 23 editions, which meant that it was used by thousands of people throughout the eighteenth and nineteenth centuries.[19]

Alongside John Wesley's commitment to natural health and wholeness was his excitement about the discovery of electricity. Patricia Fara has succinctly noted the importance of electricity in the Enlightenment when she writes: 'electricity was the greatest discovery of the Enlightenment'.[20] For John Wesley's part, he envisioned tremendous benefits about the discovery and applications of electricity. He voraciously read about its discovery and on one occasion referred to it as a 'surprising medicine', asserting that it was a 'thousand medicines in one'.[21] Having attended electrical experiments in 1747, he obtained an electrical apparatus in 1756, which he used on himself and others in order to heal various types of ailments. Excited about its prospects, Wesley proceeded to electrify thousands, carrying his portable electrical machine with him on his preaching tours. His journal entry for 9 November 1756 recorded: 'from this time I appointed, first some hours in every week and afterward hours in every day, wherein any that desired it might try the virtue of this surprising medicine'.[22] In 1760, Wesley revised and published his ideas on electricity coupled with testimonies of people who had been cured of a range of illnesses.[23] In the same year, he also revised his *Primitive Physic* to include fifty afflictions that could be treated with electricity.[24] Throughout his writings Wesley's interest in electricity was evident. He advocated its use for both the advancement of speculative science and the practical utilization of scientific knowledge, which would benefit and assist the distressed in the pursuit of health and wholeness.

II

John Wesley, however, was not naïve about the limitations of 'science' or, as it was then called, 'natural philosophy'. His understanding of healing was rooted in the love and grace of God, which was present in the matrix of human history. For Wesley, divine favour was manifested, not only in the progress of knowledge in the modern world, but also in supernatural healings, which transcended natural philosophy and science.[25] When healing occurred – especially supernatural healing – the act of God's grace was more than the absence of pain and erasure of scars. Healing was a realization of a new reference point for understanding human existence.[26] Thus, the transforming power of supernatural healing was intended to complement the natural forms, which were often realized in less spectacular ways.[27]

In both his published journals and the *Arminian Magazine*, John Wesley found a place for relating various accounts of healing miracles.[28] Always a keen editor, he strategically placed certain accounts in his journals that were intended to make an explicit theological statement about the love of God thereby reinforcing a rhetorical agenda against Enlightenment sceptics. For example, in the section for 24 May 1749, a story of a boy who had been ill with distemper from the previous summer, received pardoning love and was immediately healed of his physical condition. In the same paragraph, Wesley includes a letter that he had sent to 'N.D.', who had written a critical appraisal of Wesley to the *Bath Journal* on 17 April. In Wesley's letter he noted the criticism of Conyers Middleton in the healing of William Kirkman, who suffered from a cough for over 60 years. John Wesley acerbically concluded: 'I do not know that any "one patient yet had died under my hands"'.[29] The long enduring success of Wesley's journals and *Arminian Magazine* suggests that the appeal of his belief in supernatural healing resonated with readers. Furthermore, the space that Wesley allowed for supernatural healing corroborates, on one level, the importance of the invisible world for Methodists and their self-understanding in the eighteenth century. Another indication of the importance of the supernatural in Wesley's works can be traced, at least in regard to healing, to the fact that he had experienced healings in his own life too. Usually Wesley was reluctant about sharing events of a personal nature. When it came to healing, however, he included in his journals and letters examples of his own illnesses and recoveries. One such instance occurred while he was in Ireland in 1775.[30] While on a preaching tour during Holy Week he developed a strong cold that caused him to be weak and fatigued. On 13 June, he recorded in his journal: '...I took to bed, but I could no more turn myself therein than a new-born child. My memory failed as well as my strength, and well-nigh my under-standing.'[31] Fervent prayer was offered for him by a small group who claimed Hezekiah and his 15-year reprieve from death in 2 Kings 20:6 as their biblical precedent. At the same time, one of Wesley's most famous preachers, Alexander Mather, read an erroneous newspaper report of Wesley's death. Mather opened his Bible *sortes biblicae*, and his eyes fell on Isaiah 38:5: 'behold, I will add unto thy days fifteen years'. Several others saw their leader's recovery as providential and a direct result of intercessory prayer. Interestingly enough, like Hezekiah of the Old Testament, John Wesley lived another fifteen years and eight months, passing away on 2 March 1791.

The above account demonstrates that for Methodists prayer was a spiritual activity that exerted great power in the believer's life. On another occasion, when John Fletcher was asked to define a Methodist, he simply responded: 'Why, the Methodists are a people that do nothing but pray. They are praying all day and all night.'[32] Throughout his life, Wesley viewed intercessory prayer as a discipline that should be inculcated by the Methodist societies. With prayer, Methodists envisioned a whole uncon-verted world on the horizons, and the possibility of touching men, women, and children with the grace of God; supernatural demonstrations would be the logical consequence of such an encounter. With regard to healing, Wesley unabashedly asserted that prayer was the key. In the Preface to his *Primitive Physic* he exhorted: 'above all, add to the rest, (for it is not labour lost) that old unfashionable medicine prayer'.[33] Sometimes prayer was utilized alongside natural remedies, but at other times prayer was seen by John Wesley as sufficient medicine in itself. Such was the case of a Mr Kingsford who, like Jane Wildbore, had lost the functional use of one of his legs. He contemplated calling on a physician, but reasoned within himself: 'God can do more for me than any physician'.[34]

Immediately, he sensed strength in his leg and began to walk. Other examples of supernatural healing displayed an unapologetic commitment to the discipline of prayer and members of the Methodist societies learned from the very beginning that a central part of their identification was an active and devout life of prayer.

Next to the activity of prayer for a Methodist during this period was the discipline of fasting.[35] From his early days in the Oxford Club, John Wesley embraced fasting as a necessary component of Christian life. On one occasion, in a letter to Charles, John wrote disparagingly about his brother's abandonment of the discipline, 'some of our Preachers here', he wrote, 'have peremptorily affirmed that you are not so *strict* as me . . . I suppose they mean those which condemn "needless self-indulgence", and recommend the means of grace, fasting in particular – which is well nigh forgotten throughout this nation. I think it would be of use if you wrote without delay and explain yourself at large'.[36] In 1733, John Wesley had made the acquaintance of the Manchester physician and non-juror, Thomas Deacon, who encouraged the young Wesley to undertake a serious examination of fasting in primitive Christianity. Later, Deacon enlisted Wesley as a contributor on fasting in a work which compiled a collection of devotions using material from the early church.[37] What remained clear for Wesley throughout his life was that fasting enabled the believer to wait on the appearance of God, which at times occurred in mundane fashion and at other moments was revealed in demonstrable ways. Additionally, Wesley wrote a sermon on fasting in which he boldly declared that it was through supernatural assistance that Moses, Elijah, and Jesus were able to fast for 40 days.[38] When fasting and prayer were joined together, Wesley maintained the believer might experience another realm of existence that was intangible to the human senses. Wesley argued in a sermon: 'a more weighty reason for fasting is that it is an help to prayer . . . Then especially it is that God is often pleased to lift up the souls of his servants above all things in earth, and sometimes to rap them up, as it were, into the third heaven.'[39] Moreover, throughout his life Wesley was quick to give evidence of the power of fasting for healing and wholeness. At the end of *Primitive Physic*, for example, Wesley listed fasting-spittle as a possible cure for various ailments and diseases.[40]

Despite Wesley's endorsement and encouragement of supernatural healing there were tensions and problems that developed in the Methodist societies. William Warburton had made a direct attack on Wesley in a book that examined the characteristics of fanaticism. Warburton considered Methodism to be the best example of perfidious 'enthusiasm'. After a detailed evaluation of 1 Corinthians 13, where Warburton concluded that the gifts of the Holy Spirit had ceased with the apostolic period of Christian history, the noted religious leader assaulted Wesley's belief in miracles. Warburton wrote: 'I purpose to TRY, in him, chiefly, THE SPIRITS of all modern Pretenders to supernatural powers'.[41] The foundation of discerning the claims of Wesley, argued Warburton, was in understanding to what extent Wesley went in claiming the experiences of apostolic Christianity for himself and his followers. In the end, Warburton considered Wesley to be a 'good Actor' who fits into the role of an Apostle.[42] For Wesley's part, he denied having been imbued with any special divine grace but contended that a Christian minister could know and experience the miraculous power of God. In his response to Warburton, Wesley maintained: 'I do not pretend to any *extraordinary* measure of the Spirit, I pretend to no other measure of it than may be claimed by every Christian minister'.[43] To argue his point, Wesley delineated eight different cases where he believed the healing of individuals came, not through natural, but supernatural means. Wesley's conclusion: 'but what does all this prove? Not that I claim any gift above other men; but only that I believe God now hears and answers prayer, even beyond the ordinary course of nature.'[44] A few pages later, Wesley gets to the essence of his argument. The occurrence of miracles and healings was not an issue of whether the gifts of the Holy Spirit had ceased, but whether the miraculous is an identifying mark of Christianity itself. Citing James 3:17, Wesley averred: 'I desire to be tried by this test. I try myself by it continually; not indeed whether I am a *prophet* (for it has nothing to do with this) but whether I am a *Christian*'.[45] For Wesley, then, to deny the possibility of the miraculous was to defame the character of Christianity.

However, there were definite and specific problems within Methodism. In various issues of the *Arminian Magazine*, Wesley had sympathetically included stories of miraculous healings that had occurred at the hands of George Bell. One instance was Mary Spread, who claimed she was healed of breast cancer by the prayer and touch of Bell. When Bell determined that Spread had sufficient faith, he touched her breast and prayed for healing; the haemorrhage, immediately stopped. The pain returned on the following day, but after more prayer her breast was healed of its cancerous scars.[46] Also, in a lengthy letter that was sent to Charles Wesley by the converted Irish deist, John Walsh, Bell claimed healing powers for himself, and even asserted that he had raised individuals from the dead.[47] George Bell and his supporters in the London societies saw the gift of healing both as a miraculous cure and a sign of the restoration of the New Testament χαρισματα in the life of believers, and consequently, a prolepsis to the imminent end of the world, because the gift, according to Bell, was peculiar to those who manifested spiritual perfection in the latter days. This, John Wesley claimed, was a distortion of the New Testament idea of healing because it separated the alliance of nature and grace in God's plan of the redemption. Furthermore, Wesley never thought that prayer or fasting was a technique that could manipulate the hand of God, but rather continued to record instances of various healing miracles as an empirical method of showing the grace of God for sinful humanity in human history.

A more positive aspect of John Wesley's view of the healing presence of God in the world was his belief in the healing efficacy of the Eucharist. From early Christian times there had been those who attested to the supernatural dimensions of the Lord's Supper.[48] Amongst Protestants in the eighteenth century, though, few emphasized the healing nature of the Eucharist as the Methodists did.[49] Both in England and North America, the Methodist societies participated in the Lord's Supper with anticipation and expectation. In the celebration of both Eucharist and Love Feasts, Methodists were, according to Lester Ruth, 'staggered by the graciousness of God they experienced in the sacrament and by the overwhelming sense of God's presence'.[50] For the Wesleys, fundamental to the idea of that power experienced by communicants was an image of the crucified Jesus. Throughout various Methodist narratives for this period, visions of the horrific nature of Christ's death caused relief and healing to Methodist votaries.[51] In a sermon John Wesley wrote during his Holy Club days in Oxford, which was published over 50 years later, he addressed the idea of the death of Christ, remembered in the sacrament, and underscored his dedication to constant communion and the power of the crucified Saviour for healing body and soul:

> Whatever way of life we are in, whatever our condition be, whether we are sick or well, in trouble or at ease, the enemies of our souls are watching to lead us into sin. And too often they prevail over us. Now when we are convinced of having sinned against God, what surer way have we of procuring pardon from him than the 'showing forth the Lord's death', and beseeching him, for the sake of his Son's sufferings, to blot out our sins?[52]

Wesley himself received communion weekly, and during special times in the Christian calendar, like Holy Week, communicated daily. In journals that he prepared for publication, Wesley included supernatural events, which he directly linked to the Eucharist. On his Georgia missionary journey, for instance, he recounted how a pregnant woman contracted a fever and desired to receive communion before she died, 'at the hour of her receiving', recorded Wesley, 'she began to recover, and in a few days was entirely out of danger'.[53] Eighteen months later, as his brother lay sick in bed suffering from pleurisy, John Wesley went on Whitsunday and received the Eucharist. The irony of this episode was apparent: 'the next day, being Whitsunday, after hearing Dr. Heylyn preach a truly Christian sermon . . . and assisting him at the Holy Communion (his curate being taken ill in the church), I received surprising news that my brother had found rest to his soul. His bodily strength returned also from that hour. "Who is so great a God as our God?"'[54]

III

Although a natural part of life, the encounter with death was an ominous experience in the eighteenth century, and society grappled with the meaning of death in various ways. In France, for example, dying individuals who often used the deathbed as an opportunity for promoting Christian virtues began to decline in favour of a more secular understanding of death, devoid of religion.[55] In England, despite the general secular movement of Enlightened thinking, the writing and reading of theological books continued to be a competitive and controversial activity.[56] Charles Drelincourt's *The Christian's Defence against the Fear of Death* (trans. 1675) went through several editions in the seventeenth and eighteenth centuries and was widely read both in France and England.[57] Also William Sherlock, the non-juror theologian and dean of St Paul's, was well received.[58] His famous work, *A Practical Discourse Concerning Death*, first published in 1689, went through 50 editions and was translated into French and Welsh.[59] Sherlock, as others in his day, saw a direct correlation between a life lived in the visible world, and the existence anticipated in the invisible world.[60] For Sherlock, the nexus was indisputable and historical existence should be scrutinized. He wrote: 'and when we only consider, that after a short continuance here, man must be removed out of this world, if we believe, that he does not utterly perish when he dies, but subsists still in another state, we have reason to believe that this life is only a preparation for the next'.[61] Many throughout the eighteenth, and well into the nineteenth century, took these ideas and sought to examine and arrange their lives in a manner that prepared them for existence in the afterlife.[62]

Several accounts during the eighteenth century also show the fascination that Methodists had with death.[63] Not the least were those in the death of their founder and leader – John Wesley.[64] Various accounts show the Methodists utilizing the inevitability of death to convey their belief in an invisible world that affected and influenced their daily experiences. Sometimes the horror of death would be portrayed, as when a Mrs Clarke instructed her servants not to disturb her after dinner; but after a knocking in her room was heard, her servants rushed to find her consumed in flames. The commentary on her tragic demise was passionate and instructive:

> She express'd no concern about her Soul, though conscious she should die; nor any desire of being pray'd by; her greatest uneasiness was about a purse of money that she had left behind her chair. The circumstances of her Death I think are as disagreeable as the motive of it, but we must leave her to the infinite Mercy of God: And may our souls be profited by this & every other alarming Providence.[65]

Most of the stories about death from Methodists relate to the idea of a good death, where the deathbed became an opportunity for the dying saint to declare a parting testimony to the goodness of God. 'Effectively the deathbed', writes D. Bruce Hindmarsh, 'was to be one's final pulpit, from which one could speak with a unique authority.'[66] Sometimes the demonstration of supernatural healing clearly showed the mercy of God, and provided an unregenerate individual with another opportunity for faith and redemption. Such was the case of a man John Pawson visited, who was on the verge of death.[67] After some conversation and prayer, Pawson told the man that he was in need of the atoning work of Christ. The results were included by John Wesley in the *Arminian Magazine*: 'He [the sick man] then was something distressed; and began to pray as well as he could . . . till, either that night or the following, the Lord spoke to his soul: and what was very remarkable, his body was healed at the same time.'[68]

At other times, though, there was a strong sense of resignation to death and the invisible world; here, a life of faith would enhance the transition into heaven with little or no trauma. From the early days of the Holy Club, John Wesley and the Methodists had been intrigued with Jeremy Taylor's *Holy Living and Holy Dying*.[69] In the second part of Taylor's *magnum opus*, he gave advice as to how an individual might die well and prepare for his or her deathbed in advance.[70] In many of the Methodist accounts, a good death was transparent through the prayers and visions of dying individuals. The account of Hannah Richardson's death, which was written by Charles Wesley, became a model in this genre. Wesley wrote the account of her death in 1741, and it was published repeatedly throughout the eighteenth century.[71] Her reputation before and after her conversion was also noted in Methodist literature; John Nelson, for example, a renowned Methodist preacher, wrote to John Wesley, outlining her life and character. Later, the Methodist leader inserted this letter into a published extract of his journal.[72] Initially, Richardson had been violently opposed to Methodism and, in fact, threatened to stone to death several Methodist preachers that came into her town of Briestfield.[73] After hearing Charles Wesley preach, she experienced justifying grace, though doubts lingered in her heart as she gave place to the 'reasoning Devil', who reminded her of her past sins and wickedness. As time passed, however, Richardson found that she did not fear death and, troubled by this, she continued to hope that her previous experience with Christ was authentic and that she would be validated by God's sanctifying presence. This episode of Richardson's life and testimony solicited amazement from Charles Wesley: 'see here a Pattern of true Mourning! A Spectacle for Men and Angels! A Soul standing up under the intolerable Weight of Original Sin!'[74] In this state, according to Charles Wesley's account, Richardson remained until her final hours. Sensing her demise, she earnestly read the Bible and prayed until she was 'constrained to take her bed'. Richardson pleaded for Wesley's visitations, and upon arrival he found her in despair. 'I am dying', she cried to Charles Wesley, 'without Pardon, with a Saviour, without Hope'.[75] After prayer, Wesley assured her: 'my soul for yours . . . if you depart hence, before your Eyes have seen his Salvation'.[76] After each and every visit (there were four), the misery of her soul increased until, on the last of Wesley's visits, Richardson experienced the freedom of her faith: 'now I know that Christ died for *me*'.[77] Significantly, prior to Wesley's final visit, Richardson had shared a moment of ecstasy and vision with her sisters by her bedside:

Heaven is open! I see JESUS CHRIST with all his Angels and Saints in White. And I am join'd to them. I shall never be parted more. I see what I cannot utter or express! Cannot you see JESUS CHRIST? There, there He stands, ready to receive you all. O do not doubt of the Love of Jesus: Look on me! If He has taken me into his Bosom, who need dispair? [sic] Fear not, fear not. He is loving unto every Man. *I believe Christ died for All.*[78]

On 17–20 April 1741, Charles Wesley recorded in his journal the events surrounding Richardson's death and funeral. On first hearing of her death, Charles Wesley asserted that he too desired to follow Richardson in death. This was a common sentiment surrounding the deathbed and some even went so far as to chastise their fellow Methodists if they prayed for healing and recovery.[79] Though departed, Richardson's life testified to the greatness of God's presence. In his account of the funeral, Charles Wesley noted: 'she, being dead, yet spoke words of faith and love, which ought to be had in remembrance'.[80] At her funeral, the whole society followed a procession to Richardson's grave, despite being pelted with dirt and stones by inhabitants of the town along the way. After the burial, at graveside, they sang a hymn:

> Come, let us who in Christ believe,
> With saints and angels join,
> Glory, and praise, and blessing give,
> And thanks to grace divine.
>
> Our friend, in sure and certain hope,
> Hath laid her body down,
> She knew that Christ will raise her up,
> And give the heavenly crown.
>
> To all who his appearing love,
> He opens paradise,
> And we shall join the hosts above,
> And we shall grasp the prize,
>
> Then let us wait to see the day,
> To hear the welcome word,
> To answer, Lo, we come away,
> We die to meet our Lord.[81]

IV

For John Wesley, then, the healing ministry of the church took on various roles in the life and mission of its members. Never one to abdicate his belief in the efficacy of primitive Christianity, John Wesley was always quick to assert the power of the means of grace. The numerous accounts that testified to the occurrence of supernatural healing validated in the eyes of Wesley and his Methodist followers that the invisible intersected with the visible at various junctures. In this way, the Methodists continued to promote the idea that God's healing presence was available for all individuals in society. Thus their embracing of supernatural healing had a social and religious impact during the Enlightenment.[82] However, all the advances of science and medicine were gifts of God's grace and should not be disparaged or discarded in the pursuit of health and wholeness. The absence of complete wholeness was not always a moment of despair for the Methodists. Often, Wesley would write in correspondence as he did to Matthew Lowes on 13 October 1770: 'health you shall have, if health be best: if not, sickness will be a greater blessing'.[83] The 'greater blessing' came to those, like Elizabeth Frances, who, approaching the experience of death forbade anyone to sit with her during her last hours. Her reasoning was simple: 'Jesus Christ shall be my Nurse'.[84]

Notes

1 See *Letters* (Telford), vol. 6, p. 318.

2 John Wesley, 'Journals and Diaries II (1738–1743)', *Works*, vol. 19, p. 438. Two months later Wesley wrote in his diaries of having religious conversation with Wildbore.

3 John Wesley, *Works*, 19, p. 164.

4 John Wesley, *The Arminian Magazine: consisting of extracts and original treatises on Universal Redemption*, 14 vols, London, J. Fry, 1778–91, vol. 8, pp. 200–1.

5 We shall deal briefly with John Wesley's involvement in medical science and theory only briefly in this article. For more on this see Chapter 3, 'Pastor and Physician', by Deborah Madden in this volume. See also, Deborah Madden, '"A Cheap, Safe and Natural Medicine": Religion, Medicine and Culture in John Wesley's *Primitive Physic*', *Clio Medica* 83, Amsterdam and New York, Rodopi, 2007.

6 John Wesley, *Primitive Physic*, 18th edition, Bristol, 1780, pp. vii–viii.

7 John Wesley, *Letters* (Telford), vol. 4, p. 108. See also, John Fletcher's 'First Check to Antinomianism' in John Fletcher, *The Works of John Fletcher*, 4 vols, Salem, Schmul Publishers, 1974, vol. 1, p. 35: 'In a word, they must own themselves sick, and renounce their physicians of no value, before they can make one true application to the invaluable Physician.'

8 See Randy Maddox, 'John Wesley on Holistic Health and Healing', *Methodist History* 46 (2007), p. 11, who correctly asserts: 'even a brief perusal of his correspondence will show that he was always quick to encourage use of medical care'.

9 John McManners, *Death and the Enlightenment: Changing Attitudes to Death in Eighteenth-century France*, Oxford, Oxford University Press, 1985, p. 5.

10 In addition to the chapters in this volume see John Cule, 'The Rev. John Wesley, M.A. (Oxon.), 1703–1791: "The Naked Empiricist" and Orthodox Medicine', *The Journal of the History of Medicine and Allied Sciences* 45 (1990), pp. 41–63; R. Jeffrey Hiatt, 'John Wesley & Healing: Developing a Wesleyan

Missiology', *The Asbury Theological Journal* 20 (2004), pp. 89–109; E. Brooks Holifield, *Health and Medicine in the Methodist Tradition*, Nashville, Abingdon Press, 1986; Deborah Madden, 'The Enlightened Empiricism of John Wesley's Primitive Physic', *British Journal for Eighteenth-Century Studies* 26 (2003), pp. 41–53; Madden, 'Medicine and Moral Reform: The Place of Practical Piety in John Wesley's Art of Physic', *Church History* 73 (2004), pp. 741–58; Madden, '"A Cheap, Safe and Natural Medicine"'; and Phillip Ott, 'Medicine and Metaphor: John Wesley on Therapy of the Soul', *Methodist History* 33 (1995), pp. 178–91.

11 See Robert Webster, *Methodism and the Miraculous: John Wesley's Contribution to the Historia Miraculorum*, Oxford DPhil thesis, 2006, pp. 254–5.

12 Steven Shapin, *A Social History of Truth: Civility and Science in Seventeenth-Century England*, Chicago and London, University of Chicago Press, 1994, p. 6.

13 John Wesley, 'Journal and Diaries IV (1755–1765)', *Works*, vol. 19, p. 290.

14 John Wesley, 'Sermons III 71–114', *Works*, vol. 3, p. 397.

15 John Wesley, *Primitive Physic; Or, An Easy and Natural Method of Curing Most Diseases*, London, 1747. On this important work, see Deborah Madden, *John Wesley's 'Cheap, Safe and Natural Medicine for Health and Long Life'*; G. S. Rousseau, 'John Wesley's Primitive Physic (1747)', *Harvard Library Bulletin* 16 (1968), pp. 242–56; and John Tuck, '"Primitive Physic": An Interesting Association Copy', *Proceedings of the Wesley Historical Society* 45 (1985), pp. 1–7.

16 Throughout the work Wesley would indicate which recipes he had indeed tried on himself.

17 John Wesley, *Primitive Physic*, pp. 95–6.

18 John Wesley, *Primitive Physic*, p. v.

19 Randy Maddox, 'John Wesley on Holistic Health and Healing', p. 4: '. . . his *Primitive Physic*, went through twenty-three editions in Wesley's lifetime – among the highest number of anything that he published – and stayed in print (and use!) continuously into the 1880s'.

20 Patricia Fara, *An Entertainment for Angels: Electricity in the Enlightenment*, Cambridge, Icon Books, 2003. See also Michael Brian Schiffer, *Draw the Lightning Down: Benjamin Franklin and Electrical Technology in the Age of Enlightenment*, Berkeley, CA, University of California Press, 2003.

21 John Wesley, 'Journals and Diaries IV (1755–1765)', *Works*, vol. 21, p. 81; Wesley, 'Journals and Diaries V (1765–1775)', *Works*, vol. 22, p. 117.

22 John Wesley, 'Journals and Diaries IV (1755–1765)', *Works*, vol. 21, p. 81.

23 John Wesley, *The Desideraturm: Or, Electricity Made Plain and Useful. By a Lover of Mankind, and of Common Sense*, London, 1760.

24 Samuel Rogal, 'Electricity: John Wesley's "Curious and Important Subject"', *Eighteenth-Century Life* 13 (1989), pp. 78–90, p. 83.

25 See John Wesley, *Primitive Physic*, pp. xii–xiii, where the love of God is identified with preventive medicine: 'The love of God, as it is the sovereign remedy of all miseries, so in particular it effectually prevents all the bodily disorders the passions introduce, by keeping the passions themselves within due bounds. And by the unspeakable joy and perfect calm, serenity, and tranquility it gives the mind, it becomes the most powerful of all the means of health and long life'.

26 Andrew Sung Park, 'Holiness and Healing: An Asian American Voice

Shaping the Methodist Traditions', in Joerg Rieger and John J. Vincent eds., *Methodist and Radical: Rejuvenating a Tradition*, Nashville, Kingswood Books, 2003, pp. 95–106.

27 E. Brooks Holifield, *Health and Medicine in the Methodist Tradition*, p. 28: 'Healing in Wesley's view, could be either natural or supernatural, and it could occur through both medication and prayer'.

28 On the success of the *Arminian Magazine* see John Hampson, *Memoirs of the Late Rev. John Wesley, A.M. with a Review of His Life and Writings, and a History of Methodism, from its Commencement in 1729, to the Present Time*, 3 vols, Sunderland, printed for the author by J. Graham, 1791, vol. 3, p. 155: 'The sale of this work is a remarkable proof of the authority of his name. Standing, as it did, under every possible disadvantage; groaning under the load of a religious controversy, of which every one had been long weary; of hundreds of letters, dull as dullness itself, and with scarcely any variation, either of sentiment or expression; this magazine, with little pretension to literary merit, is in great demand; many thousands have been annually disposed of, and the demand is continually increasing.'

29 John Wesley, 'Journal and Diaries III (1743–1754)', *Works*, vol. 20, pp. 274–7. W. R. Ward notes on p. 276, n. 85 that the letter was omitted by John Wesley from his 1774 *Works*. After having published it in pamphlet form, however, he included it in his journal.

30 See Luke Tyerman, *The Life and Times of the Rev John Wesley, M.A., Founder of the Methodists*, 3 vols, London, Hodder and Stoughton, 1870, vol. 1, p. 203.

31 John Wesley, 'Journal and Diaries V (1765–1775)', *Works*, vol. 22, p. 455.

32 Quoted by John Wesley, 'Sermons III 71–114', *Works*, vol. 3, p. 615.

33 John Wesley, *Primitive Physic*, pp. vii–viii.

34 John Wesley, 'Journal and Diaries VII (1787–1791)', *Works*, vol. 24, p. 63.

35 For a treatment of fasting and miracles in eighteenth-century British religion see Jane Shaw's *Miracles in Enlightenment England*, New Haven and London, Yale University Press, 2006, pp. 51–73. For an analysis of John Wesley's view of fasting see my article entitled 'The Value of Self-Denial: John Wesley's Multidimensional View of Fasting', *Toronto Journal of Theology* 19 (2003), pp. 25–40.

36 John Wesley, 'Letters II 1740–1755', *Works*, vol. 26, p. 498.

37 Thomas Deacon, *A Compleate Collection of Devotions both Publick and Private: Taken from the Apostolical Constitutions, the Ancient Liturgies, and Common Prayer Book of the Church of England*, 2 vols, London, 1734.

38 John Wesley, 'Sermons I 1–33', *Works*, vol. 1, p. 595.

39 John Wesley, 'Sermons I 1–33', *Works*, vol. 1, p. 600.

40 John Wesley, *Primitive Physic*, pp. 126–7. Contrary to some, like Bridget Bostock, John Wesley never became interested in healing in itself but saw in it a sign of a broader theological programme. See *Oxford Dictionary of National Biography*, 'Bostick, Bridget' and Henry D. Rack, 'Doctors, Demons, and early Methodist Healing', in W. J. Shields ed., *The Church and Healing*, Oxford, Blackwell, 1982, pp. 65–87. See also, Owen Davies, 'Charmers and Charming in England and Wales from the Eighteenth Century to the Twentieth Century', *Folklore* 109 (1998), pp. 41–52.

41 William Warburton, *The Doctrine of Grace: or, The Office and Operations of the Holy Spirit Vindicated from the Insults of INFIDELITY, and the Abuses of FANATICISM: with Some Thoughts (humbly offered to the consideration of the ESTABLISHED CLERGY) REGARDING the Right Method of Defending Religion against the Attacks of Either Party. In Three Books*, 3rd edn, London, A. Millar, 1763, p. 79.

42 William Warburton, *The Doctrine of Grace*, p. 96.

43 John Wesley, 'A Letter to the Right Reverend The Lord Bishop of Gloucester', *Works*, vol. 11, p. 468.

44 John Wesley, 'A Letter to the Right Reverend The Lord Bishop of Gloucester', *Works*, vol. 11, p. 474.

45 John Wesley, 'A Letter to the Right Reverend The Lord Bishop of Gloucester', *Works*, vol. 11, p. 476. See also my *Methodism and the Miraculous*.

46 John Wesley, ed., *Arminian Magazine* 13 (1790), p. 42.

47 For the complete letter see my article, 'The London Disturbances: John Walsh's letter to Charles Wesley, 1762', *Bulletin of the John Rylands University Library of Manchester* (forthcoming).

48 See, for example, Eamon Duffy, *The Stripping of the Altars: Traditional Religion in England 1400–1580*, New Haven and London, Yale University Press, 1992, pp. 102–7.

49 For more on this aspect of Wesley's healing ministry see my *Methodism and the Miraculous*, pp. 277–82.

50 Lester Ruth, *A Little Heaven Below: Worship at Early Methodist Quarterly Meetings*, Nashville, Kingswood Books, 2000, p. 135.

51 Henry Rack, 'Early Methodist Visions of the Trinity', *Proceedings of the Wesley Historical Society* 46 (1987), pp. 40–1. See also, Henry Rack, *Reasonable Enthusiast: John Wesley and the Rise of Methodism in the Eighteenth Century*, 3rd edn, London, Epworth, 2002, p. 406.

52 John Wesley, 'Sermons III (71–114)', *Works*, vol. 3, p. 429.

53 John Wesley, 'Journal and Diaries I (1735–1738)', *Works*, vol. 28, p. 141.

54 John Wesley, 'Journal and Diaries I (1735–1738)'. *Works*, vol. 18, p. 241.

55 Laurence Brockliss and Colin Jones, *The Medical World of Early Modern France*, Oxford, Oxford University Press, 1997, repr. 2004, pp. 398–410.

56 Brian Young, 'Theological Books from The Naked Gospel to Nemesis of Faith' in Isabel Rivers, ed., *Books and their Readers in Eighteenth-Century England: New Essays*, London and New York, Continuum, 2000, pp. 79–104.

57 Charles Drelincourt, *The Christian's Defence Against the Fears of Death with Seasonable Directions How to Die Well*, trans. Marius D'Assigny, London, printed for T.N. by John Starkey, 1675. I am grateful to John Walsh for this reference.

58 See *Oxford Dictionary of National Biography* 'Sherlock, William'.

59 William Sherlock, *A Practical Discourse Concerning Death*, London, printed for W. Rogers.

60 For an analysis of the concept of life after death in Christian tradition see Alan F. Segal, *Life after Death: A History of the Afterlife in Western Religion*, New York and London, Doubleday, 2004 and John McManners, *Death and the Enlightenment*, pp. 191–233.

61 William Sherlock, *A Practical Discourse Concerning Death*, p. 31.

62 See Terry K. Basford, *Near-Death Experiences: An Annotated Bibliography*, New York and London, Garland Publishing, 1990, pp. 129–47.

63 Henry D. Rack, 'Evangelical Endings: Death-Beds in Evangelical Biography', *Bulletin of the John Rylands University Library of Manchester* 74 (1992), pp. 39–56.

64 The Methodists of London were first informed of Wesley's death in the commissioned account of Elizabeth Ritchie. See 'Elizabeth Ritchie's Account of Wesley's Last Days' in John Wesley, *The Journal of John Wesley: Standard Edition*, ed. Nehemiah Curnock, 8 vols, London, Epworth, 1938, pp. 131–44. For new accounts of Sarah Wesley discovered in the Bodleian Library, Oxford University see John Walsh, 'John Wesley's Deathbed: Sarah Wesley's Account', *Proceedings of the Wesley Historical Society* 56 (2007), pp. 1–9.

65 Thomas Betts to Charles Wesley, 28 January 1761, *Manchester Methodist Archives*, EMV/31. References to the Manchester Methodist Archives will subsequently be abbreviated as *MARC*.

66 D. Bruce Hindmarsh, *The Evangelical Conversion Narrative: Spiritual Autobiography in Early Modern England*, Oxford, Oxford University Press, 2005, p. 259. See also Hindmarsh's '"My chains fell off, my heart was free": Early Methodist Conversion Narrative in England', *Church History* 68 (1999), pp. 910–29.

67 See Kenneth Collins, 'John Wesley and the Fear of Death as a Standard of Conversion' in Kenneth Collins and John Tyson, eds., *Conversion in the Wesleyan Tradition*, Nashville, Abingdon Press, 2001, pp. 56–68.

68 John Wesley, ed., *Arminian Magazine*, 5 (1781), p. 243. For other spiritual healing occurrences in the life of John Pawson, see John Pawson's 'Some account of the life of Mr John Pawson', *MARC*, Diaries Box, 27.

69 Jeremy Taylor, *Holy Living and Holy Dying*, ed. P. G. Stanwood, 2 vols, Oxford, Clarendon Press, 1989. V. H. H. Green, *The Young Mr. Wesley: A Study of John Wesley and Oxford*, London, Edward Arnold, 1961, p. 310, notes that Wesley was reading Taylor's work in 1729.

70 Jeremy Taylor, *Holy Living and Holy Dying*, vol. 2, pp. 49–53.

71 Charles Wesley, *A Short Account of the Death of Mrs. Hannah Richardson*, 7th edn, London, printed and folded at the Foundry near Upper-Moorfields, 1754. See Richard Green, *The Works of John and Charles Wesley. A Bibliography: Containing an Exact Account of all the Publications issued by The Brothers Wesley Arranged in Chronological Order, with a list of the Early Editions, and Descriptive and Illustrative Notes*, London, C. H. Kelly, 1896, p. 18, cites this publication going through ten editions in the eighteenth century.

72 John Wesley, 'Journal and Diaries IV (1755–1765)', *Works*, vol. 21, pp. 132–3.

73 Most notably the Methodist itinerant, Enoch Williams.

74 Charles Wesley, *A Short Account of the Death of Mrs. Hannah Richardson*, p. 6.

75 Charles Wesley, *A Short Account of the Death of Mrs. Hannah Richardson*, p. 6.

76 Charles Wesley, *A Short Account of the Death of Mrs. Hannah Richardson*, p. 6.

77 Quoted by Charles Wesley, *A Short Account of the Death of Mrs. Hannah*

Richardson, p. 6. As with John Wesley's Aldersgate experience, many of the Methodist conversion narratives emphasize with italics the personal pronoun when writing about their experience of salvation.

78 Charles Wesley, *A Short Account of the Death of Mrs. Hannah Richardson*, p. 8.

79 'Account of the death of Betty Appleton, 1776', *MARC*, EMV/21: 'She said you grieve me much when you pray for my recovery'.

80 Charles Wesley, *The Journal of Charles Wesley*, ed. Thomas Jackson, 2 vols., London, John Mason, repr. Kansas City, Beacon Hill, 1980, vol. 2, p. 268.

81 Charles Wesley, *The Journal of Charles Wesley*, vol. 2, pp. 268–9.

82 David Harley, 'Rhetoric and the Social Construction of Sickness and Healing', *Social History of Medicine* 12 (1999), p. 430: 'Although mechanical explanations did tend to exile the passions to the realm of psychological states, there was a continuing tradition of discussing the physical effects of belief'.

83 John Wesley, *Letters* (Telford), vol. 5, p. 205.

84 Quoted by John Wesley, *Arminian Magazine* 10 (1785), p. 25.

Index

Made in the USA
Columbia, SC
02 August 2021